MIGRATION AND
REMITTANCES

MIGRATION AND REMITTANCES

Eastern Europe and the Former Soviet Union

Edited by
Ali Mansoor
Bryce Quillin

THE WORLD BANK

Europe and Central Asia Region
2006

©2007 The International Bank for Reconstruction and Development/The World Bank
1818 H Street NW
Washington DC 20433
Telephone: 202-473-1000
Internet: www.worldbank.org
E-mail: feedback@worldbank.org

ISBN-10: 0-8213-6233-X
ISBN-13: 978-0-8213-6233-4
eISBN: 0-8213-6234-8
DOI: 10.1596/978-0-8213-6233-4

Cover photo: Karen Robinson ©Panos Pictures.

Library of Congress Cataloging-in-Publication Data
Mansoor, Ali M.
   Migration and remittances : Eastern Europe and the former Soviet Union / [Ali Mansoor,
Bryce Quillin].
      p. cm.
   Includes bibliographical references and index.
   ISBN-13: 978-0-8213-6233-4 (alk. paper)
   ISBN-10: 0-8213-6233-X (alk. paper)
   ISBN-13: 978-0-8213-6234-1
   ISBN-10: 0-8213-6234-8
   1. Migrant labor—Europe, Eastern. 2. Migrant labor—Former Soviet republics. 3. Migrant
remittances—Europe, Eastern. 4. Migrant remittances—Former Soviet republics. I. Quillin, Bryce,
1976– II. World Bank. Europe and Central Asia Region. III. Title.
HD5856.E852M36 2007
304.80947—dc22

Contents

Boxes

Figures

Tables

Foreword

The countries of Eastern Europe and the former Soviet Union have been reintegrating into the world economy following the dissolution of the Soviet economic network. The Europe and Central Asia Region of the World Bank has undertaken a multivolume analysis of the processes that have influenced this transition period. This volume, *Migration and Remittances: Eastern Europe and the Former Soviet Union,* focuses on international migration. The core of the report documents the history of migration and remittances since transition and discusses the determinants of migration. A final chapter lays out some tentative policy interventions that might enhance the gains from migration and remittances for net immigration and emigration countries and for migrants and their families.

Migration is important for the economies of this region because many of the world's largest international migration flows emanate from and flow to the countries of Eastern Europe and the former Soviet Union. The distinctive patterns of migration experienced since transition will continue to exert an important impact on growth and development in the near future.

The early years of transition witnessed high levels of cross-border migration as populations that were previously unable to move due to Soviet restrictions relocated to their ethnic or cultural homelands. These "diaspora" flows emerged simultaneously with refugee movements that resulted from the eruption of civil and transborder conflicts among the newly emergent countries of the area. However, as conflicts abated and economic reforms took root in the last five to seven years, economic motivations became the key driver of migratory flows.

The result of these trends has been a broad biaxial pattern of migration flows among the transition economies: one axis from the western part of the region to the European Union (EU) and another axis from the southern to the northern countries of the Commonwealth of Independent States (CIS). However, this broad generalization should not obscure the more complex patterns of movement. Although the majority of migrants from the poorer CIS countries travel to the middle-income CIS countries, many also move west in search of higher earnings, toward the EU and Turkey. A number of CIS migrants may spend short or long periods in Central and Eastern European countries or Turkey in the hope of moving to Western Europe.

Migration creates challenges and opportunities for sending and receiving countries. For many net emigration countries in ECA, household income and national output are strongly tied to the incomes of migrants living and working abroad. Cross-country growth studies conducted for this report indicate that remittances have a positive impact on long-term economic growth. Migration can allow migrants to learn new skills and can facilitate cross-border trade and investment linkages. Moreover, labor-importing CIS economies and the neighboring EU rely on migrant labor from the region to maintain rates of economic growth and standards of living.

Yet, working abroad can expose migrants to risks of abuse or trafficking, particularly those that work abroad illegally and do not have recourse to legal channels. Migration can also create social dislocation by separating families for long periods. For the sending countries, large-scale migration can deprive the economy of needed skills. For the receiving country, migration can create social friction and possibly security risks.

This study finds that the benefits that sending countries and migrants secure from migration and associated remittances are at least partly conditional on the quality of economic, social, and political institutions and policies in those countries. Improvements in the overall quality of life in sending countries have the potential to (a) reduce out-migration rates, (b) induce migrants in the diaspora to return home, and (c) provide incentives for migrants to use the human and financial capital, including remittances, accumulated abroad at home.

Migration sending and receiving countries could more closely coordinate migration policy so that the supply of international migrant labor can better meet demand through legal channels that respect the rights of migrants and are politically and socially acceptable to migrant-receiving countries. Though bilateral labor agreements represent a promising route for enhancing the gains to migration in this region, the nature and content of these agreements need to reflect the actual demand for migrant labor.

In particular, managed-migration programs between sending and receiving countries might combine short-term migration with incentives for return or circular migration. Circular migration programs may be an important step in resolving a key migration paradox: there is demand for migrant labor yet often little public support for permanent migration—particularly unskilled migration—in the many European and middle-income CIS countries in demographic decline. Moreover, circular migration may have the potential to facilitate development in migration-sending countries by increasing migrants' human and financial capital, facilitating international skills transfers, building cross-border trade and investment, and preventing the long-term separation of families.

There are no ready-made solutions for migration reform in the Europe and Central Asia region. The complexity of migration and the poor data on migration and remittances require that policy recommendations be qualified. The exact mix of international and domestic policies needed to balance supply and demand varies according to the demographic and economic characteristics of the countries in question. In addition to the benefits that a stable and equitable business and social climate and good quality of governance have for economic growth and poverty reduction generally, such policies will improve the returns to migration for migration-sending and receiving countries and migrants themselves.

The study, part of a new series of regional studies, is intended as a contribution to the World Bank's goal to work more effectively with clients and partners in the Region to reduce poverty and foster economic growth by enhancing gains from international labor migration. It complements recent studies on growth, poverty, and inequality, job opportunities, and on trade and integration in the Region. I hope that these studies stimulate debate, promote better understanding, and spur action to bring about prosperity for all.

Shigeo Katsu
Vice President
Europe and Central Asia Region

Acknowledgments

This study was prepared by a core team led by Ali Mansoor and Bryce Quillin, who were the main authors, and comprising Anders Danielson, Timothy Heleniak, Kathleen Kuehnast, Theodore Lianos, Rainer Münz, Maria Stoilkova, Philippe Wanner, and Alessandra Venturini. It also draws on the inputs of Pritam Banerjee, Natalia Catrinescu, Taras Chernetsky, Carine Clert, Betsy Cooper, Shushanik Hakobyan, Elena Kantarovich, Elaine Kelly, Ben Klemens, Marek Kupiszewski, Marianne Kurtzweil, Miguel Leon-Ledesma, Diana Marginean, Margaret Osdoby-Katz, Eric Livny, Panagiota Papaconstantinou, Chris Parsons, Marina Lutova, Matloob Piracha, Sherman Robinson, Makiko Shirota, Valerie Stadlbauer, and Saltanat Sulaimanova.

The study was supported by the essential guidance of Pradeep Mitra, Chief Economist of the Europe and Central Asia Region. The team gratefully acknowledges suggestions and comments from Arup Banerji, Nora Dudwick, Willem van Eeghen, Alan Gelb, Daniela Gressani, Ellen Hamilton, Jariya Hoffman, Robert Holzmann, Nadir Mohammed, Fernando Montes-Negret, Jaime de Melo, Dominique van der Mensbrugghe, Irena Omelaniuk, Caglar Ozden, Pierella Paci, Martin Raiser, Dilip Ratha, Maurice Schiff, Dennis de Tray, Merrell Tuck-Primdahl, Alan Winters, and Ruslan Yemtsov. The team benefited from advice and comments provided by Yuri Andrienko (Center of Economic and Financial Research, Russia), Lev Palei (International

Monetary Fund), Louka Katseli (Organisation for Economic Co-operation and Development), Gregory Maniatis (Migration Policy Institute), Demetrios Papademetriou (Migration Policy Institute), Alexandros Zavos (Hellenic Migration Policy Institute, Greece), Alexander Sarris (Food and Agriculture Organization of the United Nations), and Thomas Timberg (Nathan Associates Inc.). The team thanks participants of the 2005 Migration Policy Institute–Hellenic Migration Policy Institute conference on "Capturing the Benefits of Migration in Southeastern Europe" held in Athens October 11–12.

Helpful comments and suggestions were provided during the presentation of earlier drafts of this report in 2005 to the European Commission; the Organisation for Economic Co-operation and Development; the Kennan Institute at the Woodrow Wilson International Center for Scholars; the International Organization for Migration; the International Labor Organization; the U.K. Department for International Development; the Centre on Migration, Policy and Society at Oxford University; and the Development Studies Institute at the London School of Economics.

Book design, editing, and production were coordinated by the World Bank's Office of the Publisher. Ian McDonald edited the manuscript.

Abbreviations and Glossary

BOP	balance of payments
CEECs	Central and Eastern European Countries, consisting of Albania, Bosnia and Herzegovina, Bulgaria, Croatia, the Czech Republic, Estonia, Hungary, Latvia, Lithuania, the former Yugoslav Republic of Macedonia, Moldova, Poland, Romania, Serbia and Montenegro, the Slovak Republic, and Slovenia
CES	constant elasticity of substitution
CGE	computable general equilibrium
CIS	Commonwealth of Independent States
CPIA	country policy and institutional assessment
DPD	dynamic panel data
EBRD	European Bank for Reconstruction and Development
ECA	The Europe and Central Asia region of the World Bank is an administrative regional country grouping. It consists of Albania, Armenia, Azerbaijan, Belarus, Bosnia and Herzegovina, Bulgaria, Croatia, the Czech Republic, Estonia, Georgia, Hungary, Kazakhstan, Kyrgyz Republic, Latvia, Lithuania, the former Yugoslav Republic of Macedonia, Moldova, Poland, Romania, the Russian Federation, Serbia and Montenegro, the Slovak Republic, Slovenia, Tajikistan, Turkey, Turkmenistan, Ukraine, and Uzbekistan.

EU	European Union
EU-15	Austria, Belgium, Denmark, Finland, France, Germany, Greece, Ireland, Italy, Luxembourg, Netherlands, Portugal, Sweden, Spain, and the United Kingdom
EU-8	The Czech Republic, Poland, Hungary, the Slovak Republic, Slovenia, Latvia, Lithuania, and Estonia
FSU	Former Soviet Union
FYR	Former Yugoslav Republic (of Macedonia)
GATS	General Agreement on Trade in Services
GDP	gross domestic product
GMM	generalized method of moments
GNP	Gross National Product
GTAP	Global Trade Analysis Project
IDP	internally displaced persons
ILO	International Labour Organization
IMF	International Monetary Fund
IOM	International Organization for Migration
OECD	Organisation for Economic Co-operation and Development
PPP	purchasing power parity
UN	United Nations
UNHCR	United Nations High Commission for Refugees
WTO	World Trade Organization
Western ECA	The Czech Republic, Poland, Hungary, the Slovak Republic, Slovenia, Latvia, Lithuania, Estonia, Romania, Bulgaria, Bosnia and Herzegovina, Serbia and Montenegro, Albania, Croatia, and FYR Macedonia

Overview

Migration has been an important part of the transition process in Europe and Central Asia (ECA),[1] and continues to be relevant as these countries move beyond transition. Labor migration is likely to gain in importance in view of the aging of populations in Europe and some parts of the former Soviet Union.

Migration in the region is unique and significant: ECA accounts for one-third of all developing country emigration and Russia is the second largest immigration country worldwide. Migrants' remittances, as a portion of gross domestic product, are also large by world standards in many countries of the region.

Economic motivations currently drive migration flows in ECA. This was not the case in the initial transition period, which unlocked large flows reflecting the return of populations to ethnic or cultural homelands, the creation of new borders, political conflict, and the unwinding of restrictions placed on movement by the Soviet system. Nor will it be the case in about a decade, when demographics will begin to dominate motivations for migration. However, for now market opportunities and the reintegration of ECA countries into the world economy spur labor migration.

Incentives for permanent and large quantities of undocumented migration may exist because of the structure of many of the immigration policies governing migration from ECA to Western Europe and the migration-receiving countries of the Commonwealth of Independent States (CIS). Immigration policies distinguish between skilled and unskilled labor and the policies increasingly recognize the value of skilled labor, which is partly covered by the World Trade Organization's General Agreement on Trade in Services (GATS). However, policies on unskilled labor often focus too heavily on controlling a very large supply through border controls without looking to efficiently match this supply with the domestic demand for low-skilled migrant workers. As a result, such policies can fail to contain a large and growing population of undocumented migrants. The report focuses, where distinctions are relevant, on the case of unskilled labor migration because existing international migration policies often poorly address this form of cross-border movement.

Migration-sending countries can contribute to the slowing of out-migration by accelerating economic and political reforms and thus the associated expectation that the quality of life will rapidly improve. Receiving countries could increase the payoff from migration by accepting and factoring the demand side of the equation into policies designed to minimize undocumented migration. In doing so, the negative consequences of undocumented migration—including the inefficient distribution of resources, hindrances to sending remittances, and the inhibiting of circular migration patterns—could be avoided.

The core focus of this report is on documenting the trends of international migration and remittances in this region since the period of transition (chapters 1 and 2) and discussing the determinants of migration in this region (chapter 3). A final chapter (chapter 4) reviews the organization of international migration policy in the region. It details the nature and types of bilateral migration schemes in place between ECA countries and between ECA and Western Europe and identifies some of their limitations. The final section of chapter 4 suggests some avenues through which bilateral migration agreements could be improved. The ambition of this section is explore how bilateral migration agreements could reduce the incentives for undocumented migration while minimizing the cultural and social frictions from increased migration in the receiving country. The viability of this proposal has not been tested so it is suggested that this proposal could form the basis for pilot programs in the future.

This overview chapter summarizes the main findings that are developed in much greater detail in later chapters of *Migration and Remittances: Eastern Europe and the Former Soviet Union*.

Nature and Evolution of Migration, 1990–2006

Migration in Eastern Europe and the CIS is large by international standards. If movements between industrial countries are excluded, ECA accounts for over one-third of total world emigration and immigration. There are 35 million foreign-born residents in ECA countries. Overall, several ECA countries are among the top 10 sending and receiving countries for migrants worldwide. Russia is home to the second largest number of migrants in the world after the United States; Ukraine is fourth after Germany; and Kazakhstan and Poland are respectively ninth and tenth.

The collapse of communism encouraged a massive increase in geographic migration in the ECA region, including internal movements, cross-border migration within ECA, outflows from ECA, and some inflows from other regions. The formation of many new countries following the breakup of the Soviet Union "created" many statistical migrants—long-term, foreign-born residents who may not have physically moved, but were defined as migrants under UN practice.

Migration flows in ECA tend to move in a largely bipolar pattern. Much of the emigration in western ECA (42 percent) is directed toward Western Europe, while much emigration from the CIS countries remains within the CIS (80 percent). Germany is the most important destination country outside ECA for migrants from the region, while Israel was an important destination in the first half of the 1990s. Russia is the main intra-CIS destination. The United Kingdom, in particular, is becoming a destination for migrants from the ECA countries of the European Union (EU) who are temporarily barred from legal access to many of the other EU-15 labor markets.

The number of undocumented migrants from ECA countries in Western Europe and the CIS is believed to be large but, by definition, is difficult to quantify. Currently, there are estimated to be upward of 3 million undocumented immigrants in the EU, and between 3 million and 3.5 million in Russia.

Migration and Population Change

ECA countries display significant variation in terms of the direction of migration flows and their impact on net population changes. From 2000 to 2003, ECA countries were about evenly split between those that registered a natural decline in population—in which the number of deaths exceeded births (13)—and those that registered population increases (14). In the EU, both Germany and Italy already have

declining populations and many other EU countries are expected to
show natural decreases in the future as their populations age.

Of the 14 ECA countries with a natural increase in population,

- Nine countries registered net emigration during 2000–03 with
  Turkey achieving near parity (that is, having nearly equal amounts
  of emigrants and immigrants). We anticipate that within this group
  migration pressures will persist unless economic reforms can lead
  to rapid increases in the quality of life and standard of living.

- Three countries appear to have an increase in population not only
  due to demographic causes, but also owing to a positive net migration balance.

Of the 13 ECA countries with a natural decline in population,

- One group of seven comprises countries experiencing population
  declines owing to both more deaths than births and more emigration than immigration. This group includes Bulgaria, Latvia,
  Lithuania, Moldova, Poland, Romania, and Ukraine.

- A final group comprises net-immigration countries with declining
  populations, in which immigration is insufficient to offset the natural population decline. This group includes Belarus, Russia, and
  the Central European countries that are new EU members.

Internal displacement continues to be substantial within the ECA
region. Internal displacement refers to migration within the country
owing to strife or economic motivation. In 2003, the largest concentrations of internal displacement resulting from conflict were in Azerbaijan (576,000) and Georgia (262,000). These numbers are down
only slightly from peaks in the mid-1990s as the conflicts that gave
rise to them continue to persist without any permanent settlement.

Internal displacement for economic reasons can also have substantial repercussions. Concentrations of direct foreign investment, trade,
and other economic opportunities leading to greater urban agglomer-
ation can draw in large numbers of people, leaving other parts of the
country somewhat depopulated. For example, according to the 2002
Russian census, Moscow has grown from 1.5 million inhabitants at
the start of transition to 10.4 million. This growth arises because the
bulk of both domestic and foreign investment, overall job growth,
and job creation in sectors of the "new economy" are concentrated in
Russia's capital. At the other end of the urban spectrum are a large
number of "ghost towns"—population settlements where census tak-
ers expected to find people but on census day discovered they were
completely depopulated.

In recent years, migration may have declined for many ECA countries compared with the period following transition. Immigration countries, such as Russia, receive less net immigration, while emigration countries register lower outflows. This is consistent with the view that the early period of transition was marked by ethnic and conflict-driven migration, while later, as the situation stabilized, migration became mainly economically motivated. The one exception is Ukraine, where transit migration may have increased.

The total population of the EU-8 accession countries and the Balkans declined overall by 1.1 million and by more than 2.7 million, respectively. This decline is related both to a natural population decrease and to migration. While all these countries had negative net natural-population growth, in the Czech Republic and Slovenia the total population grew because of net gains from migration. Labor migration in these states is still relatively small when compared with both population size and the size of the workforce. Furthermore, the great majority of migrant workers come from neighboring countries and regions. EU membership and the rise in sustained foreign investment, however, will create the demand for additional, most probably foreign, labor.

With the breakup of the Soviet Union in 1991, there was a rapid shift in the causes and patterns of migration. Russia gained 3.7 million persons through migration and became a net recipient of migration from all the other states of the CIS and the Baltics, except for Belarus. At the same time, 15 percent or more of the populations of Armenia, Albania, Georgia, Kazakhstan, and Tajikistan migrated permanently, many of them the better-educated and younger elements of society.

Future Trends

While economic factors will continue to be important drivers of migration (see chapter 3), demographic patterns will also play an increasingly important role. Migration flows that are generated in the short term may be unsustainable in a decade owing to the medium-term population dynamics in most of the ECA region. With the exception of Albania and Turkey, all Central and Eastern European countries are forecast to experience population declines, many of them greater than in the destination countries.

The decline in the working-age population will create a demand for workers that can only be sourced from abroad. The more prosperous EU-8 countries and middle-income CIS countries may be able to obtain some of these workers from the rest of the region. However, for the region as a whole, demand will have to be met from else-where, probably from Africa and Asia. Whether these flows are legal or undocumented will depend on future immigration legislation.[2]

Migrant Remittances

Relative to GDP, remittances are significant in many ECA countries. In 2004, officially recorded remittances to the ECA region totaled over US$19 billion, amounting to 8 percent of the global total for remittances (US$232.3 billion) and over 12 percent of remittances received by developing countries (US$ 160.4 billion).[3]

For many ECA countries, remittances are the second most important source of external financing after foreign direct investment. For many of the poorest countries in the region, they are the largest source of outside income and have served as a cushion against the economic and political turbulence brought about by transition. Migrants' funds represent over 20 percent of GDP in Moldova and Bosnia and Herzegovina, and over 10 percent in Albania, Armenia, and Tajikistan (figure 1).

FIGURE 1
Remittances as a Portion of GDP in Eastern Europe and the Former Soviet Union, 2004

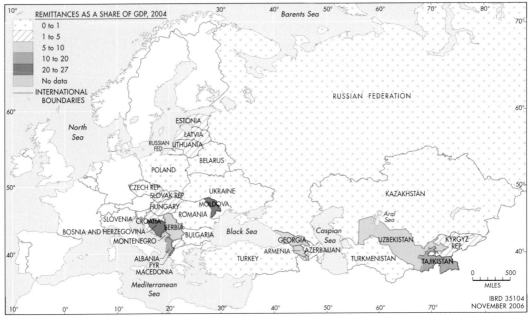

Source: IMF, *Balance of Payment Statistics.*

Notes: 1. Received remittances = received compensation of employee + received worker's remittances + received migrants' transfer.
2. Albania and Slovak Republic are 2003 data, other countries 2004 data.
3. GDP is $ converted current price.

Generally remittance flows in ECA follow the same two-bloc pattern as migration. The EU and the resource-rich CIS are the main sources of remittances, with the EU accounting for three-quarters of the total and the rich CIS countries for 10 percent. The amount contributed by the EU-8 and accession countries is also significant, just below the 10 percent level.

Remittances recorded in the balance of payments undercount transfers between migrants and their families. According to surveys with returned migrants prepared for this study, between one-third and two-thirds of migrants, depending on their country of origin, used informal channels—or methods outside of the formal financial system such as bank transfers—to transmit remittances at some point.[4] Specifically, the surveys indicated that an average of 41 percent of ECA migrants reported using an informal channel to transfer remittances, such as public transportation drivers, friends, or family. Only two countries in ECA—Moldova and Russia—attempt to capture remittances sent through these informal channels in the balance of payments statistics.[5] Thus, official remittances figures tend to undercount the actual flows by the amount sent through these informal networks in most instances.

Remittances can exert a positive impact on macroeconomic growth. Cross-country regressions indicate that remittances can have a positive, although relatively mild, impact on long-term growth. Moreover, remittances have a positive impact on poverty reduction for the poorest households. Household budget surveys indicate that remittances constitute over 20 percent of the expenditure of households in the poorest quintile.

Remittances represent an important source of foreign exchange for several ECA countries.

- The high-migration countries earn from remittances over 10 percent of the amount exports of goods and services bring in.

- In Moldova and Serbia and Montenegro, remittances bring in foreign exchange equivalent to almost half of export earnings.

- For Albania and Bosnia and Herzegovina, the contribution of remittances is almost as large as that of exports.

At the same time, the inflow of remittances may serve to raise the real exchange rate, harming competitiveness.

Unrecorded remittances appear to be crucial in explaining the continued high current-account deficit in many ECA high-migration countries. For Albania, Bosnia and Herzegovina, Moldova, Serbia and Montenegro, and Tajikistan, the current account was large but unrecorded remittances were estimated to be significantly larger than the negative balances on the current account.

Because they are a significant source of foreign exchange, remittances can improve creditworthiness and access to international capital markets for many ECA countries. For example, if remittances are included as a potential source of foreign exchange, the ratio of debt to exports falls by close to 50 percent for Albania and Bosnia and Herzegovina. Unlike capital flows, remittances do not create debt servicing or other obligations. As such, they can provide financial institutions with access to better financing than might otherwise be available. Among ECA countries, Turkey has been in the lead in using such remittance securitization, but Kazakhstan has also used this instrument to raise financing (World Bank 2006).

Because remittances per se do not lower anyone's income, the impact on poverty is beneficial. A recent analysis by Adams and Page (2003) finds that a 10 percent increase in the share of migrants in a country's population will lead to a 1.9 percent decline in the share of people living on less than US$1 a day. A review of the urban-rural distribution of remittances for selected ECA countries indicates that different countries are characterized by different patterns. Information from Household Budget Surveys suggests that in Central Asian countries, most remittances go to rural areas, while in the Caucasus the bulk go to metropolitan areas and cities. The pattern is dictated by the different regions from which migrants originate (figure 2). In the Caucasus, it appears that families that receive a higher income as a result of remittances tend to move to urban areas, which are considered safer and more convenient.[6]

Remittances to the ECA region have the potential to improve income levels and standards of living for both individuals and nations. The greatest potential benefit is enhanced economic growth, driven by consumption and investment. Increasing the volume of remittances sent through formal channels involves lowering the cost of regular payments. The extent to which increased remittance flows can deliver sustainable economic growth will depend partly on the quality of institutions and institutional development in the migrants' home countries. It is, therefore, crucial to address institutional weaknesses and governance if remittance income is to be translated into sustained advances in economic development.

Determinants of Migration

Despite the great variation in the migration patterns across the region and the extremely complex combination of economic and social moti-

FIGURE 2

Percent Distribution of Remittances and Population by Location in 2002

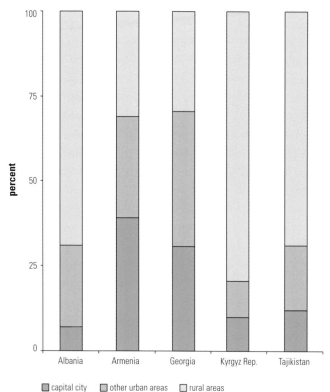

Source: World Bank, Household Data Archive for Europe and Central Asia.

Note: Tajikistan data are from 2003.

vations for migration, a number of similar motivations seem to underpin the decisions to migrate. International migration is often
explained by a basic push-and-pull model: economic conditions,
demographic pressures, and unemployment ("push factors") in the
sending countries work in coordination with higher wages, demand
for labor, and family reunification ("pull factors") in the migration-
receiving countries (Smith 1997).

Disparities in GDP per capita have widened considerably in the
ECA. One simple explanation for migration trends among the ECA
countries, based on traditional migration theory, is that widening disparities in GDP per capita drive migrants from lower-income to
higher-income countries. Countries such as those of the former Soviet
Union have attempted to equalize incomes among social groups and
also among regions, which was accomplished through a massive and
elaborate system of subsidies, transfers, and controlled prices. With
independence and economic transition, levels of GDP per capita have

widened considerably among the ECA countries, and have become a factor driving migration where this was not the case previously. According to figure 3, the coefficient of variation in per capita GDP among the ECA countries for the period 1990–2002 increased from 0.43 in 1990 to 0.70 in 1997, before declining slightly.

Yet, GDP per capita disparities do not fully explain migration trends in ECA. The links between flows and income differentials are too weak to make such differentials a viable explanation without additional qualifiers such as ethnic and political considerations, expectations of quality of life at home, and geography. Though the above data are illustrative of the widening income levels among ECA countries during transition, they are somewhat misleading because the two countries with the highest and lowest per capita GDPs in 2002 were Slovenia and Tajikistan. Given the distance between the two countries and various other factors, there is not expected to be much migration from Tajikistan to Slovenia. More telling are the income disparities between migration spaces of geographically adjacent groups of countries, in this case the CIS and Europe, the latter including both Eastern and Western Europe.

The perceptions of (potential) migrants of economic possibilities at home and abroad contribute to population movements. What emerges from this study is a complex picture indicating that expected income differences, the expected probability of finding employment abroad, and expected quality of life at home play a strong role in

FIGURE 3

Disparities in GDP per Capita in the CEE-CIS States, 1990–2002
(PPP current international dollars)

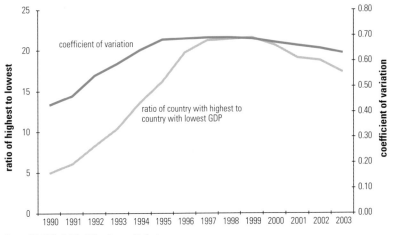

Source: World Bank, World Development Indicators.

Note: CEE = Central and Eastern European; PPP = purchasing power parity.

many cases but a role tempered by the influence of numerous other variables. Evidence for the importance of these noneconomic drivers of migration is partly given by statistical tests, yet the poor nature of migration data in the region of the period since transition may cast doubt on the utility of these results. More robust information on the drivers of current trends and forecasts of the future is provided through looking at the history of migration from the Southern European countries and Ireland and through simulations.

Experience of Southern Europe and Ireland

The migration histories of Southern Europe and Ireland—which realized a shift from being net emigration to net immigration countries during the post–World War Two period—are useful for understanding and predicting patterns of migration for the Central and Eastern European countries. First, these western ECA countries, like Ireland and all Southern European countries, are geographically near the EU. This proximity is not only physical but also cultural—languages and social traditions are comparable. Additionally, Southern European countries and Ireland, as we see with ECA countries now, were poorer than their destination countries. While there are clearly distinctions between the Southern European countries and Ireland and the ECA countries, the similarities are sufficient that a study of the migration history of the former may provide a reasonable amount of evidence about current and future trends.

The history of migration from the Southern European countries and Ireland to the wealthier European Community members during the period of the 1960s through the 1980s suggests the importance of expected income differentials and expected improvements in domestic policy in motivating migration. In Southern Europe and Ireland, for example, emigration rates initially accelerated as these countries became more integrated into the regional economy, as has occurred for many ECA countries since transition. However, this increase was also associated with a shift from long-term to shorter-term migration, suggesting greater interest in return migration which, in fact, then materialized.

Looking at the patterns illustrated in figure 4, the surge in Italian emigration to the United States at the beginning of the last century was due not to an increase in poverty but to an increase in income and employment growth at the beginning of Italian industrialization (Hatton and Williamson 1994). The surge of Spanish emigration to other European countries in the period 1960–74 was the result of a growth rate higher than in the other European countries.[7] The peak of Portuguese emigra-

FIGURE 4

Postwar Emigration from Southern Europe, 1960–88

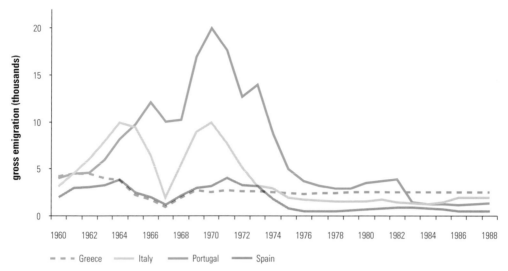

Source: Venturini 2004.

tion in the 1970s also took place during a growth phase, and Greece's emigration rates rose during the economic boom of the 1960s.

Possibilities of EU membership may also influence the desire to migrate. The slowing emigration from Southern Europe in the second half of the 1970s was the result of lower incentives to migrate owing in part to the large investments made by the EU in these countries before their accession (figure 4). Such investments in turn led to expectations of a higher quality of life in these countries. Membership in the EU also played a role in Italy's turnaround from a net emigration to a net immigration country. First, in the period before Italy's entry into the EU, the country implemented reforms that increased the quality of life and facilitated the development of its goods market. Second, transfers from the European Structural Fund after entry were an additional source of growth and improvement in the quality of life and delivery of public services. This growth also increased domestic demand for labor in Italy. Third, expectations of future growth may have been as important as current jobs in modifying the expectations of potential migrants. Fourth, the freedom to move can actually reduce migration in the short term because potential migrants are free to put off the move until later.

Simulations

The results from a simulation of the determinants of migration suggest that an improving quality of life at home can slow out-migration even when income differentials between countries exist. In other words, the policies of migration-sending countries create the incentives for migration and return migration.

The results show that with an increase in the quality of life in sending countries, migration flows into the EU are reduced from all ECA regions. For western ECA countries, legal migration flows fell between 0.6 and 1 percent. Migration also fell for the countries of the former Soviet Union and Turkey though by a reduced amount.

The model also suggests that the possibility of improvements in the quality of life increased return migration or circular migration—the process in which migrants return home for short periods before migrating again. An improvement in the quality of life in ECA countries led to increased flows from the EU-15 to all ECA countries. Migration flows from the EU-15 into western ECA increased around 1 percent and around 0.5 percent for the former Soviet Union and Turkey.

Regulatory Framework for International Labor Migration

Multilateral efforts to address migration have been related almost exclusively to the Mode 4 framework of the General Agreement on Trade in Services (GATS). Mode 4 addresses the provision of services through the cross-border movements of citizens of the World Trade Organization (WTO) member countries. Its introduction generated initial optimism that a broader liberalization of labor markets could follow. A commitment to deepen the coverage of Mode 4, however, has not yet emerged. Even though services represent over 70 percent of the GDP of developed economies, only a very small portion of international migrants qualify as "service providers" by WTO standards. WTO provisions currently focus on extending freedom of passage to a limited subset of international migrants in multinational firms. Thus, the provisions and any proposed revisions to them have little consequence for unskilled migrants at present.

Unlike trade liberalization in products and other services, providing for the free movement of people generates a number of negative externalities stemming from the values, rights, responsibilities, and risks that migrants may pose. As a result, GATS protections are only extended to "natural persons" who intend to relocate temporarily or provide a service abroad.

Most legal labor migration is facilitated by direct agreements between migration-sending and receiving countries. The current system is a series of several types of bilateral agreements that appear

largely uncoordinated between recipient countries. Only a few countries account for most of the agreements on both the sending and the
receiving sides in ECA.

Like the migration flows they regulate, bilateral agreements have a
strong bipolar regional orientation. Most of the agreements involving
western ECA (82 percent) are with Eastern European countries. Like-
wise, a large majority (64 percent) of CIS bilateral agreements are
with other CIS members, particularly Russia. The overall number of
bilateral agreements increased rapidly in the 1990s, largely as a result
of the collapse of the Soviet Union and the breakup of Yugoslavia. Of
the existing 92 agreements, 75 percent were signed after 1989. On
the EU side, half of the existing bilateral agreements covering labor
migration have been signed by Germany, the largest destination for
western ECA migrants. Of the EU-15 as a whole, 14 countries have
bilateral agreements with the western ECA countries (Denmark is the
only exception).

The need for bilateral agreements between the countries of Western and Eastern Europe will expire as the former obtain membership
in the EU's single labor market. Since the accession of the EU-8 countries to the EU in May 2004, only eight countries have opened their
labor markets to the new member states. Ireland, Sweden, and the
United Kingdom never had restrictions on workers from the EU-8.
Greece, Finland, Spain, and Portugal lifted restrictions in May 2006.
Italy ended the transitional arrangements in July 2006. France, Belgium, and Luxembourg softened their restrictions on workers from
the EU-8. The transitional arrangements following the enlargement
of the EU^8 allow the EU-15 to postpone the opening of their labor
markets for up to seven years. As a result, bilateral agreements may
retain some importance in facilitating intra-European migration for
the short term.

The current regulatory framework of legal migration flows in the
CIS is characterized by a series of regional and bilateral agreements on
labor activity and social protection of citizens working outside of their
countries. The main regional agreement is the "Agreement on cooperation in the field of labor migration and the social protection of migrant
workers," accepted in 1994 by all of the CIS states. This agreement,
however, did not come into force because it must be implemented
through bilateral agreements, which were never signed (IOM 2002).

Russia has concluded the most bilateral agreements (with nine out
of the eleven CIS member states). Belarus has concluded the next
largest number of bilateral agreements, with six other CIS countries.
Kazakhstan and Ukraine have concluded four each. Kazakhstan, the
main receiving country in Central Asia, has no agreements with its

Central Asian neighbors except for an agreement with the Kyrgyz Republic on the labor activities and the social protection of labor migrants working in the agricultural sector in the border areas.

The bilateral agreement frameworks may fail to meet their stated objectives in many instances. To the degree that the objective of these agreements is to facilitate legal international migration, these do not appear to be always successful as indicated by the high levels of undocumented migration in the region (chapter 1). Large amounts of irregular migration can impose significant social, economic, and national security costs on receiving and sending countries (see box 1). Moreover, undocumented migrants are more likely to be subject to abuse.[9]

The failure of these agreements to stem undocumented migration may reflect several weaknesses. First, there may be high bureaucratic costs for migrants to bear in applying for many of these programs. Also, the high demand for undocumented labor in the receiving countries in the EU and CIS suggest that these agreements may have insufficient quotas.

Finally, most agreements do not contain mechanisms to encourage temporary or circular migration. If it is costly for potential migrants to apply for a space on a temporary migration program, they may well have an incentive to remain abroad—even if through illegal channels by overstaying their visas—for longer periods than they prefer. Surveys with returned migrants conducted for this report found that most migrants would prefer to spend shorter times abroad then return home. Agreements that facilitate this temporary migration while opening up the option to migrate abroad at a later stage with relatively low transactions costs might represent an improvement over the current system.

The Role for International Public Policy: The Contours of a Policy Proposal

The final section of the report identifies some general means through which bilateral migration agreements could be improved, yet all policy suggestions must be heavily qualified. As the United Nation's Global Commission on International Migration detailed, migration involves a complex series of political, economic, and social factors.[10] Given the complexity of migration, it is difficult to provide a "one size fits all" selection of policies to better match the supply and demand for international labor. Further study and perhaps policy experimentation is required to better understand how to improve upon the limitations of the existing framework. Policies will need to be strongly

BOX 1

Possible Costs and Externalities of Illegal Immigration

1. With the exception of sales tax, the income earned by illegal immigrants is not taxable. This represents forgone fiscal revenue.

2. Illegal migrants offer an unfair competitive advantage to firms that employ them over firms that do not.

3. Irregular migrants are not covered by a minimum wage or national and industry wage agreements. They are therefore more likely to undercut the wages of the low skilled.

4. Whether entry is legal or illegal may affect the quality of migrants, even if the legal migration scheme does not select on the basis of skill. Skilled workers or professionals are much more likely to enter if there is a legal channel, even if their qualifications are not a condition of entry.

5. Employers may decide not to abide by health and safety regulations, leading to the potential for migrant death and injury. Police and health services may be called upon to rescue or treat the injured, to investigate the reasons for death, or to bury the dead.

6. Illegal migrants are not screened for diseases and viruses upon arrival, and have little access to health services during their stay. At the same time, they risk having been exposed to illnesses on their journey, especially if they have been smuggled or trafficked. This has the potential to generate large public health externalities because diseases can spread to the native population. Particularly important examples include tuberculosis, which seems to be reemerging in parts of Europe, and HIV, as many trafficked women become involved in the sex industry. By way of illustration, in 2002–03, those apprehended on the Slovak–Ukraine border were found to be suffering from respiratory tract infections, tuberculosis, and scabies.

7. Forced to live underground, and with little access to legitimate employment, migrants are more likely to be exposed to the world of crime.

8. Stigmatization of illegal migrants can undermine social cohesion if it spreads to cover those who entered legally.

9. Illegal migrants may be encouraged to stay longer than they might desire and to remain even when unemployed because of the risks of detection and associated costs of entering and leaving.

Source: World Bank staff.

tailored to the migration-sending and receiving countries in question. Here we detail some elements that could be included in international migration policy to improve the returns to migration for sending and receiving countries and migrants and their families.

The findings of this report suggest that the international governance of migration could be more coherent, and involve closer coordination between migration-sending and -receiving countries. Revised bilateral migration agreements could recognize, organize, and facilitate unskilled labor migration, while acting on both demand and supply to limit undocumented migration. The outcome could be an improvement in the protection given to temporary workers while still offering migration-receiving countries needed labor.

Given variations in national attributes and preferences, such a temporary framework could take a variety of different forms and be organized bilaterally, regionally, or internationally. Yet there are a number of common elements that such policies might include:

• Recognize that the labor market, like any other market, needs to balance supply as well as demand. The framework could explicitly target measures at the supply of low-skilled labor as well as the demand for such labor.

• The new regime could channel migrant labor to sectors or subsectors with little native labor to ensure that migrants are complements to and not substitutes for domestic labor.

• On the demand side, receiving countries need policies that limit the employment of undocumented migrants by offering employers the means to hire legally the workers they need. To promote development and coordinate with the preferences of many ECA migrants to go abroad temporarily, an alternative regime could emphasize circular migration. World Bank surveys for this report found that the majority of migrants would prefer to spend shorter times abroad and then return home (see figure 5).

• To ensure that employment under the new regime is temporary and not permanent, the incentives could be designed to encourage return home when not employed. For example, unemployment and pension benefits could both be portable and only payable in the country of origin.

• Policies should respect the rights of migrants to be treated with dignity while abroad, including clear and transparent rules regarding remuneration, work conditions, or dismissal procedures. Moreover, migrants' rights to appeal to receiving country authorities to adjudicate disputes and protect themselves from crime could be communicated and enforced.

Bilateral migration agreements that include some or all of these features could have a number of advantages over many existing policies:

FIGURE 5
Migrants' Preferences for Short versus Long-Term Migration

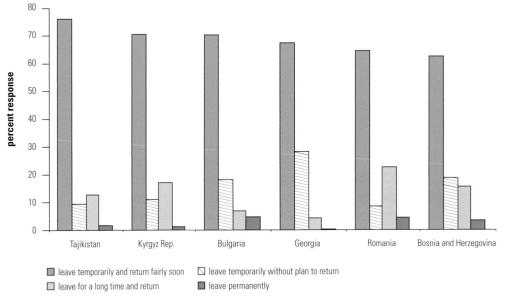

Source: World Bank surveys with returned migrants.

- Agreements could stimulate circular migration, allow employers in receiving countries to obtain affordable nontraded services while respecting the law and reduce incentives for potential migrants to use illegal means of entry.

- Such an approach seems commensurate with migrants' preferences to spend shorter periods abroad and the need for receiving countries to obtain labor services but not necessarily absorb a permanent population of migrants.

- Moreover, in the sending country, increased circular migration, encouraged by the lowering of transportation costs, could reduce many of the negative social effects that result from the separation of families during long-term migration[11] and reduce the incidence and degree of 'brain drain" from migration-sending countries in ECA.[12]

- For undocumented migrants, a regime with these features—with creative incentives for legal migration—could strengthen the rights that migrants receive in the receiving country and allow them to obtain social protection benefits that are out of reach today. Undocumented migrants have no access to adjudicative processes when abroad and hence have no legal recourse to oppose abuse. By drying up the incentives and opportunities for undocumented hiring, legal protections for large stocks of foreign workers could be expanded.

Methodology

Like all studies on migration, the analysis in this report is supported by a relatively poor and inconsistent base of underlying data and information. The problems with counting international migrants and measuring workers' remittances are notoriously difficult. Official estimates are known to contain very large errors in both overstating and understating actual stocks and flows. Such problems are exacerbated by the prevalence of undocumented migration and, as an artifact unique to the ECA, by the problem that many people who had lived permanently in one location suddenly were counted as "foreign-born" and hence as migrants when national boundaries were adjusted after the dissolution of the Soviet Union, Yugoslavia, and Czechoslovakia. These limitations make it difficult to document migration, draw inferences on its impact, and prescribe policies to optimize the role of migration in enhancing growth and poverty reduction.

This report addresses the data problem by employing a multidimensional approach that draws conclusions and inferences from several different methods (see box 2). Findings rely on cumulative evidence from the various elements that each alone suffers from weaknesses but when combined provide some degree of confidence in the results.

The Report in Perspective

This report is part of a series of World Bank studies that take stock of the state of the transition economies of Eastern Europe and the former Soviet Union as well as Turkey almost 15 years after the start of the transition. It is designed to advance understanding, promote debate, and initiate a dialogue on the role that policy could play in optimizing the returns from migration[13] for (a) the migration-sending countries; (b) the receiving countries; and (c) migrants themselves by

- Assessing the importance and characteristics of migration in Eastern Europe and Central Asia and documenting the trends of the last 15 years;

- Explaining the economic, political, and social drivers of labor migration and how they may impact migration in the near term (next 10–15 years) before demographic influences dominate;

BOX 2
<hr>

Methodology

The report relies on five different methodologies:

1. Cross-country statistical analyses of migration flow and stock levels and rates. In collecting a database of migration statistics, several different sources are drawn upon:
   a. Administrative data obtained from national population estimates
   b. Decennial population censuses

2. Comparative historical analyses of the Southern European countries' experiences with international migration to develop some insight into migration from ECA countries.

3. Statistical estimations of the determinants of migration and the economic impact of remittances.

4. Model-based simulations of the impact of adjusting economic and labor-market policies on creating the incentive for circular migration while drying up the market for undocumented migration.

5. The results of on-the-ground surveys with returned migrants in six ECA countries: Bosnia and Herzegovina, Bulgaria, Georgia, the Kyrgyz Republic, Romania, and Tajikistan.[a]

Each of these methods has fairly well-established strengths and weaknesses. The poorness of migration and remittance data makes statistical testing difficult. Comparative historical analysis may yield valuable qualitative insights, yet the past may not be a reliable guide to understanding the future, particularly in a volatile transitioning environment. Model-based simulations are a useful and flexible tool but themselves rely on the underlying migration data and a set of assumptions regarding the expectations of how international labor markets behave. Finally, the surveys of returned migrants provide a rich base of information yet the surveys may not be representative of all migrants.

When two or more of these methods indicate a particular conclusion or inference, however, some confidence is lent to the results. This report attempts, wherever possible, to draw conclusions when more than one method supports the statements and to report those instances where the application of more than one method produces contradictory evidence. In this way, it hopes to establish as firm an empirical base as possible for the conclusions drawn.

a. Further information on the survey methodology and the data will be made available through the Web site for the Europe and Central Asia Region of the World Bank (www.worldbank.org/ECA).

- Evaluating the current framework of programs to manage international labor flows among the ECA economies and between these economies and Western Europe and the key migration-receiving countries in the CIS; and

• Suggesting the broad contours of reforms to enhance the gains from migration by modifying international agreements and strengthening the policies and institutions of the migration-sending countries.

Endnotes

1. This report uses the World Bank's delineation of the zone of formerly centrally planned economies in Europe and Central Asia. Countries included in this region include Albania, Armenia, Azerbaijan, Belarus, Bosnia and Herzegovina, Bulgaria, Croatia, Czech Republic, Estonia, FYR Macedonia, Georgia, Hungary, Kazakhstan, Kyrgyz Republic, Latvia, Lithuania, Moldova, Poland, Romania, Russian Federation, Serbia and Montenegro, Slovak Republic, Slovenia, Tajikistan, Turkey, Turkmenistan, Ukraine, and Uzbekistan. Although the Czech Republic and Slovenia graduated from World Bank borrower status in 2005 and 2004, respectively, they are included in this analysis because we analyze trends spanning the entire transition process. The glossary spells out terminology, including country groupings associated with the different names used.
2. A full statistical appendix is found in appendix 1.2.
3. World Bank 2006.
4. See appendix 1.1 for a discussion of the survey methodology.
5. See De Luna Martinez (2005).
6. Studies using household survey data in Mexico suggest that while both internal and international remittances have a positive impact on incomes in rural areas, international migration has a greater impact. These studies also suggest that remittances tend to have an equalizing effect (in terms of income inequality) in high-migration areas but not so in low-migration areas. For more information see Ozden and Schiff (2006), which refers to Mora and Taylor (2004), and Lopez Cordoba (2004).
7. The rapid growth rate produced a reduction of 1,900,000 persons active in agriculture, and 800,000 emigrants (INE).
8. According to the transitional arrangements (2+3+2 regulation) the EU-15 can apply national rules on access to their labor markets for the first two years after enlargement. The diverse national measures have resulted in several legally different migration regimes. In May 2006, the second phase of the transitional period started, which allowed member states to continue national measures for up to another three years. At the end of this period (2009) all member states will be invited to open their labor markets entirely. Only if countries can show serious disturbances in the labor market, or a threat of such disturbances, will they be allowed to resort to a safeguard clause for a maximum period of two years. From 2011 all member states will have to comply with European Commission rules regulating the free movement of labor.
9. See appendix 4.3 for further information on undocumented migration and some of the risks that it poses to migration sending and receiving countries and migrants themselves.

10. UN 2005.
11. For further information on the impact of longer-term migration on communities left behind, see appendix 4.4.
12. To date, there is not a good understanding of the prevalence and impact of brain drain in the ECA region. For a summary of the existing state of knowledge, see appendix 4.5.
13. This report considers anyone who is not native born to be a migrant, owing to the limitations of UN data.

CHAPTER 1

Overview of Migration Trends in Europe and Central Asia, 1990–2004

Some of the trends and motivations for migration in the Europe and Central Asia (ECA) region are similar to those found elsewhere in the world. However, many of the migration movements that have taken place since 1990 are unique to the region, given the circumstances of economic transition, political and social liberalization, and the breakup of three federal states. Figure 1.1 shows how the factors influencing migration have changed from the communist period to the present. This chapter provides an overview of some of the main migration trends that have taken place across the region over the past 15 years, with a focus on international movements among countries.

Migration in the ECA region is both large by international standards and unique in that the region is both a major receiver and sender of migrants. Figure 1.2 exhibits the ECA region and selected ECA countries in terms of their shares of foreign-born populations. Excluding movements between industrial countries, ECA accounts for over one-third of world emigration and immigration. There are 35 million foreign-born residents in ECA countries, including 13 million in the Russian Federation, 7 million in Ukraine, 3 million in Kazakhstan, 3 million in Poland, and 1.5 million in Turkey. Furthermore, several ECA countries are among the top 10 sending and receiving countries of migrants worldwide. Russia is home to the second largest number of migrants in the world after the United States; Ukraine is

FIGURE 1.1

Transition of the Migration System in the Europe and Central Asia Region

Migration under Central Planning in the Europe and Central Asia Region	Migration during the Transition Period in the Europe and Central Asia Region
Eight countries in the region (only five remain in their pretransition borders)	Twenty-seven countries following the breakup of three federal states
Migration was very tightly controlled	Much less control over migration
Prices were administratively set and wages and income were not very differentiated across sectors or regions	Prices are market determined and income is increasingly distributed among people, sectors, and regions
A massive and elaborate system of subsidies caused certain sectors and regions to be "over-valued" and others to be "under-valued"	Wages and prices have adjusted to their market-clearing value
Migration control efforts were aimed mainly at keeping people in a country	Migration control is aimed at both keeping people in and outside a country and, in general, migration control systems are poorly developed
Little involvement in international institutions and foreign trade	Open economies, involvement with international institutions, and "globalization"

Source: World Bank staff.

fourth after Germany; and Kazakhstan and Poland are respectively ninth and tenth.

Migration patterns in the region follow a broad biaxial pattern: on one axis a migration system developed among the countries of Western, Central, and Eastern Europe and on the other a system of movement arose among the countries of the Commonwealth of Independent States (CIS). However, this system is not exclusively bipolar. Though the majority of migrants from Central and Eastern European countries move into Western Europe, the same is true for many migrants from the poorer CIS economies, particularly Moldova. While the majority of migrants from Central Asia travel to the resource-rich CIS countries (particularly Russia and Kazakhstan) many move west in search of higher earnings, toward the European Union (EU) and Turkey.

The creation of many new countries following the breakup of the Soviet Union produced "new" migrants (long-term, foreign-born residents) who may not have physically moved, but were defined as migrants under UN practice. In addition to the issue of these "statistical" migrants, there are numerous other problems in analyzing migration trends across the region based on available data. This chapter and the report in general are an attempt to pull together and analyze all available migration data to gain as complete a picture as possible of migration trends over the past 15 years; thus, the issue of the veracity of migration data is a constant theme.

The chapter begins with a description of some of the problems involved in measuring migration among the ECA countries during

FIGURE 1.2

Migration in Top 10 Sending and Receiving Countries and by Region, 2003

Immigration into the top 10 receiving countries and by Region, 2003 (stock of immigrants)

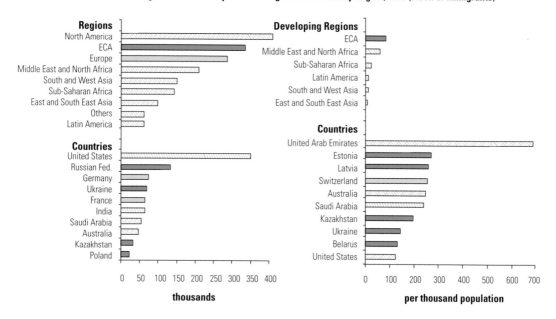

Emigration from the top 10 sending countries and by Region, 2003 (stock of immigrants)

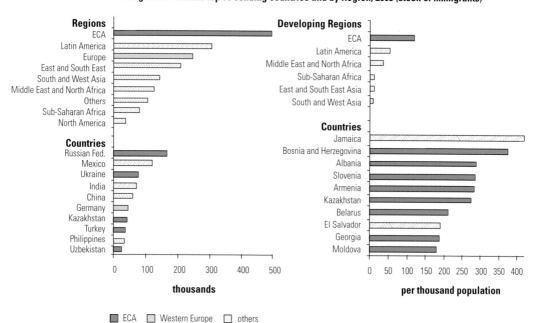

Sources: UN Population Division 2003 and Walmsley, Ahmed, and Parsons 2005.

the transition period. Then using the data that are available, it analyzes the impact of migration on overall levels of population change in the ECA countries. The next section provides a broad overview of migration flows across the ECA region during the period 2000–03, a recent period when most of the ethnic migration had already taken place and flows were dominated by the economic migration flows that are expected to predominate in the future. Following this are discussions of refugee and internally displaced population movements, and transit and irregular migration. A further section looks at the main migration partners of each ECA country. Finally, the chapter looks at possible future migration trends in the region.[1]

Problems with Measuring Migration in ECA

There are three main sources for migration data in the ECA countries, as well as in countries outside the region. These are population censuses, usually conducted once a decade; administrative statistics of persons crossing international borders; and surveys. This final category includes surveys targeted directly at migrant populations, as well as surveys designed for other purposes where migration-related questions are asked.

Population censuses usually include questions that measure lifetime migration. For instance, the last Soviet census, conducted in January 1989, included questions on place of birth, whether the respondent had been living in his or her present residence continuously since birth, and if not, when he or she had migrated to that place. All of the ECA countries conducted population censuses between the years 1989 and 1992 and most conducted another census between 1999 and 2002. The more recent round of censuses typically included a question on citizenship, though this question was frequently not posed in the censuses conducted around 1990. Some also included questions about persons temporarily absent. The 2002 Russian census also included a set of questions for those persons temporarily residing in Russia, although the total of a quarter million persons enumerated were thought to significantly underestimate the true figure.

Whereas censuses attempt to count stocks of migrants, administrative statistics are counts of flows of migrants. In most cases, data on total international border crossings also record information on the age, sex, and country of previous residence or intended destination, and other characteristics of migrants. It is the change, and in some cases breakdown, of systems for measuring migration flows where the ECA countries have suffered the most.

Surveys are useful for obtaining qualitative information about migrants and to serve as a check on the veracity of flow statistics from administrative sources. An increasing number of surveys of migrants have been conducted across the ECA region, both by the countries themselves as well as by international organizations such as the International Organization for Migration (IOM).

Several reasons make migration flows in ECA challenging to capture. First, the type, direction, and magnitude of the flows in the region have changed dramatically since the beginning of economic transition, liberalization of societies (including increased freedom of movement), and the emergence of 22 new states. What had previously been internal boundaries have now become international borders. Migration in ECA, which was once subject to considerable state control within several self-contained migration spaces, now rests in the hands of individuals who have the ability to transit across new and rather porous international boundaries. In the former Soviet Union, the propiska or resident permit system required persons to register before being allowed to migrate to a new location. However, the visa-free travel among the CIS countries for most of the 1990s contributed to an environment of porous borders, which made the recording of migration flows difficult. The extent to which the successor states have instituted systems to properly measure total migration flows and to disaggregate these flows by age, gender, nationality, and other characteristics useful for analysis and policy making varies considerably.

The previous systems for measuring migration in the centrally planned countries of the ECA are wholly inadequate for capturing movements across the newly independent states. In their initial years, the newly independent states had to erect the elements of government apparatus, including independent statistical systems to measure social and economic trends such as migration movements. With other elements of state building causing greater concern, building systems for measuring migration often received low priority. Many of these issues in migration measurement are unique to the newly independent states of the ECA region.

A second set of problems with proper migration measurement is endemic to all countries. Definitions, underlying concepts, sources, and reporting systems differ significantly between countries, making available migration statistics fragmentary. The boundaries between extended travel, seasonal work, and economic migration are blurred. In most cases it is not clear whether an individual reported as "migrant" is a long-term mover, a temporary mover, a seasonal worker, someone on the move to another destination, an individual transitioning through a territory, a returning migrant, a member of a family already residing abroad with no intention to work, a student (who may or may not undertake part-time employment), a refugee, a member of the staff of a foreign company in the country, or some other category of migrant.

Third, undocumented migration plays an important role in today's migrant flows to, from, and within ECA, as well as in many other parts of the world. Reported data refers to legal migrants, based most often on residence or work permits. Even countries in the region with seemingly well-developed statistical systems often are not able to record migration completely. Decennial population censuses are used to adjust and calibrate population totals. For instance, in Lithuania, there was a downward adjustment of the population by over 200,000, or more than 5 percent of the population, following the census conducted there in April 2001. Roughly the same magnitude of adjustment took place in Estonia following its March 2000 census, when it adjusted the population total downward by 67,000, or about 5 percent. Similar post-census adjustments downsizing the resident population were made in the Czech Republic, Poland, and the Slovak Republic. Among the surprises in the Russian census conducted in October 2002 was that the total population was 1.2 million higher than the previous estimate, mainly because of an undercount of migration.

These differences between population estimates and census figures in the ECA countries are worth comparing to the experience of the United States, long a traditional migration destination. Before the 2000 census in the United States, the population was estimated at 275 million. That census revealed a count of 281 million, a difference of 6 million, almost all attributable to an undercount of the huge migration into the United States during the 1990s.[2] The United States has long grappled with an issue that the ECA states are only beginning to deal with in trying to estimate temporary or circular migration. Until recently, most of the ECA states recorded only long-term or permanent moves and much of the movements over the past decade are of a temporary or circular nature.

The breakup of the Soviet Union, Yugoslavia, and Czechoslovakia created a large number of "statistical migrants." The commonly accepted UN definition describes a "migrant" as a person living outside his or her country of birth. As used here, statistical migrants refers to persons who migrated internally while those countries existed, thus not qualifying as a migrant under the UN definition at the time, but who began to be counted as migrants when those countries broke apart even though they did not move again. Having a large number of these statistical migrants has hampered analysis of migration patterns across the ECA region because of the difficulty of separating those who moved during the communist period, before the start of transition and independence, and those who moved later for ethnic or economic reasons. However, with data that are available from population censuses, it is possible to get a fairly good idea of the total number of statistical migrants and changes in their numbers since the breakup of the countries.

Table 1.1 shows the population of the Soviet Union by place of birth in 1989, at the time of the last Soviet census. At that time, 2.4 million persons or 0.8 percent of the population had been born outside the Soviet Union.[3] This low figure is not surprising because for most of the period between the end of World War II and the breakup of the Soviet Union, there was little migration either into or out of the Soviet Union and little shifting of international borders. In fact, the listed figure of the Soviet population being classified as migrants is likely a considerable overestimate because it also includes those not indicating their place of birth. If similar data from the 2002 Russian census is any guide, about one-quarter had actually been born outside the former Soviet Union and about three-quarters did not indicate their place of birth. Thus, the true figure of the migrant population was likely less than 1 million or only about 0.3 percent of the population.

TABLE 1.1

Population by Place of Birth in the USSR, 1989

(thousands)

Place of permanent residence	Born in republic of current residence	Born elsehwere in USSR	Born outside USSR	Total population	Born in republic of current residence	Born elsehwere in USSR	Born outside USSR
USSR	255,409	27,955	2,378	100.0	89.4	9.8	0.8
RSFSR	135,550	10,478	994	100.0	92.2	7.1	0.7
Ukrainskaia SSR	44,332	6,665	455	100.0	86.2	13.0	0.9
Belorusskaia SSR	8,883	1,213	55	100.0	87.5	12.0	0.5
Uzbekskaia SSR	18,108	1,649	53	100.0	91.4	8.3	0.3
Kazakhskaia SSR	12,715	3,536	214	100.0	77.2	21.5	1.3
Gruzinskaia SSR	5,039	349	13	100.0	93.3	6.5	0.2
Azerbaidzhanskaia SSR	6,604	398	19	100.0	94.1	5.7	0.3
Litovskaia SSR	3,299	356	19	100.0	89.8	9.7	0.5
Moldavskaia SSR	3,739	579	18	100.0	86.2	13.3	0.4
Latviiskaia SSR	1,975	678	14	100.0	74.0	25.4	0.5
Kirgizskaia SSR	3,586	638	34	100.0	84.2	15.0	0.8
Tadzhikskaia SSR	4,650	433	9	100.0	91.3	8.5	0.2
Armianskaia SSR	2,570	267	467	100.0	77.8	8.1	14.1
Turkmenskaia SSR	3,205	311	7	100.0	91.0	8.8	0.2
Estonskaia SSR	1,155	403	8	100.0	73.7	25.7	0.5

Source: Eastview Publications and CIS Statistical Committee; USSR Census Results 1989 CD-ROM.

Note: Data are as of January 1989.

However, there was considerable migration among the states of the former Soviet Union. In 1989, there were 28 million persons who were residing in a republic other than the one in which they were born. This figure amounted to 9.8 percent of the Soviet population, which should be regarded as the number of "statistical migrants" that were created by the breakup of the Soviet Union, greatly contributing to the increase in the world stock of migrants. The bulk of these individuals were in the three Slavic states, Uzbekistan, and Kazakhstan. In percentage terms, the countries with the largest migrant stock populations were Estonia, Latvia, and Kazakhstan. All of these countries were prime destinations for Russian and Russian-speaking migrants during the period after World War II.

Migration and Population Change

An analysis of migration and population change among the ECA states begins at a broad level by dividing the countries into groups according to their recent patterns of migration and natural increase in population (figure 1.3; data underlying this figure are in appendix 2). Natural increase is the difference between the number of births and deaths and is a function of the age structure of the population and levels of fertility and mortality. As will be discussed below, differential rates of natural increase among countries are a major driver of migration within the ECA region and elsewhere. A positive natural increase occurs where the number of births exceeds the number of deaths, which is the situation in nearly all countries in the world. Negative natural increase is where the number of deaths in a population exceeds the number of births. The 14 ECA countries shown below with a negative natural increase or a natural decrease, along with Italy and Germany, are among a small group of countries where this is occurring. So many ECA countries are part of this group because fertility levels have fallen steeply during the transition period, to 1.3 children per woman or less; such levels are unsustainable for natural population increase.[4] These figures are compared to net migration, which is the difference between the number of immigrants to a country and emigrants from a country.

There are two countries in the ECA region that have both a natural increase and positive net migration; however, neither truly belongs in this category because both suffer from data problems that affect their migration counts. Turkmenistan has some rather unrealistically high population estimates, which cause net migration figures to appear unrealistically high. Bosnia and Herzegovina suffers from

FIGURE 1.3

Natural Increase (Decrease) and Net Migration in the ECA Region, 2000–03

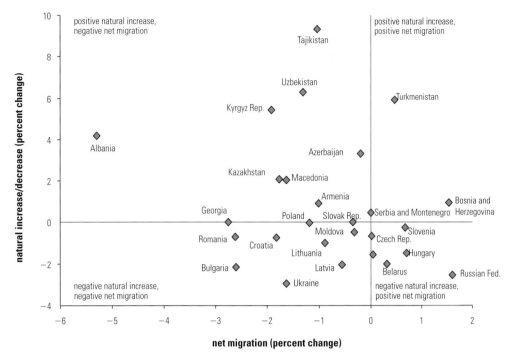

Source: National statistical office of the ECA countries and UNICEF, TransMONEE Database.

incomplete and inconsistent counts of migration, with some years showing emigration and some immigration. Furthermore, in recent years, there has been an undetermined amount of return migration of some of the refugee populations that left during the mid-1990s. Based on this evidence, both of these countries should probably be grouped in the category of countries with positive natural increase and negative net migration.

There are 10 ECA countries that combine natural increase and net emigration (12 if the two mentioned above are included). This is the pattern for most of the world's countries. This includes the countries of Central Asia, the Caucasus, and many of the former Yugoslav states. With their faster-growing populations, especially youth populations, migration pressures in these countries will likely persist into the future.

A third group of countries comprises those that combine having more deaths than births and more immigrants than emigrants. These are Russia and Belarus in the CIS and four of the smaller new EU member states. While all have had more immigrants than emigrants over recent years, in all but Russia, the population increases as a result of net migration are small, amounting to less than 1 percent of their populations. As pointed out elsewhere in this report, Russia has become a major migration magnet within the CIS, with a measured population increase from migration of 4 percent since 1990 and perhaps an equal amount of undocumented migration.

A fourth group are nine ECA countries where populations are declining because they experience both more deaths than births and more emigrants than immigrants. This includes Ukraine and Moldova, the three Baltic states, and four Central European countries, including the largest, Poland. In all of these countries, both trends are expected to continue well into the future, causing large population declines as well as rapid aging of their populations.

Figures 1.4a and 1.4b show the net population change from migration over the period 1989–2003 for the CIS and western ECA countries, respectively.[5] From this figure, one part of the region's bipolar migration story of the past decade and a half can be clearly seen, with Russia showing by far the largest population gain from migration. The impact on those other few countries with population gains from migration has been minimal. Most of the migrants into Russia consist of persons migrating from the other states of the former Soviet Union, which show large population declines from migration. There have been several countries in the region that have transitioned from net emigration to net immigration including Belarus, Slovenia, Hungary, Croatia, and Serbia and Montenegro.

Of the five ECA countries with population declines of over 15 percent, four are in the southern tier of the former Soviet Union. The three Baltic states have had considerable out-migration in large part because of the emigration of large numbers of Russians and Russian-speakers in the years immediately following the breakup of the Soviet Union. In southeast Europe, Albania and Bulgaria have also had emigrations of large portions of their populations.

These figures are based on counts of the long-term, permanent migration of the populations and do not include short-term or undocumented counts of population movements. These figures also understate the potential impact of migration because it is usually the better-educated segments of the population and those in the early stages of their working lives who migrate in the largest numbers.

Major Migration Flows in the ECA Region

As mentioned often throughout this report, proper measurement of migration is difficult, even for high-income countries with well-devel-

FIGURE 1.4

Net Migration in Western ECA and the CIS

a. Net migration in the CIS, 1989–2003

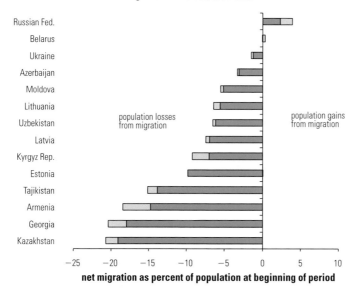

net migration as percent of population at beginning of period

b. Net migration in Western ECA, 1989–2003

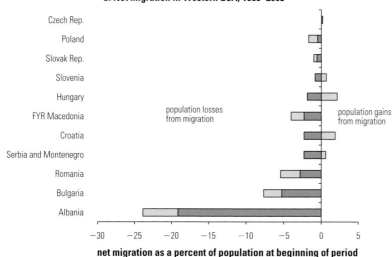

net migration as a percent of population at beginning of period

■ 1989–99   □ 2000–03

Source: National statistical offices and UNICEF, TransMONEE Database.

oped statistical systems. For the ECA countries, measuring migration during this period of rapid social, economic, and political change has been especially difficult. However, by compiling migration data from several different sources and triangulating, a fairly complete picture of the major flows taking place within the region can be obtained. It is helpful to keep in mind that international migration involves a flow between two countries and that when a person migrates, that person ideally should be recorded twice, by both the sending and receiving country. Even so, there is considerable variation in how countries record migrants; some countries track movements of people by place of previous or next residence, some by citizenship, and some by various other methods.

Table 1.2 shows the migration flows among major blocs of ECA countries and origins and destinations of flows outside the region for the years 2000 to 2003. This was a period after much of the ethnic-induced migration associated with the breakup of the Soviet Union, Yugoslavia, and Czechoslovakia had already taken place and the magnitude of migration flows had settled into a more "normal" pattern influenced primarily by economic incentives. The table was compiled by collecting all available data on migration by origin and destination country according to both residence and citizenship definitions; this was followed by calculating a "maximum" matrix of the highest of each pair of flows. Migration data for 52 countries were collected, comprising the 28 ECA countries, 21 countries in Western Europe, plus Canada, Israel, and the United States. Sufficient data were available to fill about 90 percent of the matrix. Most of the cells that were not able to be filled represented flows between pairs of countries for which there is not known to be substantial migration (for example, between Iceland and Turkmenistan). Thus, the assembled data are thought to be a fairly complete representation of migration involving ECA countries during this period.

The data partially support the story that two major migration blocs have developed involving migration of the ECA countries. As suspected by other and anecdotal evidence, there has been considerable migration from western ECA to Western Europe and considerable migration from the rest of the CIS into Russia. At the same time, there are other flows developing that were not suspected and not that readily apparent from other data. About equal percentages of migrants from the CIS countries other than Russia (other CIS) travel to Russia as to Western Europe, with Ukraine and Kazakhstan being the major sending countries and Germany the major receiver. Over 70 percent of migrants from western ECA go to Western Europe. At the same time, there is also considerable flow from Western Europe to western ECA. Flows between Germany and three countries make up the bulk of this overall total, that is, flows from Germany to Poland, Serbia and Montenegro, and Turkey. These figures not only represent the return of persons who had previously migrated but also indicate considerable "churning," as for each of these three flows, there are also large flows in the opposite direction.

TABLE 1.2
Migration Flows Involving ECA Countries, 2000–03

TABLE 1.2A
Total Migration Flows Involving ECA Countries and Major Partners, 2000–03

From	To					
	Russia	Other CIS	Western ECA	Western Europe	U.S., Canada, Israel	Total (emigration)
Russia	0	272,929	17,882	85,468	53,539	429,818
Other CIS	319,514	159,652	85,104	280,843	90,265	935,378
Western ECA	22,896	32,820	274,762	1,300,289	149,045	1,779,812
Western Europe	74,460	82,705	640,052	2,808,366	269,253	3,874,837
U.S., Canada, Israel	8,466	6,342	16,973	457,664	142,762	632,207
Total (immigration)	425,336	554,448	1,034,773	4,932,630	704,864	

TABLE 1.2B
Percent of Total Emigration

From	To					
	Russia	Other CIS	Western ECA	Western Europe	U.S., Canada, Israel	Total (emigration)
Russia	0	63	4	20	12	100
Other CIS	34	17	9	30	10	100
Western ECA	1	2	15	73	8	100
Western Europe	2	2	17	72	7	100
U.S., Canada, Israel	1	1	3	72	23	100

TABLE 1.2C
Percent of Total Immigration

From	To					
	Russia	Other CIS	Western ECA	Western Europe	U.S., Canada, Israel	
Russia	0	49	2	2	8	
Other CIS	75	29	8	6	13	
Western ECA	5	6	27	26	21	
Western Europe	18	15	62	57	38	
U.S., Canada, Israel	2	1	2	9	20	
Total (immigration)	100	100	100	100	100	

Source: See text for explanation of how data were compiled.

Note: "Other CIS" consists of Armenia, Azerbaijan, Belarus, Georgia, Kyrgyz Republic, Kazakhstan, Moldova, Tajikistan, Turkmenistan, Ukraine, and Uzbekistan. "Western ECA" consists of Albania, Bosnia and Herzegovina, Bulgaria, Serbia and Montenegro, the Czech Republic, Estonia, Croatia, Hungary, Lithuania, Latvia, FYR Macedonia, Poland, Romania, the Slovak Republic, Slovenia, and Turkey. "Western Europe" consists of Austria, Belgium, Switzerland, Cyprus, Germany, Denmark, Spain, Finland, France, Greece, Ireland, Iceland, Italy, Liechtenstein, Luxembourg, Malta, the Netherlands, Norway, Portugal, Sweden, and the United Kingdom.

On the immigration side, Russia receives 75 percent of its immigrants from other CIS countries. There are minimal flows from the CIS states in the western ECA, with over half consisting of migrants from Ukraine to the Czech Republic and from Moldova into Romania; Ukraine and Moldova are thus unique in having significant migrant flows both to Western Europe and to resource-rich CIS countries. The largest flows into Western Europe are from other Western European countries, making up about half of the total. However, flows into Western Europe from western ECA make up about one-third of the total.

Figure 1.5 shows the largest country-to-country migration streams involving a CIS country for the period 2000–03. Much of this is driven by the gravity of proximity and population size; thus, it is not surprising that Russia is either a source or destination of most of these flows. The largest flows that do not include Russia are flows from Kazakhstan to Germany and Ukraine to Germany. The flow from Ukraine to Germany can be explained by proximity, population size, and large differences in per capita income, while the flow from Kazakhstan to Germany can be explained by the fact that Kazakhstan was home to the largest concentration of Germans in the former Soviet Union and, initially, Germany had a rather liberal law for the return of the *Aussiedler.* The pull of Russia from the other CIS countries is clearly evident from the map.

Figure 1.6 shows the largest country-to-country migration streams involving a western ECA country for the same period. A quite different pattern emerges than among CIS states, with a country outside

FIGURE 1.5

Largest Migration Flows Involving a CIS Country, 2000–03

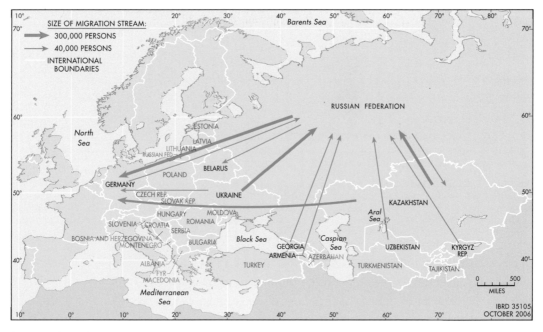

Source: World Bank staff estimates based on analysis of migration statistics from a variety of sending and receiving countries.

Erratum

Migration and Remittances: Eastern Europe and the Former Soviet Union

The map below should have appeared as figure 1.6 on page 37.

FIGURE 1.6
Largest Migration Flows Involving a Western ECA Country, 2000–03

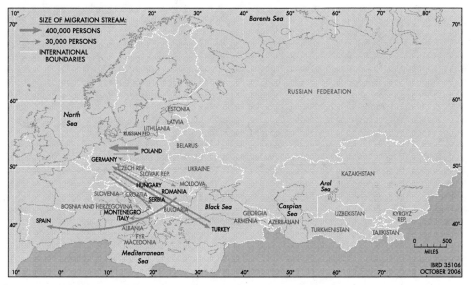

Source: World Bank staff estimates based on analysis of migration statistics from a variety of sending and receiving countries.

FIGURE 1.6

Largest Migration Flows Involving a Western ECA Country, 2000–03

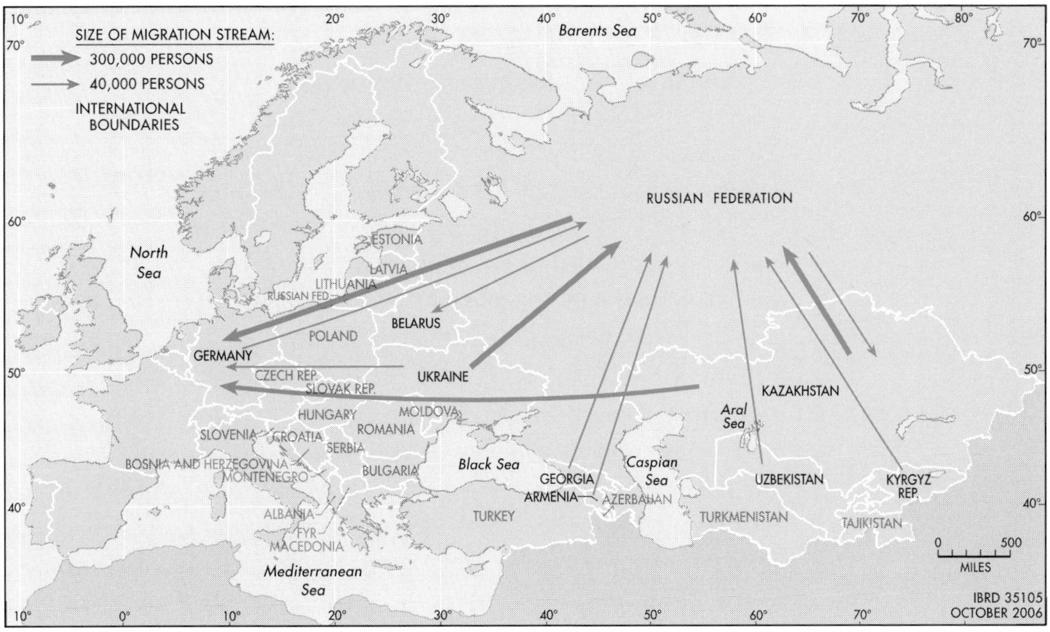

Source: World Bank staff estimates based on analysis of migration statistics from a variety of sending and receiving countries.

the region, Germany, being the major driver of migration for these countries. Again the gravity of migration encompassing proximity, population size, and the size of the German economy explains many of the notable patterns. None of the largest flows involved two countries within the region because there are only two countries, Turkey and Poland, that can be considered sizable (or at least medium-sized comparable to the largest Western European countries). What is interesting is that all of the largest flows involving Germany are two-way flows with large amounts of return migration.

Refugees and Internally Displaced Persons

Each of the ECA countries is an ethnic homeland. However, many other ethnic homelands exist at the subnational level. The boundaries of many of these were drawn arbitrarily by outside authorities and do not necessarily coincide with what different ethnic groups regard as their rightful homelands. During the communist period, there was considerable migration of different ethnic groups to regions or countries outside of their homelands. When Yugoslavia and the Soviet

Union broke apart, they did so along their ethnic seams. Most of this occurred peacefully but was accompanied by some diaspora migration. However, in some cases these cleavages instigated considerable ethnoterritorial conflict; as a result, forced migration became the predominant form of migration in some parts of the region. Figure 1.7 shows the major displacements that took place in the former Yugoslavia in 1995 at about the peak of the conflict there. Figure 1.8 shows the same for the former Soviet Union for the mid-1990s.

Figure 1.9 shows the temporal trends in the numbers of refugees and internally displaced persons (IDPs) across the ECA region between 1989 and 2003.[6] The figure shows a combination of actual and statistical trends. During the late communist period, the numbers of refugees and IDPs were rather small. However, estimates rely on imperfect data counting measures; none of these countries had acceded to the 1951 Geneva Convention on Refugees and hence did not have mechanisms in place for recognizing and counting refugees. As the newly independent states in the region and others began to erect institutions capable of enumerating refugees and asylum seekers, their numbers began to increase. Thus, part of the rise from 1989 to the mid-1990s is statistical. However, a large part of the increase is real, brought about by the increase in the number of persons dis-

FIGURE 1.7

Main Displaced Populations from the Former Yugoslavia, December 1995

Source: Humanitarian Issues Working Group HIWG06/6, December 11, 1996.

FIGURE 1.8

Main Displaced Population from the Former Soviet Union, Mid–1990s

Source: Based on IOM, CIS Migration Report 1996.

Note: Map is designed to broadly illustrate major refugee and IDP flows at the time, based upon best available information, and is not intended to be authoritative or precise.

FIGURE 1.9

Refugees and Internally Displaced Persons in the ECA Region, 1989–2003

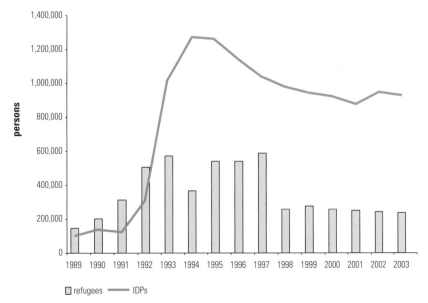

Source: UNICEF, TransMONEE database.

placed as a result of the breakup of the Soviet Union and Yugoslavia and the resultant ethnoterritorial disputes.

The number of refugees increased from 145,000 in 1989 to over a half million during the years 1992 to 1997 (with the exception of 1994), but fell to about 237,000 in 2003. It should be kept in mind that these figures refer to the numbers of refugees and IDPs *within* each of the ECA countries, *not* from the countries. Refugees, by definition, have crossed an international border, whereas IDPs have not. If the number of refugees *from* the ECA countries were counted instead, the number would certainly be higher because many of those from the former Yugoslav states fled to Western Europe. Partly for these reasons, the number of IDPs is comparatively much higher than for the number of refugees, rising from about 100,000 in 1989 to over a million during the years 1993 to 1997 before declining slightly to 927,000 in 2003. In 2003, the largest concentrations of IDPs were in Azerbaijan (576,000) and Georgia (262,000). These numbers are down only slightly from peaks in the mid-1990s because the conflicts that gave rise to them continue to persist without any permanent settlement.

Figure 1.10 shows the countries in the ECA region with the largest concentrations of refugees, IDPs, and "others of concern" at the end of 2004, according to the UNHCR. Overall, the ECA region accounts for 7.4 percent of the world population in total but contains 19 percent of

FIGURE 1.10

Largest Numbers of Refugees, IDPs, and Others of Concern in the ECA Region, 2004

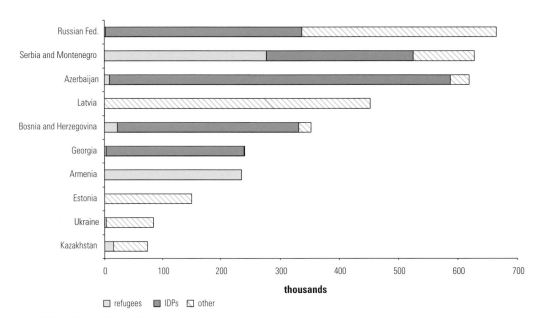

Source: UNHCR, 2004 Global Refugee Trends (http://www.unhcr.org).

the total number of asylum seekers, refugees, and others of concern. In particular, the ECA region accounts for a disproportionate share of the world's total number of IDPs (32 percent), because of past or ongoing conflicts in Russia, Georgia, and Azerbaijan in the CIS, and in Serbia and Montenegro and Bosnia and Herzegovina in the former Yugoslavia. Substantial proportions of ECA migrants also fall into the category of "others of concern," which generally includes asylum seekers, returned refugees, returned IDPs, and various other categories of (usually forced) migrants. In ECA countries, this includes various categories of stateless persons and, in Latvia and Estonia, the large Russian-speaking groups of noncitizens. Aside from those two countries, the ECA countries with the largest numbers of persons of concern are mostly those where there has been or continues to be conflict. The region also accounts for a disproportionate share of others of concern because of the large number of stateless or noncitizens living in various countries. Many of the original ethnoterritorial conflicts that gave rise to these groups of forced migrants remain unresolved more than a decade after they first arose.

Transit and Undocumented Migration in the ECA Region

With the opening up of the ECA countries to the rest of the world and the liberalization of migration, transit, illegal, and undocumented migration has become an issue for countries in the region, and particularly for those that were not previously under communist rule. Some migrants (from within and outside ECA) hoping to migrate to the United States, Japan, or Western Europe seek transit through ECA countries. Some transit migrants then conclude that this hope is unrealistic and settle in the transit country, which typically is poorer than the West but more developed than their home country. Russia is emerging as a transit as well as a key sending and receiving country. Ukraine, Romania, and Azerbaijan are examples of other countries in the ECA region that have significant transit migrant populations. This section first considers the motivations of migrants who come to the ECA. It then considers the experience of the host countries from two perspectives: the statistical frequency of undocumented migration (a figure notably difficult to calculate), and the policy decisions of ECA states for regulating this phenomenon.

Migration Experiences

The decision to migrate, as well as the choice of destination, reflects a careful calculation of relative risks and income-earning potential for those who end up in ECA countries. A U.K. Economic and Social Research Council survey of Fujianese Chinese finds that Europe was the second choice for refugees unable to get to Japan or the United States but who wanted to make money abroad within a set time. Fujianese migrants choose their preferred migration destination based on the likelihood of successfully getting there, expected income, and the presence of relatives or friends. Availability of legal residence status seems to be less important, although visa requirements, perceived ease of obtaining refugee status, and amnesties for undocumented migrants are all important in directing Fujianese (and other Chinese) migrants to particular countries at particular times (Economic and Social Research Council 2002).

A survey conducted from May to October 2003 of transit migrants in Azerbaijan (IOM 2004) also determines that the motivations for migration are the result of careful contemplation. Most such transit migrants depart from developing countries in Asia and the Middle East and aim to settle in North America or Western Europe. Some would like to return home when the political and economic situations in their home countries stabilize. Some entered and reside in Azerbaijan legally, while others migrated illegally. Most undocumented entries were through Iran, and were frequently assisted by middlemen. "Push factors"—including conflict and economic difficulties in the countries of origin—were the main motivations for migration. For many, Azerbaijan was attractive owing to its geographical proximity to and cultural similarities with their homeland.

Countries with generous immigration provisions, such as Ukraine, also have the potential to become important crossroads for the transportation of undocumented migrants. A Kennan Institute study (Kennan Institute 2004) focusing on nontraditional immigrants from Asia and Africa identified a set of migrants heading for Western Europe who took advantage of the relatively open immigration system in Ukraine (at least before 1999). They entered both legally and illegally, and hoped to stay a short time before crossing to Western Europe. Some had been duped by traffickers who promised safe passage to Western Europe and then dumped them in Ukraine. In this case as well, migration decisions were greatly influenced by available information from government, extended family, business ties, friends who had studied in Ukraine during Soviet times, communities of compatriots in Ukraine, and organizers of undocumented migration. The majority of Chinese immigrants stated that they relied primarily on small business owners and traders, individuals who were first to take advantage of favorable conditions for entering Ukraine after the breakup of the Soviet Union. Many such migrants had legalized their status and launched businesses, especially in the food industry and trading at Kiev markets. In contrast, many African migrants were informed about Ukraine as an "easy" transit country to Western Europe by countrymen who had studied in Ukraine during Soviet times.

Profiles of undocumented migrants demonstrate that young, middle-level educated men are more likely to migrate illegally. Most respondents to the Azerbaijan survey were between the ages of 18 and 34 and the majority had completed secondary or vocational schools (with legal migrants having more education on average than irregular migrants) and had worked as low-skilled workers. Among legal migrants, men and women were about equally numerous, whereas most irregular migrants were men (Economic and Social Research Council 2002). The survey of undocumented transit migrants in Ukraine found that about 15,000 such migrants, many young Muslim men, may be located in Kiev. Many were married to Ukrainian women. Two-thirds had a high level of education and had lived in large cities or capitals in their home countries before migrating (Kennan Institute 2004).

Despite the careful calculations made in decisions to migrate, the migration process is long and difficult for most transit migrants. Those interviewed in Azerbaijan had all spent at least one year there, and most were uncertain how much longer they would stay in transit. Few expected to depart for their final destinations within the next year and 11 percent had decided to stay in Azerbaijan if possible. Transit migrants faced a number of difficulties—including shortages of finance, unemployment, poor access to housing and health care, and language barriers—yet were largely satisfied with the overall attitudes of government officials and the local population. More irregular migrants had employment in Azerbaijan than did legal migrants (Economic and Social Research Council 2002).

A major factor inhibiting the further movement of so-called transit migrants was their lack of information. The intended final destinations of most irregulars were the United States, Canada, and Western Europe, whereas most legal migrants intended either to return home (especially to Russia) or to continue on to Western Europe. Most were poorly informed about the rules and regulations for entry to their planned destination countries and living conditions there. Furthermore, illegal migrants who intended to return home were often dependent on outside assistance to do so. Most legal migrants planned to leave Azerbaijan on their own, while most irregular migrants were hoping for assistance from humanitarian organizations, travel agencies, and middlemen (Economic and Social Research Council 2002).

Thus, clearly the migration experience is substantially influenced by the legal status of those who undertake it.

ECA Country Experiences and Policies

Undocumented immigration is by definition difficult to quantify. Currently, there are estimated to be upward of 3 million undocumented immigrants in the EU, and between 1,300 and 1,500 in Russia. The International Organization for Migration reports that "99 percent of labor migration in the Eurasian Economic Union formed of Tajikistan, Kyrgyz Republic, Kazakhstan, the Russian Federation, and Belarus is irregular. Due to their irregular situation, most labor migrants do not benefit from the same protection rights other regular citizens enjoy and are thus more vulnerable to exploitation by underground employers" (IOM 2001, p. 11). Legal status not only affects the relative migration costs and expected benefits, but also changes the underlying economic incentives. Table 1.3 provides a range of estimates of undocumented migration in selected ECA countries, Western Europe, and the United States.

ECA countries act as source, host, and transit countries for undocumented migrants. The concerns associated with the illicit movement, transit, and trade in people are therefore salient across the region. The major host is Russia, most of whose undocumented workers are from the rest of the CIS. However, following accession of the EU-8 to the EU, undocumented migration from western CIS, Russia, the Balkans, and Turkey is becoming an increasing issue for the EU-8 and other countries along its borders. Demographic change is generating a demand for workers in certain sectors and regions, while other migrants are becoming "stuck" as they fail to cross the EU-15 borders. The status of the EU-8 is in transition, but the slowdown in westward emigration in most countries, as well as the opening up of labor markets in some parts of the EU-15, is increasingly regularizing flows. In fact, the expansion of the Schengen Agreement to cover the EU-8 is extending the problem eastward, as irregular migrants are now becoming stuck in the Ukraine.[7] Turkey hosts a number of undocumented workers mainly from ECA, but also from the Middle East. Taking into account these factors and the role of the ECA as the main overland route to Western Europe, the whole of the region is a major transit route. Transit migrants may come from the region itself, or from the Middle East, Africa, or Asia. It is thought that of the 500,000 trafficked women in Eastern Europe, 300,000 originated in or were transported through the Balkans.

The growth of undocumented migration in the ECA region may be closely tied to the migration policies used to regulate it, and particu-

TABLE 1.3
Estimated Irregular Migrants

(thousands)

Country	Total number of migrants	Estimated number of irregular migrants		Year of estimation	Average % of total migrants
		Max	Min		
North America and Canada					
United States	34,988	10,300	—	2004	29.44
Canada	5,826	200	100	2003	3.43
High-income Europe					
Greece	534	320	—	2003	59.87
Portugal	233	100	—	2003	42.96
Italy	1,634	500	—	2003	30.59
United Kingdom	4,029	1,000	—	2003	24.82
Spain	1,259	280	—	2003	22.24
Belgium	879	150	—	2003	17.06
Germany	7,349	1,000	—	2003	13.61
Switzerland	1,801	180	—	2003	9.99
Netherlands	1,576	163	112	2003	8.72
France	6,277	400	—	2003	6.37
Ireland	310	10	—	2003	3.23
Finland	134	1	—	2003	0.75
Total	26,015	4,104	—		15.78
ECA countries					
Poland	2,088	600	—	2000	28.73
Ukraine	6,947	1,600	—	2000	23.03
Tajikistan	330	60	—	2002	18.16
Czech Republic	236	40	—	2003	16.98
Slovak Republic	51	8	—	1998	15.69
Turkey	1,503	200	—	2001	13.31
Russia	13,259	1,500	1,300	2000	11.31
Kazakhstan	3,028	300	220	2002	9.91
Belarus	1,284	150	50	2000	11.68
Kyrgyz Republic	572	30	—	1998	5.24
Uzbekistan	1,367	30	—	2000	2.19
Lithuania	339	2	—	1997	0.59

Sources: Pew Hispanic Center; IOM; ILO; World Bank; ISTAT; Home Office in United Kingdom; Jimenez (2003); Center on Migration, Policy and Society of the University of Oxford; EU Business Council of Europe; Ministry of Labor in Finland; Sadovskaya (2002); Migration Policy Group; Jandl (2003).

Note: — = not available. Estimation methods are different for each country. Total number of migrants is at the point in 2000 and is estimated by UN (2003).

larly policies in the EU-15 that cap supply of labor below demand. The flow of labor under existing migration agreements is regulated through quotas, as well as a maximum residency period allowed in the receiving country. Quotas often appear small both in relation to the perceived need for labor and in relation to the actual flow of labor migrants. Thus, for instance, Jandl (2003) notes that while 1.11 million foreigners had valid residence permits in Spain in 2000, the 2001 census counted 1.57 million foreigners and the Organisation for Eco-

nomic Co-operation and Development (OECD) (OECD 2005) estimates that roughly 1 million irregular migrants (around 6 percent of
the labor force) will be affected by the recent amnesty. In the United
Kingdom, Migration Watch estimates that the number of irregular
migrants—including disappeared asylum seekers, visa overstayers,
and clandestine entries—is over 100,000 a year; other sources put the
figure as high as 500,000.[8] Jandl (2003) estimates that the stock of
irregular migrants in Europe is somewhere between 2.6 million and
6.4 million and the annual number of border apprehensions in EU-15
is close to 300,000.

In light of these numbers, and assuming that most clandestine
migrants succeed in finding work, the quotas for labor migration in
the bilateral agreements between EU-15 and Central Europe and the
Balkans are very small. For example, the Italian agreement on seasonal migration concluded in 1997 with Albania allows 3,000
migrants a year; Germany's quota for guest workers is 15,500 a year
(though there are approximately 200,000 seasonal agricultural workers), and the United Kingdom allows an annual inflow of 25,000 from
all countries outside of the European Economic Area (OECD 2004).
Between the time of EU enlargement in May 2004 and November
2005, there has been an inflow of 156,165 workers from the EU into
the United Kingdom and 107,024 into Ireland. Through December
2004, there was a flow of 3,514 workers into Sweden.

Major Migration Partners of the ECA Countries

An important aspect of migration management is understanding the
patterns of migration for any particular country. Such an exercise is
similar to investigating a country's major foreign trade partners,
though usually fewer countries are major senders and receivers of
migrants to any particular country than are significant trade partners.
Furthermore, the problems with obtaining migration data in many
countries in the region make this a somewhat inexact exercise. For-
tunately, the largest country in the region, Russia, which is also the
main migration partner of most of the other former Soviet Union
(FSU) states, has a fairly complete set of migration data, although it
does not include the undocumented migrants in the country. Figure
1.11 shows that Russia has been a net recipient of migration from all
of the other FSU states except for Belarus, and a net sender to the "far
abroad" or to countries outside of the FSU (data underlying these figures are in table 1.6 of appendix 1). The countries from which Russia
has received the largest numbers of migrants are those from which

FIGURE 1.11

Russia, Net Migration by Country, 1989–2003

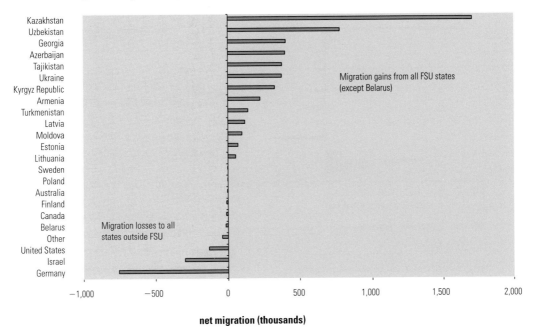

Source: Goskomstat Rossii (selected publications).

there has been a large return of ethnic Russians—Kazakhstan, Ukraine, and Uzbekistan. However, since 1994, there has been a net immigration to Russia of many other nationalities. If undocumented migrants were included, the numbers representing non-Russians would be even larger.

Three countries outside Russia are the primary destinations for Russian migrants: Germany, Israel, and the United States. Those who migrate consist primarily of Germans, Jews, and Russians, reflecting a combination of ethnic and economic factors driving their decisions to migrate.

The trends shown in the data from Belarus, Moldova, and Ukraine (see figure 1.12) are roughly consistent with the data that appear in the data from Russia. Ukraine had net migration losses to Russia while Belarus overall gained migrants. Moldova had net overall losses and net migration losses to the FSU countries, though it did gain migrants from all FSU countries except Russia, Ukraine, and Belarus. All three of these countries are net recipients of migrants from all of the other FSU states. As was the case for Russia, the same three countries outside the FSU—Germany, Israel, and the United States—are the primary destinations of migrants from Ukraine, Belarus, and Moldova. There is anecdotal evidence that an increasing number of

FIGURE 1.12

Major Migration Partners of the CIS Countries

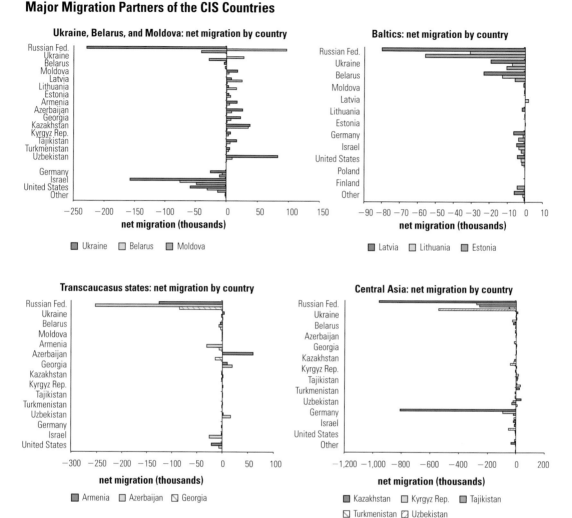

Source: National statistical offices of the ECA countries.

labor migrants from Ukraine and Moldova are departing for the countries of Western Europe.

For the three Baltic states (Latvia, Lithuania, and Estonia), mainly titular members of these states have migrated to Russia and the other Slavic states. The data do not demonstrate the fact that this ethnic migration peaked in 1992–93, just after the breakup of the Soviet Union, or that it has declined substantially since then as Russians and other minorities in the Baltics have remained as a result of faster growing economies and impending EU membership. As in other FSU countries, Germany, Israel, and the United States are the primary destinations for migrants from the Baltic states to countries outside the

FSU, although there may have been a broader dispersion of destinations after these states became EU members in 2004.

For the three Caucasus countries (Armenia, Azerbaijan, and Georgia), Russia has been the dominant migration destination. There is considerable evidence that these figures represent only a fraction of a much larger undocumented and circular migration from these countries to Russia. This is especially the case with Georgia, where the data on net migration by country only cover the period 1990 to 1992. In contrast, the 2002 population census in Georgia revealed a net migration loss of 1.1 million persons or 20 percent of the population. The migration of Armenians from Nagorno-Karabakh and the surrounding regions in Azerbaijan is shown in this data set, although such movement was confined to the early 1990s. The United States is the primary destination outside the FSU for migrants from Armenia, with most of these joining the already large Armenian diaspora community there, while Israel remains a top Azerbaijani destination.

For the five Central Asian countries (Kazakhstan, the Kyrgyz Republic, Tajikistan, Turkmenistan, and Uzbekistan), Russia again dominates as a migration destination, as migration turnover to other FSU states is rather minimal. There is, however, some tentative evidence that Kazakhstan is becoming a favored migration destination for persons from the other Central Asian countries. From both Kazakhstan and the Kyrgyz Republic, there were large migrations of ethnic Germans to Germany. From Kazakhstan, over 800,000 Germans left and from the Kyrgyz Republic, nearly 100,000. These movements were the remnants of both voluntary and forced migrations of Germans to Central Asia during the Soviet period.

Figure 1.13 shows the major migration patterns of the largest western ECA country, Poland. As can be seen, Poland is losing people to many developed countries (albeit to varying degrees) and remains a net emigration country. Its largest losses are to neighboring Germany, the United States, and Canada, where there are already large Polish diaspora populations as a result of past migrations. The figure for Germany is likely an underestimate because many Poles can travel rather easily to Germany. This figure encompasses the period before Poland became an EU member and thus does not include Poles working in the United Kingdom, Ireland, and Sweden. Many of them would not likely be included in these totals, because such labor migrants generally do not view their departure from Poland to be permanent.

Figure 1.14 provides data on the main migration partners of Hungary, Romania, the Czech Republic, and the Slovak Republic. According to these data, Hungary is a net recipient of migrants from nearly all listed countries, with especially large numbers coming from Romania,

FIGURE 1.13

Poland: Net Migration by Country, 1992–2003

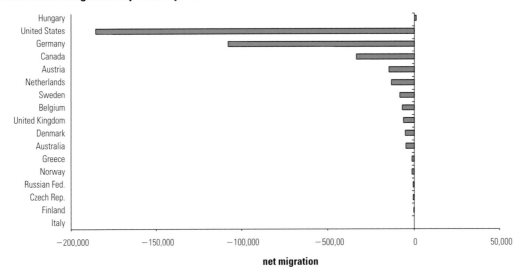

Source: Migration Policy Institute; OECD SOPEMI 2003; and German Federal Statistical Office.

Yugoslavia, and other countries that housed ethnic Hungarians after present-day Hungary was carved out of the Austro-Hungarian Empire. Romania shows population losses to nearly every other country, with especially large losses to Germany, where many Romanians have gone for work. The only country from which Romania is gaining migrants is its close ethnic neighbor, Moldova. The Czech Republic has been a net recipient of people from other countries, with the bulk of in-migration coming from the Slovak Republic (which had been a part of Czechoslovakia until 1993). The Slovak Republic itself is a net recipient from all listed countries except the Czech Republic.

Future Migration Trends in the Region

One of the themes of this report is that both economic and demographic incentives affect the motivation to migrate for ECA and neighboring countries. This section describes the demographic implications for future migration flows in this region.

Future Migration Patterns in the EU and Neighboring Countries

A combination of income convergence and demographic change suggests that the potential for large-scale migration from western ECA to

FIGURE 1.14

Major Migration Partners of Selected Western ECA Countries

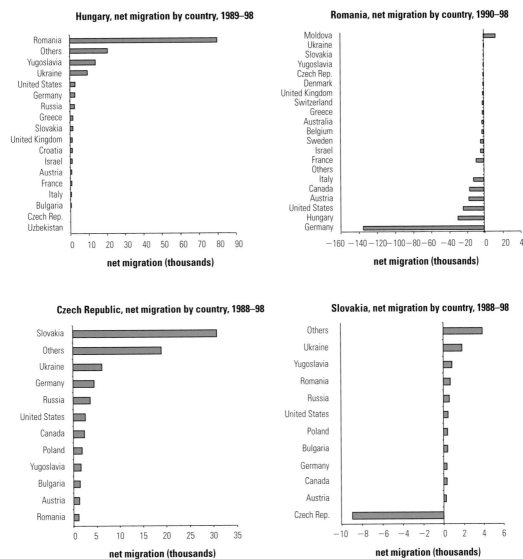

Source: Walmsley, Ahmed, and Parsons (2005).

the EU and other neighboring countries is limited. The richest countries in western ECA have already begun to be net immigration countries. This suggests that the experience of most Western European countries that are net recipients of migrants is likely to become the norm in most western ECA countries with income convergence and EU membership. Even with no convergence, changes in migration patterns appear inevitable.

With the exception of Albania, all western ECA countries are forecast to experience population declines between now and 2050. The total population of these countries peaked in 1990 at 130 million and is projected to decline by 19 percent to 104 million by mid-century. As shown in figure 1.15, western ECA source countries are often projected to have larger population declines than those in Western Europe. The population of Western Europe is expected to increase from its current size of 397 million to a peak of 407 million in 2030 before declining to 400 million in 2050. For western ECA, a decline in the working-age population and a corresponding increase in those over age 65 will create a demand for workers from abroad. The more prosperous western ECA countries may be able to source some of these workers from the rest of the region. However, for the region as a whole, demand will have to be met from elsewhere, probably CIS, Africa, and Asia. Whether these flows are legal or undocumented will depend on immigration legislation.

While the total population of Western Europe is expected to rise slightly between now and mid-century as a result of the current age structure of these countries and expected demographic trends, the working-age population in these countries is expected to decline substantially. Of course, the largest variable in future European migration

FIGURE 1.15

Population Size of Western Europe, Western ECA, and Turkey, 1950 to 2050

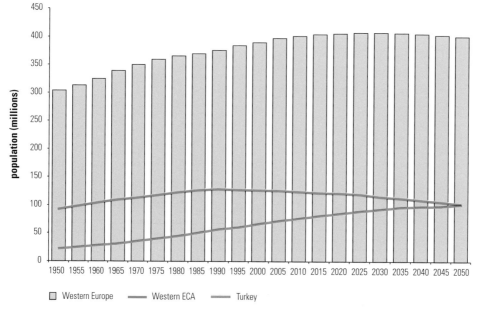

Source: United Nations Population Division, World Population Prospects: The 2004 Revision (http://www.un.org/esa/population/unpop.html).

patterns in both Western Europe and western ECA is Turkey, in which most of the future population growth and additions to the labor force in Europe are expected to take place. Because of its younger age structure and higher fertility rates, Turkey is expected to grow by 33 million between now and 2050 to a total of 101 million, nearly the size of the other western ECA countries combined. Turkey, with an increase of 16 million in its working-age population, could produce sufficient migration to cover the 12 million person population deficit in the EU.

Future Migration Patterns in the Former Soviet Union

Economic factors such as differences in per capita income drive migration patterns among the post-Soviet states in the short term. These will continue to be important, but demographic factors also will play an important role. Figure 1.16 shows the population and expected population of the FSU states over the period 1950–2050. The countries are grouped into the northern FSU—the Slavic and Baltic states and Moldova, and the southern FSU states—Central Asia and the Caucasus. The northern states as a group are characterized by continued low fertility, aging populations, an excess of deaths over births, and declining populations. The group's population peaked in 1990 and is expected to decline over the next half century by about one-third to 149 million. By contrast, the southern FSU states have younger populations, above replacement-level fertility, and continued growing populations. As a group, these countries nearly tripled in size, from 25 million in 1950 to 72 million in 2000. While growth is declining, the momentum built into the age structure of these populations will cause their continued growth to 93 million in 2050.

Differential rates of population growth (or decline) do not necessarily imply that there will be migration from the high-growth to low-growth areas but do present a precondition to that effect. While the northern FSU states will have declining working-age populations in even greater numbers than their overall population declines, most of the southern FSU states, with their "youth bulges," will have growing working-age populations with economies not growing fast enough to supply jobs. Given their geographic proximity and common historical legacy, it would be only natural that the youth of the southern FSU would look north for jobs, and as mentioned above, there is ample evidence that they are doing so. Furthermore, historical legacy contributes to the selection of migration destinations. The Soviet Union was an almost self-contained migration space; the interconnectedness of FSU countries may cause people to favor destinations in that area over others.

FIGURE 1.16

Population Size of the Northern and Southern FSU States, 1950 to 2050

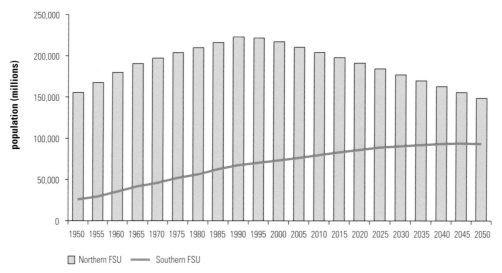

☐ Northern FSU　━━━ Southern FSU

Source: United Nations Population Division, World Population Prospects: The 2002 Revision Population Database (http://www.un.org/esa/population/unpop.htm).

Note: The northern FSU consists of Russia, Ukraine, Belarus, Moldova, Latvia, Lithuania, and Estonia. The southern FSU consists of Armenia, Azerbaijan, Georgia, Kazakhstan, the Kyrgyz Republic, Tajikistan, Turkmenistan, and Uzbekistan.

A recent United Nations study examined the issue of using "replacement migration" as a policy measure to address declining and aging populations.[9] The EU and Russia were included in the study, as were other countries—including France, Germany, Italy, Japan, the Republic of Korea, the United Kingdom, and the United States—that face similar trends of declining and aging populations. The population declines projected by 2050 in these countries range from 17 percent (Moldova) to 52 percent (Estonia). Countries with aging and declining populations face a number of policy dilemmas, including appropriate retirement ages, pension system reform, and health care for the elderly; support levels and ratios between working and pension-age populations; labor force participation; and possible replacement migration and the integration of immigrant populations. In contrast to these other possibilities, replacement migration refers to the principle of using international migration to offset declines in total population, working-age population, or population aging.

Figure 1.17 shows the combination of natural increase (the difference between births and deaths) and net migration for Russia for the period 1980–2015. During the 1980s, Russia's population was growing as a result of both demographic and migratory factors. Starting in 1992 and expected to continue for the foreseeable future, the number of deaths has exceeded the number of births. Migration into Rus-

FIGURE 1.17

Russia: Net Migration and Natural Increase, 1980–2015

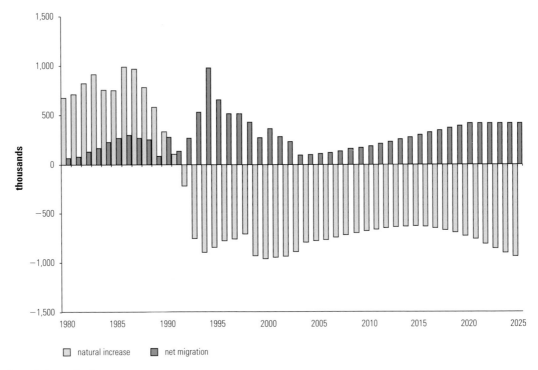

□ natural increase   ■ net migration

Source: Goskomstat Rossii.

Note: Data are actuals from 1980 to 2003 and projected from 2004 to 2015.

sia spiked sharply in the 1990s following the breakup of the Soviet
Union and has declined sharply since then (at least documented
migration). If these trends continue, Russia's population will decline
and age rapidly. For Russia to maintain the size of its total and working-age populations, allowing migration seems to be the only policy
option.

Under the medium-variant scenario used in the study, the EU is
projected to have a net migration of 13.5 million and Russia to have
a net migration of 5.4 million between 2000 and 2050. To maintain
the population size as it was in 1995 using migration alone would
require a net migration of 47.9 million into the EU and 24.9 million
into Russia during that period. Maintaining the same size working-
age population would require a net migration of 79 million into the
EU and 35.8 million into Russia. For comparison's sake, there was a
net migration of about 8.8 million into the EU and about 3.3 million
into Russia during the 1990s. Furthermore, for Russia this was a
period of extraordinary change and unprecedented migration that is
not likely to be repeated.

For the EU, Russia, and the other large aging and declining populations in the UN study, it is obvious that the needed replacement migration levels are far above levels that are politically and socially plausible. Even low levels of migration will require very careful political and social balancing acts in Russia, the other northern FSU countries, and other major migration destinations. Policies must be designed to accommodate these new migration realities in both destination and originating countries, and, most importantly, the dynamic fluctuations between the two. There is evidence that Russia and some of the other FSU states are facing up to this new migration reality in the region and taking steps to regularize it.

Endnotes

1. Much of the migration data upon which this chapter is based is contained in appendix 1.
2. Estimates as of March 2004 are that there are 10.3 million undocumented migrants in the United States and each year another 700,000 to 800,000 unauthorized enter the country, which is about the same size as those who migrate legally to the United States (Passel 2005).
3. The figure for Armenia, which includes those not indicating their place of birth, is likely a large overestimate because of the problems with the census, which was conducted in January 1989, just after the devastating earthquake in December 1988.
4. For more on the fertility decline in the ECA region, see Heleniak (2005).
5. Turkmenistan and Bosnia and Herzegovina are not included because of the suspected migration data problems mentioned above.
6. To ensure comparability, the data are taken from one source, UNICEF's TransMONEE database, which collects data from the national statistical offices of the 27 transition ECA countries, not including Turkey.
7. The Schengen Agreement originally was a state treaty to end internal border checkpoints and controls among European countries. Today the Schengen system is part of EU legislation regulating border control, visa and admission and nonadmission standards, as well as the joint Schengen Information System. The 15 current Schengen countries include Austria, Belgium, Denmark, Finland, France, Germany, Iceland, Italy, Greece, Luxembourg, the Netherlands, Norway, Portugal, Spain, and Sweden. All these countries except Norway and Iceland are EU members. The name "Schengen" originates from the small town in Luxembourg where the agreement was signed in 1985.
8. Data from the U.K. Home Office. Source at http://www.timesonline. co.uk/article/0,,2087-1572533,00.html, retrieved June 22, 2005.
9. United Nations Population Division 2001. The study uses the 1998 Revision of UN population projections as a baseline. The European Union defined in the report was the EU-15.

CHAPTER 2

Migrants' Remittances

For most countries in the Europe and Central Asia (ECA) region, remittances are the second most important source of external financing after foreign assistance and foreign direct investment. For many of the poorest countries in the region they are the largest source and have served as a cushion against the economic and political turbulence brought about by transition.

The situation is substantially different in the new European Union (EU) member countries (EU-8). Income levels are higher, cross-country income differentials are lower, and there is less need for workers living abroad to support their families' consumption. Moreover, the current and improving opportunities at home mean that there can be large gains from accumulating human and financial capital abroad, although as the economic situation at home improves, the incentives to migrate may themselves decrease.

Yet, relative to GDP, remittances are significant in many ECA countries (figure 2.1).[1] Four of the world's largest recipients of remittances as a portion of GDP are in ECA (Moldova, Bosnia and Herzegovina, Albania, and Armenia). In 2004, officially recorded remittances to the ECA region amounted to over US$19 billion, the equivalent of about 8 percent of the global total (US$232.3 billion) and 12 percent of remittances received by developing countries (US$160.4 billion).

The first section of this chapter seeks to complement chapter 1 in providing a statistical overview of migrants' remittances in ECA (figure 2.2).

FIGURE 2.1

Leading 20 Remittance-Receiving Countries in the World
(percentage of GDP in 2004)

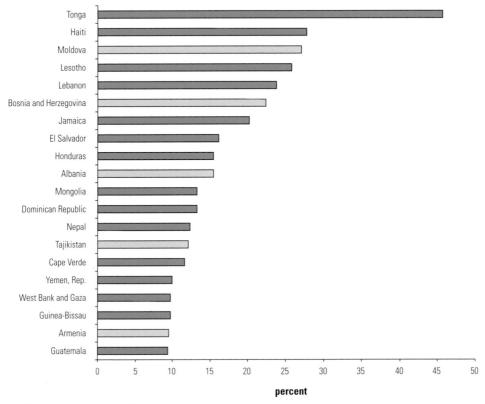

Source: IMF *Balance of Payment Statistics:*, World Bank.

Note: Received remittances = received compensation of employee + received worker's remittances + received migrants' transfer. Lighter bars in the graph are ECA countries.

As before, the problems of data quality are pervasive because of the difficulties of measuring remittances sent outside of the formal financial sector are very difficult to quantity. Further complicating these data problems are that large year-on-year increases in remittances may reflect improvements in central banks' remittance recording systems rather than changes in migrants' behaviors.

Data

While remittances have increased dramatically in a number of countries, they have slowed for others. A review of remittance flows over the past nine years demonstrates this pattern (figure 2.3). Interestingly, while remittances from migrants who have lived out of their

FIGURE 2.2

Remittances as a Portion of GDP in Eastern Europe and the Former Soviet Union, 2004

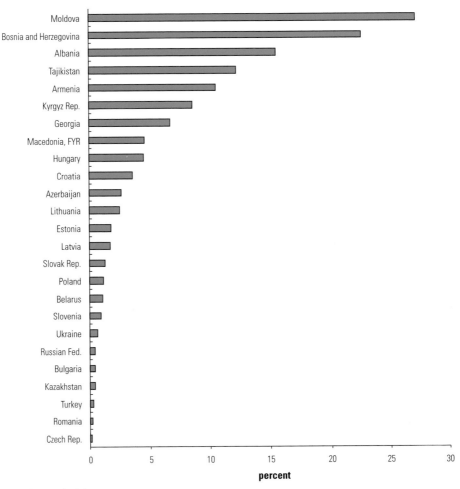

Source: IMF *Balance of Payments Statistics.*

Note: Received remittances = received compensation of employee + received worker's remittances + received migrants' transfers. Albania and Slovak Republic are 2003 data, other countries are 2004 data. GDP is $ converted current price.

home countries for more than one year represent the largest share of inflows, remittances from migrants who have lived abroad for less than a year represent an increasingly large share.

Not all migrants, however, send remittances, particularly in those cases where the stay in destination countries is short. Surveys conducted for this report found that in Bulgaria, 80 percent did not; in Bosnia and Herzegovina, 37 percent; and in Romania, 62 percent.

Generally remittance flows in ECA follow the same two-bloc pattern as migration (table 2.1). The EU and the middle-income Commonwealth of Independent States (CIS) countries are the main sources of

FIGURE 2.3

Growth Rate of Remittances in ECA: 1995–98, 2001–04
(percent)

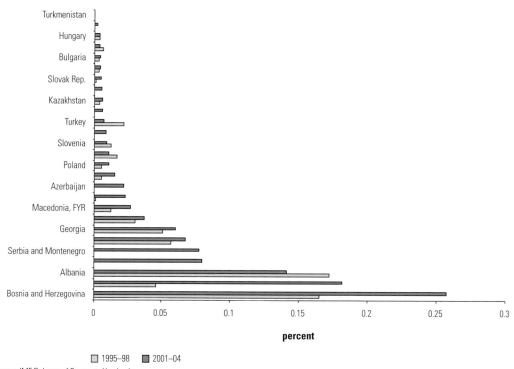

□ 1995–98   ■ 2001–04

Source: IMF Balance of Payments Yearbook.

Note: Remittances defined as the sum of received workers' remittances, compensation of employees, and migrants' transfers.

remittances, with the EU accounting for three-quarters of the total and the rich CIS countries for 10 percent. The amount contributed by the EU-8 and accession countries is also significant, just below 10 percent.

Impact of Remittances on Development

The theoretical and empirical record on the economic impact of remittances is far from clear. Remittances can reduce poverty and fuel high rates of household savings and investment (Rapoport and Docquier forthcoming; Roberts 2004). At the same time, however, remittances may exert upward pressure on the real exchange rate and reduce the competitiveness of exports (similar to arguments about the Dutch disease). Some have found that remittances can also create incentives that reduce the domestic work effort (Chami, Fullenkamp, and Jahjah 2003).

This section explores the development impact of remittances in ECA. Considering each in turn, we find that remittances are often an impor-

TABLE 2.1

Remittance Flows by Subregion, 2003

Receiving	Sending						
	EU-15	New and accession EU	Balkans	Russia and resource-rich CIS	Moldova and Ukraine	Non-resource-rich CIS	Total
	($ million)						
New and accession EU	2,813	244	1	46	18	36	3,159
Balkans	1,322	168	0.1	2	0.3	2	1,495
Russia and resource-rich CIS	357	85	1	183	200	61	886
Moldova and Ukraine	223	23	0.2	165	29	3	443
Non-resource-rich CIS	428	35	0.4	340	8	54	865
Total	5,143	555	2	736	255	156	6,848
	(percent for sending subregion)						
New and accession EU	55	44	35	6	7	23	46
Balkans	26	30	5	0	0	1	22
Russia and resource-rich CIS	7	15	30	25	78	39	13
Moldova and Ukraine	4	4	10	22	11	2	6
Non-resource-rich CIS	8	6	20	46	3	35	13
Total	100	100	100	100	100	100	100
	(percent for receiving subregion)						
New and accession EU	89	8	0	1	1	1	100
Balkans	88	11	0	0	0	0	100
Russia and resource-rich CIS	40	10	0	21	23	7	100
Moldova and Ukraine	50	5	0	37	7	1	100
Non-resource-rich CIS	49	4	0	39	1	6	100
Total	75	8	0	11	4	2	100

Source: World Bank staff calculations from migration and remittance data in chapters 1 and 4.

Note: Remittances are defined as workers' remittances and compensation of employees. Cell contents refer to the total remittance flows or percentage flows into the receiving region from the sending region. Shaded areas are 10 percent or more of receiving or sending subregion or 5 percent or more of ECA flows.

tant source of foreign exchange, domestic consumption, and investment. Unlike other international transfers, remittances may be countercyclical. Remittances also are an important and stable source of income for many households in the region, especially in the rural areas. Though the underlying remittances data are poor, our estimations of the broader, macroeconomic impact of remittances suggest that they exert a mild positive impact on long-term patterns of macroeconomic growth, while evidence on their impact on the distribution of poverty is mixed.

Remittances as a Stable Source of Foreign Exchange

Remittances often serve as a key source of foreign exchange for the countries in the region. For example, remittances have represented a key source of foreign exchange for Albania and helped to finance its rapidly mounting deficit on trade in goods and services since 1990. In contrast, both official and private financial inflows on capital account have played a relatively small role, although some increase in direct investments in Albania since the turn of the millennium has occurred. Remittances financed more than 70 percent of the deficit since 1995 (Lucas 2005). A recent World Bank study found that remittances provided similar financing of the trade deficit in Moldova since the late 1990s (World Bank 2005). In general, remittances have played an increasingly important role in the foreign exchange flows to the poorer countries in the ECA.

Figure 2.4 depicts shares of total remittances to exports of goods and services for selected ECA countries. Taking into account that in many cases exports are the major source of foreign exchange into the country, this ratio can be a good approximation of the importance of migrants' transfers for the foreign exchange revenues of the country.

Being a significant source of foreign exchange, remittances can serve as a pillar to support and improve creditworthiness and access to international capital markets for many countries in the ECA region. The ratio of external debt to exports, a common indebtedness indicator, declines substantially for some ECA countries if remittances are also included as a potential source of foreign exchange.

Because they are a significant source of foreign exchange, remittances can improve creditworthiness and access to international capital markets for many ECA countries. For example, if remittances are included as a potential source of foreign exchange, the ratio of debt to exports falls by close to 50 percent for Albania and for Bosnia and Herzegovina. Unlike capital flows, remittances do not create debt servicing or other obligations. Thus, they can provide financial institutions with access to better financing than might otherwise be available. Among ECA countries, Turkey has been in the lead in using such remittance securitization, but Kazakhstan has also used this instrument to raise financing.

Remittances are one of the defining factors of exchange rate dynamics and, as a consequence, macroeconomic policy in the small open economies. Lucas (2005) observed that from 1992 to 2002, the Albanian lek depreciated by some 7.6 percent per year on average against the U.S. dollar. Because this is less than the rate of inflation, this means a real appreciation of the lek, and this rate of real appreciation has continued at more than 7 percent on average in the five years to 2002. No doubt exports would have been stronger in the absence of this real appreciation. Even so, U.S. dollar earnings from merchandise exports grew on average by almost 20 percent in the decade to 2002, outstripping import growth even though exports started from a much smaller base (Lucas 2005).

FIGURE 2.4

Remittances as a Share of Exports in 2003
(percent)

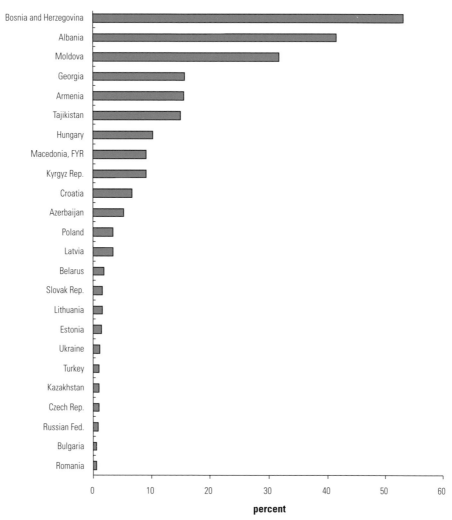

Source: IMF *Balance of Payment Statistics,* World Bank.

Note: Received remittances = received compensation of employee + received worker's remittances + received migrants' transfer.

Economic Impact of Remittances

The economic consequences of remittances are hard to disentangle—
they can affect growth through a variety of channels. Lucas (2005)
divides the discussion of remittances in two: the effects on poverty
and inequality (which are considered in the subsequent section of
this report); and the influences upon investment, growth, and macroeconomic stability, which are considered here.

Remittances augment national income and aggregate demand as a whole. Figure 2.2 provided estimates of the income received from friends and relatives abroad as a proportion of the national income. The leaders in this respect are Moldova, Bosnia and Herzegovina, Albania, Tajikistan, Armenia, and Kyrgyz Republic. It is interesting to note that in Moldova, for example, earnings abroad constitute almost one-quarter of the national income.

Like any income, remittances are partially spent on household consumption and partially saved and invested. If we subscribe to a traditional macroeconomic model, the expansionary effect of remittances will be greater if they are spent on investment or saved in the formal financial sector. Results from surveys with returned migrants in ECA found that the majority of remittances are utilized for funding consumption of food and clothing but that large quantities are also used for education and savings (over 10%). Smaller amounts are spent on business investment (less than 5%) (see figure 2.5).

Figure 2.6 provides the share of total remittances compared with total household expenditure for selected ECA countries in 2003. It is not surprising that the results are well correlated with GDP shares, given that consumption is a main component of GDP. If the propensity to consume from remittances is similar to other income, it can be

FIGURE 2.5
Expenditure Patterns from Remittances in Six ECA Countries

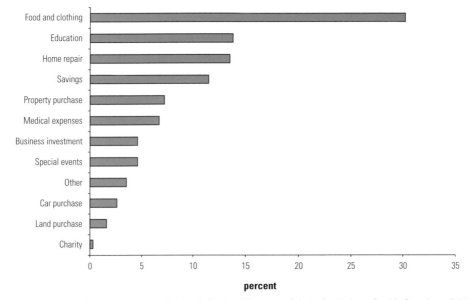

Source: Results from a World Bank survey with returned migrants in Bosnia and Herzegovina, Bulgaria, Georgia, Kyrgyz Republic, Romania, and Tajikistan. See appendix 1.1 for further information on the survey.

FIGURE 2.6

Remittances as Share of Total Household Expenditure in 2004

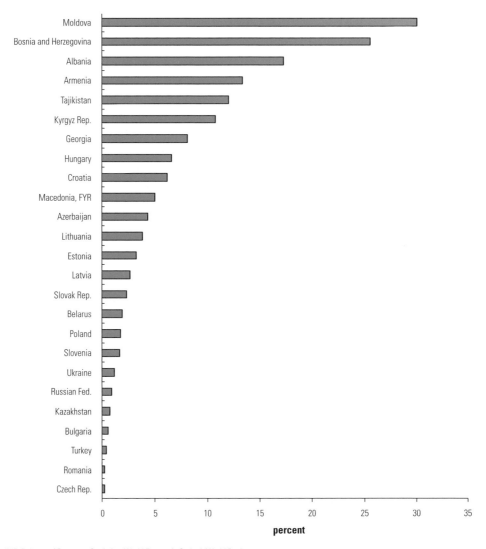

Sources: IMF, *Balance of Payments Statistics, World Economic Outlook;* World Bank.

Note: Received remittances = received compensation of employee + received workers' remittances + received migrants' transfer. Albania and Slovak Republic are 2003 data. Otherwise, in 2004 data. Household expenditures is $ converted current price.

concluded that, for some countries, remittances spurred a significant portion of total consumption. For example, in Moldova or Albania, every fifth dollar spent in 2003 came from remittances.

There is a debate over the extent to which remittances actually boost the economy of the migrant-source country, because, as the discussion above demonstrates, a substantial portion of income has been used for consumption purposes and not saved or invested (Drinkwater, Levine, and Lotti 2002). Recent strands of literature, however, indicate that remittances can lead to economic growth simply by increasing the migrant's household income, regardless of whether this additional income is spent on consumption or savings. For example, Ratha (2003) indicated that if remittances are invested, they contribute to output growth, but they generate positive multiplier effects if consumed. Research on Moldova corroborates this information, as economic growth has been strongly driven by a spike in gross national disposable income since the late 1990s, a period characterized by high levels of international remittances (World Bank 2005).

Furthermore, significant empirical evidence indicates that remittances lead to positive economic growth, whether through increased consumption, savings, or investment. Lucas (2005) cites several case studies that show signs that remittances may indeed have accelerated investment in Morocco, Pakistan, and India. Glytsos (2002) models the direct and indirect effects of remittances on incomes and hence on investment in seven Mediterranean countries, and finds that investment rises with remittances in six out of the seven countries. Additionally, the results of the analysis conducted by León-Ledesma and Piracha (2001) for 11 transition economies of Eastern Europe during 1990–99 show support for the view that remittances have a positive impact on productivity and employment, both directly and indirectly through their effect on investment. A recent study by Roberts (2004) on remittances in Armenia concludes that, overall, empirical evidence suggests that the propensity to save out of remittance income is high (almost 40 percent) and remarkably consistent across studies.

There is also evidence of important multiplier effects from remittance spending, particularly from housing construction (Roberts 2004; Lucas 2005, citing Glytsos 1993; Adelman and Taylor 1990; Zarate 2002). The multiplier effect can be high—Durand, Parrado, and Massey (1996) find that every "migradollar" that enters a local economy generates as much as $4 in demand for goods and services, though such analyses may rely on extreme assumptions. Moreover, Desai et al. (2003) indicate that additional consumption increases indirect tax receipts, thus also increasing government consumption or savings.

Therefore, there is evidence that remittances have enabled economic growth through greater rates of investment. Even more certainly, remittances have important multiplier effects, raising income levels in the economy beyond the households of remittance recipients. There are, nevertheless, at least two points of reservation regarding these optimistic conclusions. One is the possibility that countries can face a situation similar to the Dutch disease, in which the inflow of remittances causes a real appreciation, or postpones depreciation, of the exchange rate, restricting export performance and hence possibly limiting output and employment (Lucas 2005). More importantly, research by Chami, Fullenkamp, and Jahjah (2003) ascertained that income from remittances may be plagued by a moral-hazard problem, permitting the migrant's family members to reduce their work effort.

Part of the explanation for these distinct findings may be that the studies suffer from an omitted variable bias: the role of institutions. We hypothesize that the impact on remittances of macroeconomic growth and development is conditioned by the quality of the recipient country's political and economic policies and institutions. The quality of institutions might play an important role in determining the exact effect of remittances on economic growth, because institutions exert substantial influence on the volume and efficiency of investment.

Overall, estimations conducted with dynamic-panel methods find that remittances have a positive impact on macroeconomic growth. Moreover, the results are not inconsistent with the argument that institutions play a role in conditioning this relationship (see box 2.1).

Distribution, Poverty, and Inequality

In addition to absolute indicators of growth and macroeconomic stability (Lucas 2005), remittances may have distributive effects on poverty and inequality. Of the two factors, the effect of remittances on poverty seems much less controversial, because remittances per se do not lower anyone's income. Remittances contribute to household income and thus, in the short run, reduce poverty. Recent analysis by Adams and Page (2003) confirms that a 10 percent increase in the share of international migrants in a country's population will lead to a 1.9 percent decline in the share of people living on less than $1 per person per day. In addition, Adams finds that international remittances have a negative statistically significant effect on three poverty measures (poverty headcount measure, poverty gap, and squared poverty gap measure) (Adams and Page 2003).

When it comes to the overall impact of remittances on income inequality, Ratha (2003) finds the evidence mixed. Some find that remittances sharpen inequality (Stark, Taylor, and Yitzhaki 1986; Adams 1991), while others claim that in the long run, income distribution becomes more equal as a result of the liquidity provided for capital accumulation, or through trickle-down effects in the labor market (Taylor and Wyatt 1996).

Richard Adams in his "The Effects of International Remittances on Poverty, Inequality, and Development in Rural Egypt" (1991) finds

BOX 2.1

Estimating the Impact of Remittances on Macroeconomic Growth

This dynamic-panel investigation estimates the impact of workers' remittances on per capita GDP growth in a sample of developed and developing economies (for information on the estimations and alternative specifications, see appendix 2.2). The estimator used in most of the sample equations below is the Anderson and Hsiao (1981) method. The results of using the GMM estimator are also relevant because we do not have specific Monte Carlo evidence on the appropriateness of each estimator for our panel settings. In all the estimations we have used the

Worker Remittances and Growth: Dynamic Panel Estimation (1970–2003)

(dependent variable: growth of GDP per capita; endogenous variable: log (remittances/GDP)

	(i) AH	(ii) AH	(iii) AH	(iv) AH	
Growth GDPpc (t-1)	0.233*** (0.015)	0.203*** (0.018)	0.315*** (0.076)	0.051 (0.352)	
Log(remittances/GDP growth)	−0.002 (−0.003)	0.001 (0.002)	0.024*** (0.008)	0.053 (0.045)	
Log(GCF/GDP)		0.041*** (0.011)	−0.010 (−0.048)	−0.161 (−0.250)	
Log(NPCF/GDP)			−0.003 (−0.004)	−0.019 (−0.012)	
TI corruption index				−0.037 (−0.039)	
UNHDI				−1.711 (−1.257)	
Voice and accountability					
Political stability					
Government efficiency					
Regulatory quality					
Rule of law					
Corruption					
Observations	1926	1660	566	150	
Number of ID	121	108	90	51	
Wald	0.000	0.000	0.000	0.088	
Sargan	0.358	0.443	0.452	0.867	
AR(1)	0.000	0.000	0.000	0.140	
AR(2)	0.532	0.406	0.254	0.854	
Long-run remittances coefficient	−0.003 (−0.010)	0.001 (0.003)	0.035*** (0.012)	0.055 (0.054)	

Source: World Bank Staff calculations.

Note: Specifications (1) to (6) were obtained using the Anderson-Hsiao estimator (AH). Specifications (7) to (9) were obtained using the 2-steps GMM estimator of Arellano and Bond (1991) with robust standard errors.
Standard errors in parentheses.
* significant at 10 percent; ** significant at 5 percent; *** significant at 1 percent.

logarithm of the remittances/GDP ratio as our independent variable, as well as the control variables described in further detail in appendix 2.2. Finally, we provide the long-run dynamic solution for the coefficient on remittances, which is to be interpreted as the impact of remittances on growth in equilibrium.

According to the results below, remittances appear to have a positive and statistically significant impact on growth in four out of six of these specifications. We could safely conclude that we can reject the existence of a negative impact of remittances on growth and that there is some indication of a positive, albeit mild, impact.

(v) AH	(vi) AH	(vii) GMM	(viii) GMM	(ix) GMM
0.939	0.585	0.293***	0.164**	0.061
(1.432)	(1.344)	(0.071)	(0.069)	(0.090)
−0.032	0.05	0.028*	0.023*	0.043*
(−0.114)	(0.177)	(0.016)	(0.012)	(0.023)
0.336	−0.372	0.012	0.062***	0.047***
(0.441)	(−1.719)	(0.018)	(0.016)	(0.014)
−0.007	0.002	−0.003	−0.001	
(−0.106)	(0.181)	(−0.003)	(−0.002)	
	−0.033	0.001		
	(−0.096)	(0.005)		
	−1.262	−0.034		
	(−12.510)	(−0.034)		
0.688	0.011	0.018	0.008	
(0.950)	(1.450)	(0.020)	(0.019)	
−0.590	0.020	−0.023	−0.006	
(−0.676)	(0.708)	(−0.014)	(−0.007)	
0.100	0.353	−0.018	0.009	
(0.519)	(1.296)	(−0.016)	(0.012)	
−0.221	−0.147	−0.005	−0.025**	−0.023*
(−0.329)	(−0.148)	(−0.015)	(−0.012)	(−0.016)
0.285	0.431	0.025	0.024	
(0.782)	(1.668)	(0.022)	(0.018)	
0.047	0.081	0.0114	−0.027**	−0.0001
(0.514)	(0.779)	(0.016)	(−0.012)	(−0.002)
344	150	150	334	530
77	51	51	77	93
0.936	0.782	0.000	0.000	0.001
0.998	0.845	0.216	0.51	0.973
0.367	0.646	0.017	0.000	0.000
0.369	0.967	0.127	0.242	0.346
−0.536	0.12	0.040**	0.027**	0.045**
(−13.800)	(0.691)	(0.021)	(0.014)	(0.023)

that when remittances are included in predicted per capita household income, the Gini coefficient increases by 24.5 percent. He explains this by the fact that the poorest quintile of households produces a proportionate share of still-abroad migrants, the richest 40 percent of households produce more than their share, but the second and third quintiles are under represented. "It is these variations in the number of migrants produced by different income groups—and not differences in either migrant earnings abroad or marginal propensities to remit—that cause international remittances to have a negative effect on rural income distribution" (Adams 1991, p. 74).

The distribution of remittances across urban and rural as well as capital-city areas for the abovementioned case studies is presented in figure 2.7. As can be seen from the figure, different countries are characterized by different patterns. For example, in Tajikistan and Albania the bulk of remittances goes to the rural areas (almost 70 percent), while in Armenia and Georgia the pattern is the opposite—almost 70 percent of remittances channeled into the countries go to large metropolitan areas and other cities. There appears to be a link

FIGURE 2.7

Distribution of Remittances by Location in 2002

(percent)

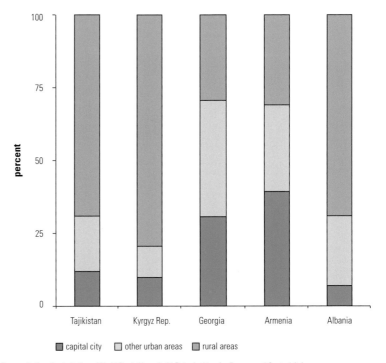

Source: Authors' calculations; World Bank, Household Data Archive for Europe and Central Asia.

Note: Data for Tajikistan are for 2003.

between such findings and population distributions; figure 2.8 demonstrates that Armenia and Georgia have proportionally less of their populations living in rural areas.

The relationship between remittances and inequality becomes even more evident when we look at the specific areas from which international migration is more prevalent. In the case of Albania, it is the poor regions in the north and other rural areas in the country that send international migrants.[2] In Armenia or Georgia, most households that report receiving remittances (and thus have relatives or other acquaintances abroad) hail from urban areas; the majority share of remittances reported by households goes into urban areas as well.

There are two explanations for the trend toward remittances to urban areas. First, individuals may find it relatively difficult to migrate abroad from rural areas. Second, most households that receive remittances might move into cities as a result of their newfound wealth. The latter situation is of special relevance to Armenia, where some portion of households may receive relatively high amounts of income from remittances from the so-called "old diaspora" on a regular basis.

FIGURE 2.8

Distribution of Population by Location in 2002
(percent)

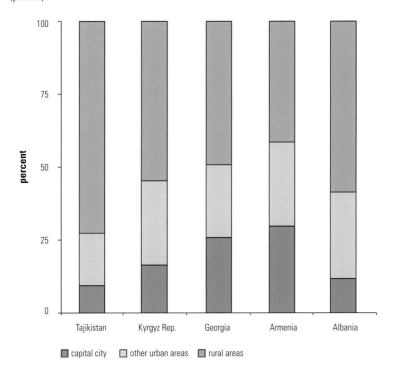

Source: Authors' calculations; World Bank, Household Data Archive for Europe and Central Asia.

Note: Data for Tajikistan are for 2003.

As a result, their incomes increase by a substantial amount, thus enabling a move to urban or capital areas, which are considered safer and more convenient to live in, though more expensive.

Table 2.2 presents estimates of average remittances and consumption per quintile for receiving and all households for the selected ECA countries. One of the key findings of the table is that richer households receive more remittances as a proportion of all households. This tendency is prevalent for all countries in the investigation, where data quality allows such investigation.

There can be several explanations for this migration bias skewed toward better-off families. First, movement internationally may be costly. Fixed costs of migration include transportation, as well as visa and work-permit fees. Furthermore, migrants likely support themselves for the first months of living abroad. Such expenditures may be relatively expensive once the differences in prices between host and sending countries are taken into account. Second, richer households have better access to information: they can employ expensive con-

TABLE 2.2

Annual Consumption and Remittances per Capita by Quintile

(US$)

Quintile	1	2	3	4	5
Albania (2002)					
Consumption per capita (all households)	283.66	425.76	560.02	761.15	1,403.13
Share of receiving households (percent)	16.87	13.23	18.08	24.31	28.37
Remittances per capita (receiving households)	147.58	186.59	261.76	294.35	541.85
Remittances/consumption (receiving households; percent)	52.03	43.82	46.74	38.67	38.62
Armenia (2003)					
Consumption per capita (all households)	135.39	194.02	244.81	312.24	547.30
Share of receiving households (percent)	16.51	16.30	16.40	17.61	21.20
Remittances per capita (receiving households)	67.88	105.36	74.30	112.47	167.51
Remittances/consumption (receiving households; percent)	50.13	54.31	30.35	36.02	30.61
Georgia (2002)[a]					
Consumption per capita (all households)	24.73	46.66	67.38	96.06	193.85
Share of receiving households (percent)	2.58	2.15	1.83	1.91	2.53
Remittances per capita (receiving households)	35.83	35.76	35.18	50.49	76.57
Remittances/consumption (receiving households; percent)	144.88	76.63	52.21	52.56	39.50
Kyrgyz Republic (2003)					
Consumption per capita (all households)	78.31	115.55	148.32	198.93	337.12
Share of receiving households (percent)	0.84	1.63	1.38	3.41	7.04
Remittances per capita (receiving households)	7.73	7.14	10.80	41.76	46.02
Remittances/consumption (receiving households; percent)	9.87	6.18	7.28	20.99	13.65
Tajikistan (2003)					
Consumption per capita (all households)	67.20	103.88	139.03	188.13	344.35
Share of receiving households (percent)	8.01	9.82	9.33	8.96	7.66
Remittances per capita (receiving households)	23.56	28.12	34.25	41.85	55.68
Remittances/consumption (receiving households; percent)	35.07	27.07	24.63	22.25	16.17

Sources: Authors' calculations; World Bank, Household Data Archive for Europe and Central Asia.

a. Quarterly.

sulting services and on average have higher education levels, factors that may facilitate migration. Third, existing social relationships help facilitate migration. Richer households with better opportunities to move initially may also pass on the knowledge and networks they obtain to households that interact with them—households that are most likely to be from the same or neighboring quintile. Finally, remittances received have an effect on household income—some households are likely in the top quintiles of income distribution precisely because they receive remittances.[3] Even so, it is likely that over time the difference in shares of remittances received for every quintile equalizes and even reverses; migrants who moved earlier on may return home to start their own businesses. Furthermore, the costs of moving will decrease in the long run through a reduction in the fees of consulting companies for migrants.[4]

Another finding of table 2.2 is that richer households receive greater remittances on average in per capita terms than poor households. Migrants in many cases remit two or three times as much to rich households. It is worth noting that this situation is present for all countries under our investigation, even those where only tiny proportions of the households surveyed report actually receiving remittances.

One of the explanations for this finding can be, as mentioned above, better access to information for richer households than for poor ones. Richer households can pay for costly consulting services to help them find better jobs, a cost that in many cases poor households cannot afford. Decisions made throughout the migration process are another reason for this phenomenon. Given expected future earnings at home and abroad, the cost of moving, and the time spent apart from family, migrants from rich households may have greater discretion over which job offers to accept than one who represents a household from a poorer quintile. It is possible that migrants from poor households have on average worse paid jobs than migrants from rich ones, at least at the beginning. A further explanation relies on connections to the "old diaspora." For example, in Armenia relatively large values of remittances are sent abroad by distant relatives or friends from the West.[5] If richer households have more connections within the old diaspora, they may have greater networks through which to receive remittances.

The third key finding from table 2.2 is that remittances constitute a considerable proportion of household expenditure and a higher portion of consumption per capita for the poor households than for the rich, suggesting that remittances are more important for poor than for rich households.

Endnotes

1. More detailed remittances data, including more extensive international comparisons, are presented in appendix 2.1.
2. For more evidence on migration patterns in Albania see Albania Poverty Assessment 2003 and A. Sarris (2004).
3. For more information on this topic, see Adams (2004).
4. Consulting companies or most of the so-called travel agencies in ECA countries assist migrants with visa documents, work permits, traveling, job search, and so forth. For many migrants this assistance is crucial in their decision to move. At the beginning of the migration era, this array of services was provided by just a few companies, which could result in price-setting power.
5. For more information on the Armenian diaspora and its role in remittances, see Roberts (2004).

CHAPTER 3

Determinants of Migration

Migration is driven by perceived differences in the utility of living or working in two geographical locations. Over time, such perceptions have changed in Eastern Europe and the former Soviet Union (FSU). In the aftermath of transition, migration was stimulated not only by economic motivations but also by the desire to escape conflict and relocate to ethnic homelands in many instances. As much of the diaspora migration ran its course and security risks diminished—with some exceptions such as in southern Russia—migration flows began "normalizing" and much current migration reflects perceived expectations about differences in income and the quality of life.

Despite the great variation in the migration patterns across the region and the extremely complex combination of microeconomic and social motivations for migration, similar motivations seem to underpin the decisions to migrate throughout the region. The most recent labor flows in Europe and Central Asia (ECA) region seem largely to be a response to poorly functioning labor markets, insufficient productive capital, the low quality of life in a number of migration sending countries, and a rising demand for unskilled labor for the nontraded services sector in the labor-importing economies in the European Union (EU) and Commonwealth of Independent States (CIS). As the neoclassic or Harris-Todaro approach argues, differences in real income or expected income clearly drive the supply of migration in a large number of cases. Yet, income differentials explain only a portion of the story. There is evidence that migration between two countries with unequal average real wages can remain low when there is an expectation that aggregate "quality of life" is improving in the lower-income country. Significant portions of any country's workforce may, all else being equal, prefer to remain at home rather than take on the risks of moving abroad and leave family and friends. Yet, many households agree to leave their familiar surroundings when their home countries do not provide for their physical protection from attack or abuse, or have poor public-service delivery and governance at the local and national level, an uncertain business investment environment, or high unemployment.

On the demand side, the migration of unskilled labor to the EU and the resource-rich CIS primarily reflects a need for labor in non-traded services resulting from rising incomes, the growth of the middle class, and the increasing number of women participating in the labor force. This demand for labor can be met by migrants for whom the market-clearing wage is superior to opportunities back home. As per capita incomes and mandated wages rise, unskilled local workers are increasingly priced out of the market, while the large excess supply of migrant labor sustains demand and the prevailing wage.

This chapter seeks to understand the motivations driving migration in ECA using three methods. The first section lays out the theoretical perspective for the chapter—it undertakes a literature review of existing research on the determinants of migration, and raises the possibility that overall quality of life expectations, in addition to wage differentials, may drive migration.

The next two sections contain a comparative historical analysis of the migration experiences of the countries of the FSU in one case and of the Southern and "cohesion" European countries from the 1960s to the 1980s. These countries' experiences in moving from net emigration to immigration countries over this period provide insights into the configurations of migrants' expectations and economic and quality-of-life motivations that shape broader national migration patterns. A key goal of this section is to provide a more refined understanding of the migration "hump" that some have observed characterizes migration from Southern Europe and other regions, as well as to identify the role that migrants' expectations play in shaping such hump patterns. Coming to grips with these countries' experiences may be instructive for understanding how migration may evolve in ECA in the future.

A final section employs an economic model to simulate international labor markets and thus judge the impact of improving quality of life in the receiving countries on patterns of migration. The simulation finds that improvements in the sending countries' policies and institutions can slow out-migration and perhaps enhance the incentives for circular migration, a form of migration where the migrant spends intermittent time at home and abroad.

Incentives for Migration: A Theoretical Perspective

The motivations for migration may be stylistically described as combinations of social, ethnic, and politically related push and pull factors (table 3.1). Yet, as chapter 1 discussed, labor migration is becoming the chief motive for migration for the majority of migrants in Central and Eastern European and Central Asian countries. This labor migration has generally been understood to be driven by differences in returns to labor, or expected returns, across markets.[1]

The simplest economic models of migration highlight that migration streams result from actual wage differentials across markets, or countries for our purposes, that emerge from heterogeneous degrees of labor market tightness. Todaro (1968, 1969) and Harris and Todaro (1970) refined this simple model into the more widely applied explanation that migration is driven by expected rather than actual wage differentials. Though their model was designed to understand internal migration in less-developed economies, their approach of explicitly modeling *expected* wage differentials has been widely generalized in formal explanations of international migration because it reflects the uncertainty that migrants will be able to successfully locate better paying jobs in another location. As Todaro (1969, p. 140) explained, "[a] 70 per cent …real wage premium, for example, might be of little consequence to the prospective migrant if his chances of actually securing a job are, say, one in fifty."

Yet as Bauer and Zimmermann (1999) observed, the predictions made by this simple economic model have had mixed success in explaining and predicting migration across a variety of regions. These authors found that in a number of studies, wage and also employment differentials (which are linked to the probability of locating a position abroad) were statistically significant predictors of migration in the expected directions only about half the time. In a number of cases, these differentials seemed to produce the opposite of the expected effect.

To some extent, these uneven results reflect the differential drivers of migration across countries at different points in time, as well as the extreme complexity of the migration process. They might also reflect

TABLE 3.1
Motivations for Migration

	Push factors	Pull factors
Economic and demographic	Poverty Unemployment Low wages High fertility rates Lack of basic health and education	Prospects of higher wages Potential for improved standard of living Personal or professional development
Political	Conflict, insecurity, violence Poor governance Corruption Human rights abuses	Safety and security Political freedom
Social and cultural	Discrimination based on ethnicity, gender, religion, and the like	Family reunification Ethnic (diaspora migration) homeland Freedom from discrimination

Source: World Bank staff.

the poor and noisy qualities of migration data. Yet, there are a number of empirical anomalies to the Harris-Todaro framework that suggest a more fundamental weakness. For example, the accession of Greece (1981), Portugal (1986), and Spain (1986) to the European Community (EC) was accompanied by predictions of massive waves of economic migration from these Southern European countries to Western and Northern Europe as barriers to free labor movements were phased out. The income differentials between these new member states and the majority of the EC raised fears that wages would be depressed and unemployment of indigenous workers would result in the older EC states while domestic social security systems would be placed under enormous pressure. Similar "doomsday" scenarios resulted when EU membership expanded into Central and Eastern Europe in 2004 (European Commission 2006). However, in both instances, the most extreme of these fears were exaggerated because migration levels were not as elastic to wage and employment differentials as some empirical estimations of the Harris-Todaro model would predict.

These anomalies indicate the importance of including broader quality-of-life considerations in the home country as an explanatory variable. Differences in political stability, human rights situations, and the general rule of law may also affect migration, because these factors serve as a proxy for the level of individually perceived insecurity. Thus, it is possible to hypothesize that broad, quality-of-life considerations drive or even inhibit migration. Though the decision to migrate for more productive and lucrative jobs is certainly related to the search for a higher-quality life, wage and unemployment differentials alone will not explain as much migration as when combined with these broad quality-of-life concerns. Risk-averse individuals and households may be less motivated to exploit spreads in earnings across countries if their day-to-day lifestyle is comfortable and stable. Yet, differentials in the pursuit of security may motivate those who would otherwise stay at home to search for a better and more secure life. This suggests that migration might be kept low even when income differentials are high if growth is rapid or the adoption of better institutions is underway (as with EU candidates adopting the *Acquis Communautaire*), but might increase when change is not occurring.

Thus, the policies that improve the incentives for business investment, financial deepening, and the exercise of entrepreneurship might be the same as those that reduce the incentives for migration. If "quality of life" policies are understood as a broad range of economic structural, social equity, and governance factors, then improving these policies creates the incentives necessary to maximize the benefits from existing migration flows.

Incentives for Migration: Empirical Evidence from Eastern Europe and the Former Soviet Union

As discussed above, neoclassical economic theory posits that it is differentials in wages among regions, or countries, that cause people to move from low-wage, high-unemployment regions to high-wage, low-unemployment regions. Extensions of neoclassical theory, called "the new economics of migration," use households, families, or other groups of related people, rather than markets themselves, as their unit of analysis. These units operate collectively to maximize income and minimize risk. Thus, they often send one or more family members to other parts of the country, usually a larger city, or abroad to increase overall family income while others remain behind earning lower but more stable incomes.

The complex system of ethnic homelands that make up the ECA countries further complicates migration patterns in several ways. For instance, when the Soviet Union broke apart, there were 53 different ethnic homelands, 15 of which became independent sovereign states. Across ECA, there were large diaspora populations living outside their ethnic homelands. Many thought that "return migration" to ethnic homelands of diaspora groups would dominate migration patterns during the early part of the transition period.

It appears from available data that these ethnic causes of migration, namely "diaspora" migration, did dominate trends in the early 1990s, but that economic motives are now becoming the major factor influencing migration. Much diaspora migration was accompanied by ethnic violence, resulting in large refugee and internally displaced populations. Appendix table 1.3 shows the nationality composition of the ECA countries based upon the 1990 and 2000 population censuses. In all but one of the 15 countries of the FSU, the titular population increased its share of the total population. The lone exception was Russia, where the percentage of the Russian population fell slightly, likely owing to the high rate of natural decrease of the ethnic Russian population. In the eight countries of the western ECA region where data are available from both censuses, the titular population increased in only three. This result is explained in part by increases in Roma populations resulting from ethnic reidentification.

Figure 3.1 shows the ethnic composition of migration into Russia since 1989. The share that ethnic Russians contributed to total migration into Russia peaked in 1992—the first year after the breakup of the Soviet Union—at two-thirds of total immigration. The Russian share has since declined to only half of total immigration into Russia as, presumably, those Russians who were going to leave the non-Russian states of the FSU did so in the early 1990s. As the number of Russians migrating to Russia has declined, total migration to Russia has declined and the number of non-Russians going to Russia has increased, presumably for economic reasons. The share of non-Russians would presumably be even higher if undocumented and temporary migration were included.

FIGURE 3.1

Nationality Composition of Migration to Russia, 1989 to 2003

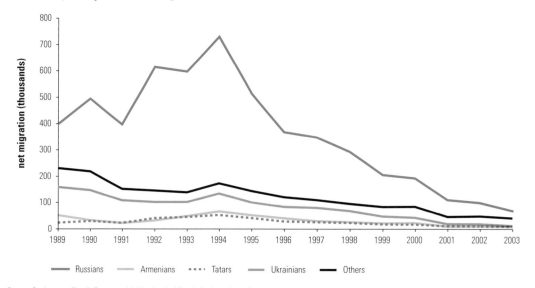

Source: Goskomstat Rossii, Demographic Yearbook of Russia (selected years).

One rather simple theoretical explanation for the migration trends among the ECA countries is the widening disparities in GDP per capita. Within countries such as the Soviet Union there was an attempt to equalize incomes among both social groups and geographic regions, which was accomplished through a massive and elaborate system of subsidies, transfers, and controlled prices. With independence and economic transition, levels of GDP per capita have widened considerably among the ECA countries, and now act as a factor. Figure 3.2 shows the coefficient of variation and the high-low ratio of per capita GDP among the ECA countries for the period 1990–2002. The coefficient of variation increased from 0.43 in 1990 to 0.70 in 1997, before declining slightly. The ratio of the country with the highest GDP to the lowest showed a similar trend, increasing from 4.9 in 1990 to 21.6 in 1999, before declining slightly.

Though illustrative of the widening income levels among ECA countries during transition, these coefficients are somewhat misleading because the two countries with the highest and lowest per capita GDPs in 2002 were Slovenia and Tajikistan. Given the distance between the two and various other factors, there is not expected to be a lot of migration from Tajikistan to Slovenia. More telling are the income disparities between migration spaces of geographically adjacent groups of countries, in this case the CIS and Europe, which includes both Eastern and Western Europe. Appendix table 1.4 shows

FIGURE 3.2

Disparities in GDP per Capita in the CEE-CIS States, 1990–2002
(PPP current international dollars)

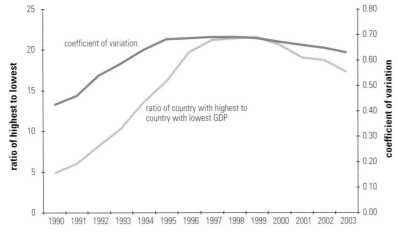

Source: World Bank, World Development Indicators.

Note: CEE = Central and Eastern European; PPP = purchasing power parity.

the income differentials between western ECA countries and Western Europe and appendix table 1.5 shows these differentials among CIS countries. Among western ECA countries, even the country with the highest income, Slovenia, has an income less than two-thirds of the Western European average. Similarly, within the CIS, the two countries with the second highest incomes, Kazakhstan and Belarus, still have incomes only about two-thirds that of Russia, while Russian GDP per capita is eight times that of Tajikistan.

The relative influence of ethnic versus economic factors partially explains the temporal trends in migration that took place across the ECA region since 1990. Yet, clearly the motivations for migration across the region have been complex and, for periods in the early 1990s, were partly driven by the dissolution of the Soviet Union. This complexity combined with the poorness of the data used for measuring these flows make the statistical estimation of the determinants very difficult. What emerges from such studies is a complex picture indicating that expected income differences, the expected probability of finding employment abroad, and expected quality of life at home play a strong role in the decision to migrate in many cases but can also be tempered by the influence of numerous other variables and the patterns vary considerably across countries (see box 3.1).[2]

Figures 3.3 and 3.4 show the trends in net migration rates for selected immigration and emigration countries, respectively. For nearly all immigration countries, net migration was much higher in the early 1990s than after 2000. As shown in figure 3.3, in Russia the net migration rate went from 0.1 per thousand in 1991, the last year of the Soviet Union's existence, to 5.4 in 1994 before falling back to almost the pretransition rate of 0.2 in 2003. Most of the other ECA countries that are now net recipients of migrants experienced a similar trend of either larger immigration or emigration in the early and mid-1990s as a result of ethnic reshuffling. However, much of the migration as a result of ethnic factors, whether voluntary or forced (or somewhere between the two), seems to have been a one-time event brought about by the increase in the number of states. Most of those who found themselves outside their ethnic homelands and who would migrate "back" home already have done so.

A similar pattern is seen among emigration countries in figure 3.4, where the large outflow of the early 1990s slowed considerably after 2000. Of the total migration of ethnic Russians to Russia over the period 1989 to 2002, over half took place in the first four years after the breakup of the Soviet Union—1992 to 1995. In the three Baltic states, which all had large Russian populations, three-quarters of return migration took place during this period. Now that these three

BOX 3.1

Estimating the Determinants of Migration in ECA

In this investigation of the determinants of migration in ECA, the model of migration developed by Hatton (1995) is used as a starting point (further information on the model and estimations is presented in appendix 3.1). This model, based on the concepts of individual utility maximization and migration as a form of investment in human capital, is delineated as follows:

$$U_t = \ln(w_d)_t + \gamma \ln(e_d)_t - \ln(w_h)_t - \eta \ln(e_h)_t - z_t \tag{1}$$

where w_d, w_h, e_d, e_h are the income and probability of employment in the countries of destination and origin, respectively, and z is the cost of migration.

The formation of expectations of the future utility of migration follows a geometric series of past values; the most recent utility streams are given greater weight.

$$U_t^* = \lambda U_t + \lambda^2 U_{t-1} + \lambda^3 U_{t-2} + ..., \qquad 0 < \lambda < 1$$

or

$$U_t^* = \lambda U_t + \lambda U_{t-1}^* \tag{2}$$

Furthermore, the immigration rate (M_t) is assumed to be a function of current and net present value levels of utility from immigration.

$$M_t = \beta(U_t^* + \alpha U_t), \ \alpha > 1 \tag{3}$$

where β stands for the aggregation parameter, and α for the extra weight given to the current utility.

Extending this basic migration model and following Zoubanov (2004) to account for the nonlinear relationship between the cost of migration and current stock of immigrants, we incorporate the squared current stock of immigrants (MST) from a given country of origin into the equation. To account for quality-of-life considerations, the same adaptive expectations structure is used as above. The European Bank for Reconstruction and Development transition index is used to account for the quality of life in the origin country. As such, the final specification is as follows:

$$\Delta M_t = \beta(\alpha + \lambda)\left[\Delta \ln(w_d / w_h)_t + \gamma \Delta \ln(e_d)_t - \eta \Delta \ln(e_h)_t - \varepsilon_1 \Delta MST_t - \varepsilon_2 \Delta MST_t^2 + \Delta EBRD_t\right] +$$
$$+ \beta(\alpha + \lambda - \lambda\alpha)\left[\varepsilon_0 + \ln(w_d / w_h)_{t-1} + \gamma \ln(e_d)_{t-1} - \eta \ln(e_h)_{t-1} + \varepsilon_1 MST_{t-1} + \varepsilon_2 MST_{t-1}^2 + EBRD_{t-1}\right] \tag{4}$$
$$- (1 - \lambda)M_{t-1}$$

The dependent variable here is the change in gross migration rates (inflows from origin to destination country divided by the population stock of origin country). Explanatory variables in the model are transformed to one-year differences and 1-year lagged levels to capture short and

(Continues on the following page.)

BOX 3.1

Estimating the Determinants of Migration in ECA (*continued*)

longer-term dynamics. The real wages w_d and w_h are approximated by per capita income data (with purchasing power parity calculations applied) of the destination and origin countries, respectively. Ignoring the labor market participation, the employment rates e_d and e_h are proxied by 100 percent minus unemployment rate in destination and origin countries, respectively. The model also incorporates distance between the capitals of destination and origin countries as a dependent variable, as well as the EBRD transition index discussed above. A summary of the results is in the table below:

Migration Rates and Current Stock of Immigrants: Extended Basic Migration Model, 1991–2003

Migration to	Changes				Lagged levels					
	PCI ratio	E in d	MST	EBRD	PCI ratio	E in d	MST	EBRD	M	D
Russia	+	−	−	+	+	0	−	−	−	−
Germany	0	+	+	0	0	+	−	−	−	−
United Kingdom	−	−	0	0	−	0	0	+	0	0
Austria	0	0	−	0	−	+	0	+	−	−
Sweden	0	+	0	0	0	+	+	−	−	−
Denmark	0	0	0	0	+	+	−	−	−	−

Source: World Bank staff estimates.

Note: + indicates that the coefficient was positive and significant at less than 10 percent; − indicates that the coefficient was negative and significant at less than 10 percent; 0 indicates that the coefficient was not statistically significant.
PCI ratio: Ratio of GDP per capita of host country to GDP per capita of home country.
E in D: Employment rate in destination country.
MST: Squared current level of migrants in host country (capturing network effects).
EBRD: EBRD Transition Index capturing quality of life related issues.

The model suggests that wage and employment differentials were statistically significant predictors of migration in the expected directions only about half the time. In a number of cases, these differentials seemed to produce the opposite of the expected effect.

In general, the results for the Russian model are broadly in line with our hypothesis that the migration rate is positively correlated with expected income differentials and negatively correlated with the expectations of improving quality of life at home. The significant negative effect of the stock of migrants seems to reject the commonly referred "network" effect in the models for Russia, Austria, and Denmark, suggesting instead that the existence of factors such as increased competition in the labor market of the destination country, anti-immigration policy, racial intolerance, and other factors may make migrant stock a poor predictor of future migrant flows. As was expected, distance is negatively correlated with the migration rate in all models.

Source: World Bank Staff estimates.

FIGURE 3.3

Net Migration in Selected Immigration Countries in ECA, 1989–2003

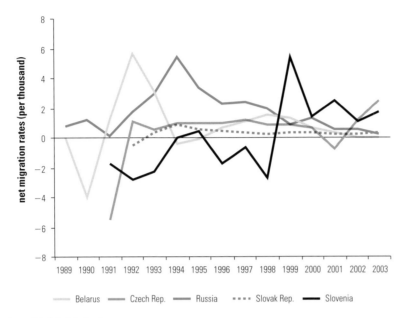

Source: World Bank Staff estimates.

FIGURE 3.4

Net Migration in Selected Emigration Countries in ECA, 1989–2003

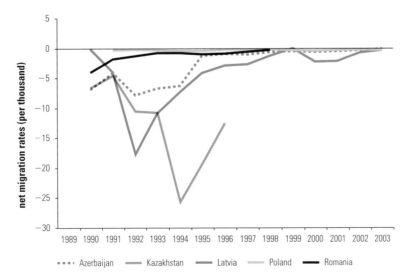

Source: World Bank Staff estimates.

countries have joined the EU and their economies are growing, net migration of Russians to Russia is less than 1,000 a year; for comparison, over 60,000 Russians left in 1992 alone. It appears that income differentials among countries will be the primary factor driving migration in the ECA region in the medium term, while demographic factors will play a role in the longer term (see chapter 1).

Despite this evidence, the temporal dimensions of these patterns do not clearly match up to those that might emerge if migrants' motivations were driven solely by cross-national income differences. The income disparities that persist fail to explain contemporary migration patterns in the ECA. The following section considers alternative explanations for determinants of migration, using the experiences of Southern Europe and Ireland as test cases.

Incentives for Migration: Lessons from Southern European Countries and Ireland

The migration histories of Ireland and Southern Europe—countries that saw many of their citizens emigrate during the postwar period—are especially useful for interpreting and forecasting patterns of emigration for the countries of Central and Eastern Europe. First, ECA countries, like Ireland and all Southern European countries, are close to their respective destination countries. This proximity is not only physical but also cultural—languages and social traditions are comparable. Additionally, Southern European countries and Ireland, as we see with ECA countries now, were poorer than their destination countries. However, in both cases the differential (especially in the last century) in fact was not extreme, particularly if the quality of human capital is the measure employed, as opposed to per capita gross national product (GNP) at purchasing power parity. Thus, while there are obvious differences between the Southern European and Irish countries and the ECA countries,[3] the similarities are sufficient that a study of the migration history of the former may provide a reasonable amount of evidence about current and future trends.[4]

To begin, some have observed that migration patterns in Southern Europe evolved as a "hump." This pattern of migration, as figure 3.5 illustrates, refers to a scenario in which emigration rates accelerate as a country's wealth increases and more households are able to fund migration. Yet as a country develops further, the motives for migration diminish and emigration rates drop.

Looking at the patterns illustrated in figure 3.5, the surge in Italian emigration during the 1960s to early 1970s was due not to an increase

FIGURE 3.5

Postwar Emigration in Southern Europe, 1960–88

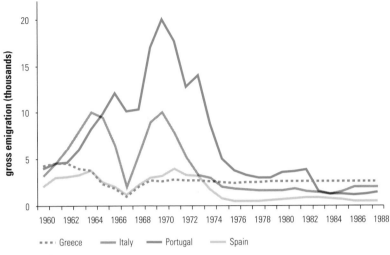

Source: Venturini 2004.

in poverty but to an increase in income and employment growth at the beginning of Italian industrialization (Hatton and Williamson 1994). The surge of Spanish emigration to other European countries in the period 1960–74 was the result of a growth rate higher than in the other European countries.[5] The peak of Portuguese emigration in the 1970s also took place during a growth phase, and Greece's emigration rates rose during the economic boom of the 1960s.

After World War II, even if the gains from intercontinental emigration were greater (given the lowering of international travel costs during this period), emigrants were affluent enough to choose a closer destination, which they viewed as a more temporary emigration solution with numerous emigrants returning home. Faini and Venturini (1993, 2001) have tested these hypotheses using gross emigration flows from Spain, Greece, Portugal, and Turkey between World War II and the end of 1980s. During that period, the per capita income differentials between these countries of origin and European destination countries were relatively stable, and increases and decreases in migration flows were due to the effects of other variables—labor market factors, the per capita income in the origin country, and the absence of a competitive business or investment environment at home. The turning point in this inverted U shape effect of the annual per capita income on the migration decision in these countries was estimated at about $3,500, after which additional economic growth discouraged emigration decisions. Similarly, Irish emigrants ceased to prefer the

United States to Britain as a consequence of the Great Depression—
80 percent of total flows went to Britain in the late 1940s—but they
did not change preferences when the American economy recovered.
Nor were their flows sensitive to the reduction in travel costs, which
again corroborates the dominance of the effect of income after World
War II (Barrett 1999).

Looking at the downward slope of migration rates in figure 3.5,
Italian outflows declined to a fractional value during the 1960s, at
which time the wage differential between Italy and the main destination countries was approximately 30 percent. This can be called the
"cost" of migration: people no longer emigrate if the return on the
investment in migration is not 30 percent higher than the wage that
they can earn in the country of origin. Yet, as was discussed above,
though wage differentials are a good first indicator with which to
understand emigration patterns, they must be combined with
employment and quality of life expectations, which are a function of
the future prospects of the economy and income levels, and these are
not always included in empirical estimates. It could be argued that
Italians reached the level of income that, all other things equal, yields
no migration incentive. The halting of Spanish and Greek emigration
to Germany in the second part of the 1970s was also the result of
lower incentives (the GDP per capita in purchasing power parity differential with Germany was about 42 percent) from both the restrictive immigration policies adopted in Northern Europe and changes in
their own governments accompanied by positive growth expectations. Such changes created strong incentives for existing migrants to
return home, and for others to postpone emigration.[6]

The history of Irish emigration is very similar to what has been
described above. The Irish have long been the United Kingdom's
"unsung gastarbeiters" (Ford 1994, p. 67). The long-run decline in
Irish migration can be accounted for by the growth of Irish income
and living standards relative to those in Britain. Irish industrial earnings rose from 70 percent of those in Britain in 1950 to 90 percent in
1990 (Ó Gráda and Walsh 1994, pp. 130–1).

Boxes 3.2 and 3.3 present two of the most recent and interesting
experiences of emigration among the EU member countries, and they
represent the opposite ends of the skill spectrum, the highly skilled
Irish and the lower-skilled Portuguese. They also represent two different patterns of emigration, though both demonstrate that migration became temporary when the home countries grew and decreased
the per capita income differential with host countries.

The above discussion supports this chapter's theory that wage or
income differentials of 30 to 40 percent are probably a necessary but

BOX 3.2

Irish Migration Dynamics

Irish emigration declined steadily until the beginning of the 1970s: the net migration rate was negative 12.7 per thousand over the period 1871–81 and declined to negative 6.3 per thousand over the period 1936–46; it increased for the last time to negative 14.0 per thousand during 1951–61, reached negative 4.0 per thousand in 1961–71, and became positive in the subsequent decade. In addition to this reversal of Ireland's net migration balance, the composition of Irish emigration changed in favor of higher skilled and educated workers.

In the late 1960s and the 1970s, the average education level increased in Ireland, and in the 1980s the workers that emigrated to the United Kingdom (44 percent), to the other EU countries (14 percent) and to the United States (14 percent, with 27 percent to the rest of the world) were better educated. As Ó Gráda and Walsh (1994) show, the proportion of emigrants among the Irish with education at the tertiary level and above was between 18 and 30 percent, while those with secondary level educations composed less than 10 percent. This was not only due to an increase in average education in Ireland, but also resulted from a more selective emigration strategy. Migration among the lower educated may have yielded returns too low to make it worthwhile, while it was still rewarding for the higher-educated as a general career strategy (Barrett 1999; Breen 1984). Thus, on the one hand, welfare discouraged emigration by the poor, while on the other, high taxes encouraged emigration by the better educated (Callan and Sutherland 1997).

As a result of trade liberalization during the 1990s and the attractiveness of foreign direct investment, the Irish economy underwent rapid growth, which induced many high-skilled emigrants to return (mainly from non-UK destinations, where the cost of migration was probably higher because of differences in culture and language). Owing to their experience abroad, return migrants were able to earn on average 10 percent more than similarly educated natives who had not moved (Barrett and O'Connell 2000). Furthermore, thanks to its rapid economic growth, Ireland became a country of immigration that attracted high-skilled EU workers and that sought to attract high-skilled ECA workers as well.

Source: World Bank staff.

not sufficient condition to determine the end of emigration. The decision to migrate depends jointly on the income differential and on other economic and noneconomic variables. However, any such discussion should be careful not to lump all migrants together; what discourages one group of migrants may encourage another. For instance, unskilled migration may be replaced by skilled, and permanent migration by temporary.

As discussed below, much of the explanation for the slowing of emigration in the mid- to late 1990s and the conversion of many

BOX 3.3

Portuguese Migration Dynamics

The case of Portugal provides a good contrast to that of Ireland (box 3.2). Portugal has a long history of emigration, and its overseas territories have served as migrants' main destinations in past centuries (Bagahna 2003). Even after World War II, the main emigrant destination was Brazil.

This picture changed during the 1960s. In line with encouraging the industrialization of the Lisbon area, the government decided that emigration had a positive impact on the labor market and contributed to the country's progress and development. Emigration took off when the country started to grow, drawing parallels to Italy; that country's emigration reached its peak with its industrialization at the beginning of the 1900s. While the Portuguese were the last of the Southern EU populations to emigrate, they followed the pattern set by Italian and Spanish workers: first to France, then to Germany and Switzerland. In contrast to the Irish, however, the average human capital of Portuguese workers was rather low, and emigrants left the country for low-skilled jobs abroad. Little by little, the Portuguese economy grew and emigration declined.

The relationship between Portugal and Germany, a major destination country for Portuguese emigrants, demonstrates the role of interacting supply and demand in the decision to migrate. When Portugal joined the EU in 1986, the GNP per capita in purchasing power parity of Germany was double that of Portugal. As a result, Germany experienced positive net immigration from Portugal. After 1993, when free mobility by Portuguese workers began (and the GNP differential was still high at about 40 percent), there was an increase amounting to 27,000 persons and only 5,000 employees.

However, the need for Portuguese labor in Germany had not disappeared. Permanent employment emigration was replaced by contracted temporary emigration or *Werkvertragsarbeiter*. These workers were employed by Portuguese companies operating in Germany and therefore did not show up in any emigration statistics. The demand for this type of worker declined when the German government obliged foreign companies to pay German wages and social security contributions.

Source: World Bank staff.

Central European countries from net emigration to net immigration status partly reflects expectations about the improvement in the quality of life in many countries in the region. However, it is first important to recognize the role of the EU in migration trends in Southern Europe, because accession of the ECA countries (or those proximate to the region) will likely affect ECA migration patterns in the future.

European Union Accession and Migration Trends

EU participation has also certainly played a major role in European migration, but probably a role different from the one expected. First, new member countries in the period before entry into the EU were required to implement a series of reforms that increased and favored the expansion of goods production. Italian development was export led, because domestic demand was too low to absorb the new production (low consumption, high savings, and the like). Similar patterns were displayed by other countries—both Ireland and Portugal also experienced export-led development—even if such development took place later on in the 1990s. Second, transfers from the Structural Fund that countries received after entry were an additional source of growth that increased domestic demand for labor, and that also helped indirectly by increasing the ability of these countries to attract foreign investments, which in turn increased the domestic demand for labor. Finally, factors in addition to strictly economic components help predict future migration trends. Expectations of future growth may be as important as current job availability in the decision to migrate, and membership in the EU has had an important effect upon potential migrant expectations

While growth prospects have traditionally been associated with increased migration, Burda (1993) points out that the freedom to move can reduce near-term immigration, because migrants are free to put off the move until later. Whereas a potential migrant would have to have taken whatever opportunities luck presented preunification, the postunification migrant can delay moving for as long as he or she wishes. If the quality of life at home shows signs of improvement, the potential migrant may decide to wait and see.

Despite the role EU membership may play in growth opportunities and migration incentives, it is important not to overemphasize its role. The emigration rates in Southern European countries had already started declining at the beginning of the 1970s, and have never regained those previous dynamics, even after EU membership. The country most at risk for large-scale emigration was Portugal. As described in box 3.3, when Portugal joined the EU in 1986, Germany's per capita GNP at purchasing power parity was double Portugal's. After 1993, when free mobility by Portuguese workers began, temporary contracts replaced permanent immigration, and even the former slowed substantially with the Portuguese economic boom of the 1990s.

This is an important finding for the ECA emigration countries and in particular for the new EU members. Joining the EU has already favored economic growth or expected growth for these countries, and both direct investment from the Social Fund and the indirect attraction of foreign investment will further enhance growth prospects. These factors, as well as higher expectations of a better quality of life at home and the reduced cost of postponing the emigration decision, will discourage emigration. Furthermore, entrance into the EU may further support the prediction of declining migrant outflows, because temporary movements may increase in comparison to permanent ones. Such a trend toward temporary movement is already taking place between Germany and Poland, for example.

Simulating the Determinants of Migration

One of the themes of this chapter is that spreads in per capita income cannot alone explain contemporary migration flows in the ECA. In addition to evidence from history and statistical estimation, an economic model was employed to further understand the role that expected quality of life at home can play in driving migration or restricting migratory flows in the face of constant income differentials among countries. Such a model provides an opportunity to test the reaction of migrants to changes in the quality of life.

The model is an extension of GTAP, a comparative-static, multiregional computable general equilibrium model developed by the Global Trade Analysis Project (see appendix 3.2 for further information on the model). Versions of this model have been used previously to look at questions relating to the impact of international migration.[7]

An extension of the GTAP model is used to examine the impact of an improvement in the general "quality of life" in ECA countries on migration flows into the EU-15 countries. The index (known as the Country Policy and Institutional Assessment or CPIA) is a World Bank index that takes a variety of a country's attributes into account, including macroeconomic policy, financial sector policy, trade, social equity, business investment environment, environmental policy, and political accountability.[8]

In this analysis, the CPIA index is treated as an exogenous factor that represents changes in overall quality of life. The impact of two simulations of improvement in the quality of life in the ECA migration-sending countries are illustrated in figure 3.6 for three groups of countries: (a) western ECA, (b) former Soviet Union, and (c) Turkey. The figure indicates the impact of increasing the quality of life on gross migration flows into the EU-15 for the western ECA countries by 10 percent and for FSU countries and Turkey by 3 per-

FIGURE 3.6

Percentage Decrease in Total Migration Flows into the EU Owing to Improvements in Quality of Life

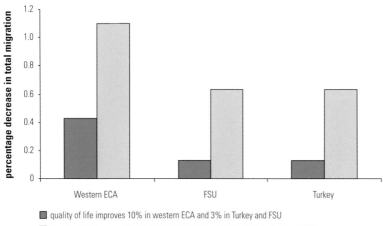

quality of life improves 10% in western ECA and 3% in Turkey and FSU
quality of life improves to EU-15 levels in western ECA and 15% in Turkey and FSU

Source: World Bank simulations. For more information on the simulations, see appendix 3.2.

Note: FSU = Former Soviet Union.

cent, and the impact on flows if quality of life in western ECA was identical to that of the EU-15 while Turkey and the FSU countries realized a 15 percent improvement.

The results indicate that migration from western ECA would fall by just over 0.4 percent with the 10 percent improvement and over 1 percent if quality of life is equalized. Flows from Turkey and the FSU also fall with an improvement of 15 percent in the quality of life index. Outflows from these two fell by about 0.63 percent.

Looking at the other side of the issue, figure 3.7 presents the results of our simulation on flows from the EU-15 countries into western ECA, Turkey, and the FSU. As before, we see the impact of improving the quality of life index in western ECA by 10 percent and to EU-15 levels, and in Turkey and the FSU by 3 percent and 15 percent. The simulations find that migration outflows do increase as quality of life improves in the ECA countries. In the case of the larger shock, the improvement of western ECA's quality of life to EU-15 levels increases migration from the EU-15 by 1 percent and into Turkey and the FSU by about 0.5 and 0.6 percent, respectively. This may very well reflect return or indeed circular migration flows from natives of these ECA countries.

Though the magnitudes of change in migration flows found with these simulations are not enormous, the results show that improvements in quality of life do have the potential to shift the direction of

FIGURE 3.7

Percentage Increase in Migration Outflows from EU-15 to ECA Countries Owing to Improvement in Quality of Life in ECA

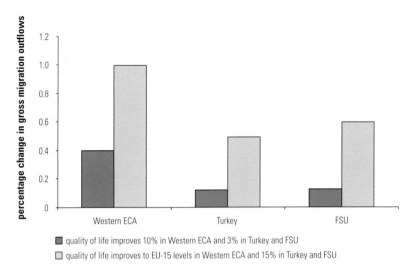

■ quality of life improves 10% in Western ECA and 3% in Turkey and FSU
□ quality of life improves to EU-15 levels in Western ECA and 15% in Turkey and FSU

Source: World Bank simulations. For more information on the simulations, see appendix 3.2.

Note: FSU = Former Soviet Union.

migration patterns in the region in such a way that improvements in economic, political, and social policies can slow outflows and perhaps encourage return flows.

Taken as a whole, the results of our simulations and the history of migration in Southern Europe and Ireland provide qualified support to the hypothesis that the quality of life in migration-sending countries matters as a determinant of migration, even in the presence of constant income differentials. Moreover, the results suggest that these policies are even capable of creating incentives for circular migration or return migration. As is discussed in chapter 3, encouraging circular migration may represent a positive step toward enhancing the returns of migration to sending and receiving countries and migrants themselves. As further simulation results in chapter 4 will indicate, these effects are magnified when immigration policies encourage temporary or circular migration.

Endnotes

1. For summaries of the migration literature, see Lucas (2005); Bauer and Zimmerman (1999).
2. Full details on the econometric estimations of the determinants of migration in ECA are presented in appendix 3.1.

3. For instance, Ireland and the Southern EU countries have long histories of international emigration (first overseas, later in Europe). This is highly different from present ECA migration, with the exception of Poland, which has only recently seen international migration on a large scale.
4. This section draws heavily from Venturini (2004).
5. The rapid growth rate produced a reduction of 1,900,000 persons active in agriculture, and 800,000 emigrants (INE).
6. By 1974 the underemployment in agriculture in Greece was reduced; between 1963 and 1973 GNP growth was about 6 percent. It is thus not very clear whether the increase in the unemployment rate in Germany or the reduction of the unemployment rate in Greece reduced the emigration rate.
7. World Bank 2006.
8. For more information, see information on the CPIA index at www.worldbank.org.

CHAPTER 4

International Regulatory Framework

International labor migration within Eastern Europe and the former Soviet Union (FSU) and between this region and Western Europe occurs within two regimes:

- For the migration of skilled workers, the General Agreement on Trade in Services (GATS) under the auspices of the World Trade Organization (WTO) has emerged as a vehicle for the multilateral relaxation of restrictions on temporary transborder labor movements.

- A set of bilateral labor agreements facilitates most legal labor migration.

The WTO provisions currently focus on extending freedom of passage to a limited subset of international migrants in multinational firms. Thus, the provisions and any proposed revisions to them have little consequence for unskilled migrants at present. Most legal unskilled migration is governed by a series of bilateral agreements on labor activity and the social protection of citizens working outside their countries.

The diverse range of bilateral policies makes it difficult to generalize about the impact of their specific provisions. If, however, one judges the impact of these agreements by looking at actual unskilled migratory flows—in particular, the very large levels of undocumented migration—it would seem that these policies often do not provide sufficient incentives for or facilitate legal migration by unskilled workers.

This chapter has two key parts. The main portion of the chapter reviews the existing framework for international labor migration in Eastern Europe and the FSU. It documents the bilateral migration agreements among ECA countries and between them and the EU-15 countries.

The second part of this chapter proposes the outlines of an alternative regime for organizing international migration. Drawing upon the information presented throughout this report and the results of simulations, this section proposes that bilateral migration agreements could be modified to encourage legal migration by unskilled workers. Though some countries may want to encourage more permanent migration, in instances where this is not preferred, circular migration may allow for the effective matching of supply and demand for international labor without necessarily creating higher rates of permanent migration. The alternative framework presented here provides the contours of incentives designed to encourage such circular migration flows.

Surveys with ECA migrants conducted for this report suggest that the shift to a circular pattern of labor migration is likely a closer match with the preferences of many migrants to spend short periods abroad—building human and financial capital—and then return home. Moreover, circular or temporary migration may have the advantage of limiting "brain or brawn drain" from the migrants' home country. Temporary migration also has the advantage of reducing cultural friction in the migration receiving country.

As the UN (2005) report on migration highlights, migration involves a complex organization of political, economic, and social forces. This complexity requires that policy prescriptions be highly qualified. The exact policies needed will certainly vary by country, whether on the sending or receiving side of the equation. This chapter suggests the rough outlines of the sorts of international cooperation that might increase the returns from migration for sending and receiving countries and migrants and their families.

Given the uncertainty of policy, the best way forward may be a stepwise "learning by doing" approach that takes the form of pilot, temporary managed-migration schemes among willing pairs of countries.

Current Regime

This section provides an overview of the existing policies for facilitating international labor movements from Eastern Europe and the FSU.

The section begins with a brief overview of the WTO provisions on labor migration. It then discusses the various bilateral agreements that have been made directly between migrant sending and receiving countries in this region.

Multilateral Arrangements and Their Limitations

The major multilateral policy effort to address international legal migration flows is the Mode 4 framework of the GATS. Mode 4 tackles the provision of services by allowing cross-border movements of certain citizens of the WTO countries. Its introduction generated initial optimism that eventually the broader liberalization of labor markets could be negotiated. A commitment to deepen the coverage of Mode 4, however, has not yet emerged. Even though services represent over 70 percent of the GDP of developed economies, only very small portions of international migrants qualify as "service providers" by WTO standards.

Unlike trade liberalization in products and other services, providing for the free movement of labor generates a number of negative externalities: the values, rights, responsibilities, and risks that the migrants bring to the receiving society and economy may create various forms of conflict.[1] As a result, GATS protections are only extended to "natural persons" who intend to relocate temporarily or provide a service abroad. Moreover, even if GATS were to progress, a large portion of ECA labor migrants would not be covered by its provisions because the framework only addresses skilled labor.

Bilateral Agreements
Given the weaknesses in multilateral agreements for cross-border migration movements, a collection of bilateral labor agreements have been negotiated between the migration-sending and -receiving countries that facilitate a great deal of the legal transborder labor flows in the region. It is difficult to generalize about the impact of these agreements, because they vary dramatically in type and scope across countries. Bilateral agreements facilitate short- to medium-term migration across countries for the purposes of seasonal employment, specific project-related employment, apprenticeships or trainee-ships, and other purposes. As with migration flows more generally, bilateral agreements have a strong, bi-axial regional orientation (table 4.1). The majority of the agreements involving the Central and Eastern European countries (CEECs) are with Western Europe or other CEECs (82 percent). In contrast, a large majority (64 percent) of CIS bilateral agreements create labor flow links with other CIS members.

TABLE 4.1

Regional Composition of Bilateral Agreements

(percentage)

Country group	CEECs	CIS	EU-15
CEECs	21	18	61
CIS	31	64	4

Source: World Bank Staff estimates.

Note: Cells indicate the percentage of agreements signed between the subregions in the rows and columns. Percentages may not sum to 100% due to rounding.

Agreements Between the EU-15 and CEECs

The number of bilateral agreements within Europe is very large and has increased rapidly during the 1990s: of the 92 agreements in existence, some 75 percent were signed after 1989. There are several reasons for this, the most important ones being the collapse of the Soviet Union and the disintegration of the former Yugoslavia. It should be stressed, however, that many bilateral agreements were signed to manage the large ethnically motivated and conflict-related migration streams during the first half of the 1990s. Because the second half of that decade saw a return to more "normal" migration volumes (see chapter 1), it is not clear to what extent existing agreements are still operational.

The need for bilateral agreements between the countries of Western and Eastern Europe will expire as the latter obtain membership in the EU's single labor market. The Accession Treaty of 2003 set out that there will be a transitional period for the free movement of workers allowing the EU-15 to postpone the opening of their labor markets for up to seven years. The so-called 2+3+2 regulation divides the transitional period into three phases. During the first phase, the EU-15 can apply national rules on access to their labor markets for the first two years after enlargement. The diverse national measures have resulted in several legally different migration regimes. Since the accession of the EU-8 countries to the EU in May 2004, only eight countries have fully opened their labor markets to the new member states: Ireland, Sweden, and the United Kingdom never had restrictions on workers from the EU-8. Greece, Finland, Spain, and Portugal lifted restrictions in May 2006. Italy ended the transitional arrangements in July 2006, while France, Belgium, and Luxembourg softened their restrictions on workers from the EU-8. Poland, Slovenia, and Hungary apply reciprocal restrictions to nationals from the EU-15 member states applying restrictions. All new member states have opened their labor markets to EU-8 workers.

In May 2006, the second phase of the transitional period started, which allowed EU-15 member states to continue national measures for up to another three years. At the end of this period (2009) all member states will be invited to open their labor markets entirely. Only if countries can show serious disturbances in the labor market, or a threat of such disturbances, will they be allowed to resort to a safeguard clause for a maximum period of two years. From 2011, all member states will have to comply with European Commission rules regulating the free movement of labor.[2] Thus, in the short-run, bilateral migration agreements may remain relevant for some countries in western ECA.

Germany is by far the most important country in terms of the number of agreements, perhaps because it is the largest destination for CEEC migrants. Over half of all existing bilateral agreements have been signed by Germany; all CEECs have agreements with Germany except Serbia and Montenegro, which has no bilateral migration agreement with any EU country (table 4.2). Out of the 15 EU countries, 14 have bilateral agreements with one or more CEEC (the only exception is Denmark). On average, each EU country has signed between two and three bilateral agreements with countries in Central and Eastern Europe.

On the CEEC side, there is a substantial variation in the number of agreements, ranging from 15 for Poland and 12 for Hungary to 7 for Bulgaria and Romania. A number of intra-CEEC agreements exist, but only for a few countries, notably Poland, the Czech Republic, and the Slovak Republic. These are mainly cross-border arrangements. Most CEECs do not have any intra-CEEC agreements.

The CEEC countries have very few bilateral agreements with Organisation for Economic Co-operation and Development (OECD) countries outside the EU. Only three non-EU countries in the OECD have bilateral agreements with CEEC countries—Canada, Finland, and Switzerland. Moreover, these agreements have mainly been

TABLE 4.2

Geographical Distribution of Bilateral Migration Agreements between CEEC and EU-15

	Germany	Luxembourg	Austria	France	Other EU-15
Poland	6	1	0	2	6
Hungary	4	1	2	1	4
Czech Rep.	5	1	2	1	0
Slovak Rep.	5	1	0	1	1
Bulgaria	3	1	0	0	3
Romania	3	1	0	0	3
Turkey	2	0	1	1	3
Serbia and Montenegro	0	0	0	0	0
Other CEECs	15	0	0	0	—

Source: Compiled from OECD (2003).

signed by the CEEC countries with relatively high per capita income, specifically the Czech Republic, Hungary, Poland, and the Slovak Republic.

Table 4.3 shows that the most common types of agreements are guest worker schemes and trainee arrangements. Together, they account for over half of all agreements. Seasonal-worker agreements and project-type agreements together account for another third.

It is useful to distinguish between agreements that target unskilled labor and those aimed at skilled labor. Typically, seasonal arrangements and cross-border agreements do not require migrants to possess specific skills; the same appears often to be true for guest worker agreements. Project-type and trainee agreements, however, often explicitly state required skills or experience that migrants must demonstrate (see Hárs 2003 for an account of Hungary's agreements with the EU-15). Table 4.3 suggests that agreements requiring skilled labor are mainly between the EU-15 and CEECs with relatively high per capita income, while seasonal and guest worker agreements are mainly between the EU-15 and the relatively poorer CEECs. Consequently, geography and CEEC income are important variables for explaining the number and the nature of bilateral agreements in the region.

The motives for migration-sending countries in the CEEC to sign bilateral agreements are at least fourfold. First, it is a way to reduce the amount of surplus labor in these countries by reducing unemployment. Second, remittances are sometimes (as detailed in chapter 2) a

TABLE 4.3

Bilateral Migration Agreements between the EU and CEECs by Country and Type

Country	Seasonal	Projects	Guest	Trainee	Cross-B	Others	Total
Austria	0	0	1	2	2	0	**5**
France	2	0	1	6	0	0	**9**
Germany	8	13	13	3	1	7	**45**
Spain	2	0	2	2	0	0	**6**
Other	4	2	4	14	1	2	**27**
Total	**16**	**15**	**21**	**27**	**4**	**9**	**92**
Czech Rep.	1	1	1	4	1	1	**9**
Hungary	1	1	1	5	1	1	**10**
Poland	3	1	3	6	1	1	**15**
Slovak Rep.	1	1	1	4	0	1	**8**
Bulgaria	3	2	1	1	0	0	**7**
Romania	2	1	2	2	0	2	**9**
Turkey	0	1	6	1	0	0	**8**
Other	5	7	6	4	1	3	**26**
Total	**16**	**15**	**21**	**27**	**4**	**9**	**92**

Source: Compiled from OECD (2003).

very large share of total income in the economy and may provide funds for savings and investment. Remittances costs or security may be higher when they are sent through formal, legal channels. Third, temporary employment in relatively wealthier countries may increase skills that can be used productively when the migrant returns home. Finally, and arguably the most important in comparison with costs of undocumented migration, a bilateral agreement may help migrants to enjoy reasonable working conditions and to get access to the social safety net in the receiving country. This would increase their human capital and make them more valuable on return.

The available migration data suggest that labor migration into the EU-15 from the CEECs is employed in sectors or activities where it does not compete with local labor. Thus, for instance, Germany received over 200,000 seasonal workers in the late 1990s while only 33,000 workers were employed as contract workers (OECD 2001, tables 2.4–2.5), and according to Garnier (2001), the number of Polish seasonal workers received in Germany is approximately eight times as large as the number of workers received under all other categories. It is important to point out that the skills or education of migrants do not necessarily provide an indication of the positions in which they will work in the recipient countries. Frequently, highly skilled migrants take jobs with low skill requirements and thus create "brain waste" (Garnier 2001).

Agreements Within the CIS

The intra-CIS agreements differ from the agreements directed at Europe by not focusing on quotas while concentrating on legal status and social protection. Also, agreements directed at Europe have more of a "migration creating" role, whereas agreements within the CIS seem to be a reaction to existing migration flows.

As a result, the current regulatory framework of legal migration flows in the CIS is characterized by a series of regional and bilateral agreements on labor activity and social protection of citizens working outside of their countries. This situation is the result of the disintegration of the Soviet Union, which obliged the newly independent states to pragmatically defend their citizens' interests. The main regional agreement is the "Agreement on cooperation in the field of labor migration and the social protection of migrant workers," accepted in 1994 by all CIS states. This agreement, however, did not come to force because it was to be implemented through bilateral agreements, which were never signed (IOM 2002). In the field of undocumented migration, the cornerstone of regional cooperation is the 1998 Agreement on cooperation in Combating Illegal Migration (IOM 2002, 2005b).

The Russian Federation has concluded the most bilateral agreements (with 9 out of the 11 CIS member states). Belarus has concluded the next largest number of bilateral agreements, with six other CIS countries. Kazakhstan and Ukraine have concluded four each. Kazakhstan, the main receiving country in Central Asia, has no agreements with its Central Asian neighbors except for an agreement with the Kyrgyz Republic on the labor activities and the social protection of labor migrants working in the agricultural sector in the border areas.

Along with the intergovernmental agreements, interagency agreements are a form of international cooperation that has emerged more recently. Since 2002, the Russian Ministry of Internal Affairs has concluded such agreements in the migration sphere with the counterpart agencies in the Kyrgyz Republic, Tajikistan, and Ukraine.

The majority of CIS labor migrants do not profit from the protection provided for in these agreements or from any other legal protection, however, because they work under an undocumented status. In both Russia and Kazakhstan, the largest recipient countries in the region, the estimated number of irregular migrants is several times higher than the number of official migrants. For example, according to IOM (2005a), Tajikistan had 16,800 legal migrant workers in Russia in 2002, while the actual number of undocumented labor migrants was estimated at more than 600,000. Uzbekistan had 16,100 legal labor migrants, while the labor emigration from Uzbekistan is estimated at between 600,000 and 700,000. Similarly, the number of foreign "licensed" workers employed in Kazakhstan was 11,800 in 2002 while IOM estimates the number of irregular immigrants to be 20 to 50 times higher. According to official estimates, from 220,000 to 300,000 migrant workers are employed now in the country while experts and official statistical analysis suggest up to 500,000 (table 4.4).

TABLE 4.4
Number of Registered Foreigners and Estimated Number of Aliens Living Irregularly in Some CIS Countries, 2000

Country	Foreigners	Irregular migrants
Belarus	94,570	50,000–150,000
Kazakhstan	81,133[a]	200,000
Russian Federation	58,200[b]	1,300,000–1,500,000
Tajikistan	—	20,000
Ukraine	456,300	1,600,000
Uzbekistan	—	30,000

Source: IOM 2002.

Note: — = not available.
a. Foreigners who settled in Kazakhstan for a period longer than six months.
b. Non-ECA aliens who were granted a residence permit at year end.

This large number of undocumented labor migrants reflects that there is a demand for labor that can be satisfied neither from the resident labor force nor from the existing legal quotas. Also, movement is facilitated by the low transportation costs (generally less than $300) and the ability of most CIS citizens (with the exception of Georgians in Russia and Turkmen in general) to travel to Kazakhstan or Russia without a visa. Moreover, a survey showed that about one of five Tajik migrants traveled and worked in Russia without passport or official document (Bokozada 2005).

At the same time, irregular status arises because migrants are required to have work and residency permits (with the exception of citizens of Belarus in Russia). Indeed, except for visa-free travel, migrants from CIS countries have no advantages over migrants from other countries in either Kazakhstan and Russia. This means that they also have to apply for work permits within the general quota established by the government. These quotas for legal immigration are allocated to each region of the receiving country, and are established on a yearly basis. In Russia, this yearly quota is on average set at 0.3 percent of the active population, in Kazakhstan it was 0.14 percent and 0.21 percent of the active population in 2003 and 2004 respectively (IOM 2005a). However, excessive bureaucracy and the small overall quotas result in most migrants never applying for work permits.

The resulting outcome is suboptimal. It leaves millions of workers without any legal protection not only from employers, but also from government agencies. Moreover, the situation causes considerable losses in terms of tax revenues to the government.

Costs of the Current Regime
The bilateral-agreement frameworks may fail to meet their stated objectives in many instances. To the degree that the objective of these agreements is to facilitate legal international migration, they often do not appear to be successful, as indicated by the high levels of undocumented migration in the region (chapter 1). Large amounts of irregular migration can impose significant social, economic, and national security costs on receiving and sending countries (see box 4.1). Moreover, undocumented migrants are more likely to be subject to abuse.[3]

Furthermore, as the previous section highlighted, the agreements are often not able to facilitate large amounts of legal, unskilled migration. The high bureaucratic costs of applying for many of these programs and insufficient quotas provide incentives for migrants to pursue other channels through which to migrate—especially undocumented options.

BOX 4.1

Possible Costs and Externalities of Illegal Immigration

1. With the exception of sales tax, the income earned by illegal immigrants is not taxable. This represents forgone fiscal revenue.

2. Illegal migrants offer an unfair competitive advantage to firms that employ them over firms that do not.

3. Irregular migrants are not covered by a minimum wage or national and industry wage agreements. They are therefore more likely to undercut the wages of the low skilled.

4. Whether entry is legal or illegal may affect the quality of migrants, even if the legal migration scheme does not select on the basis of skill. Skilled workers or professionals are much more likely to enter if there is a legal channel, even if their qualifications are not a condition of entry.

5. Employers may decide not to abide by health and safety regulations, leading to the potential for migrant death and injury. Police and health services may be called upon to rescue or treat the injured, to investigate the reasons for death, or to bury the dead.

6. Illegal migrants are not screened for diseases and viruses upon arrival, and have little access to health services during their stay. At the same time, they risk having been exposed to illnesses on their journey, especially if they have been smuggled or trafficked. This has the potential to generate large public health externalities because diseases can spread to the native population. Particularly important examples include tuberculosis, which seems to be reemerging in parts of Europe, and HIV, as many trafficked women become involved in the sex industry. By way of illustration, in 2002–03, those apprehended on the Slovak-Ukraine border were found to be suffering from respiratory tract infections, tuberculosis, and scabies.

7. Forced to live underground, and with little access to legitimate employment, migrants are more likely to be exposed to the world of crime.

8. Stigmatization of illegal migrants can undermine social cohesion if it spreads to cover those who entered legally.

9. Illegal migrants may be encouraged to stay longer than they might desire and to remain even when unemployed because of the risks of detection and associated costs of entering and leaving.

10. Trafficking is a subject that is far too large to be addressed in this report; however, the trade in many ways exacerbates the previous costs, as well as being a source of organized crime (for further information on some of the social and human costs of trafficking, see chapter 3).

Source: World Bank staff.

Finally, most agreements do not contain mechanisms to encourage circular or repeated migration. If it is costly for potential migrants to apply for a space on a temporary migration program, they may well have an incentive to remain abroad—even if through illegal channels by overstaying their visas—for longer periods than they prefer. As will be discussed below, surveys with migrants conducted for this report found that most migrants would prefer to spend shorter periods abroad, then return home. Agreements that facilitate this temporary migration while opening up the option to migrate abroad at a later stage with relatively low transactions costs might represent an improvement over the current system.

Despite these weaknesses, bilateral agreements have some advantages relative to the most-favored-nation approach used in trade negotiations, and particularly are useful for policy makers in receiving countries who are seeking to balance labor-market demand with the potential externalities of migration.[4] As discussed before, migration generates a number of social and political externalities not found in the cross-border movement of products and other services (box 4.2). Such agreements can limit adverse selection by choosing particular groups of migrants and may provide a framework to send home migrants who impose too high a cost on social benefits or are socially disruptive. Most important, however, they provide a legitimate way for nations to legally and safely supply business with the labor it demands. As a result, an alternative framework that improves upon the existing bilateral structure may represent a good direction forward for improving policy.

A Proposal for an Alternative Framework

This section details the broad contours of an alternative framework that could be employed by migration-sending and -receiving countries to facilitate the legal migration of unskilled labor. Given the complexity of migration, general policy prescriptions must be qualified. Further study and perhaps policy experimentation are required to better understand how to improve upon the limitations of the existing framework, as identified earlier in this chapter.

What follows is a collection of observations, derived from the information presented throughout this report and from economic modeling, on the sorts of elements that seem to be missing from existing international migration policies, but that could increase the payoffs to migration for sending and receiving countries and migrants and their families. Future policy experiments and analytical studies could keep these considerations in mind when moving forward.

BOX 4.2

Social Externalities Generated by Migration

This box provides a summary of some of the social externalities arising from migration.

- First, migrants from other cultures bring different values, which some sections of the native population may resent.

- Second, unlike imported goods, migrants are people who hold a package of political, social, and moral rights and obligations. While a migrant may be welcome for the labor he or she can provide, the implications of allowing a human being to enter a country go beyond purely economic functions. For example, migrants may make demands for family reunification or treatment that is different from that given to residents, for example, religious holidays, food, dress, and safety regulations. While these considerations need not in themselves be negative, they are externalities not present with the decision to import a good.

- Third, while buying an imported product is a one-time decision, bringing in a migrant could result in future labor market commitments, including the renewing of visas, paying of taxes, and provision of relevant training. Furthermore, even in conditions of temporary labor market employment, if the labor market tightens it may not be possible to send the migrant home.

- Finally, a migrant generates implicit or explicit claims for social protection that, depending on the taxation regime and the effectiveness of tax administration, may result in a net fiscal cost.

Source: World Bank staff.

The findings of this report suggest that the international governance of migration could be more coherent and requires improved capacity at the national level and closer coordination between states. Any framework to replace the existing one could recognize, organize, and facilitate unskilled labor migration, while acting on both demand and supply to limit undocumented migration. The outcome could be an improvement in the protection given to temporary workers, while still offering migration-receiving countries needed labor.

Given variations in national attributes and preferences, such a temporary framework could take a variety of different forms and be organized bilaterally, regionally, or internationally. Yet, there are a number of common elements that such policies might include:

- Recognize that the labor market, like any other market, needs to balance supply as well as demand. The framework could explicitly target measures at the supply of low-skilled labor as well as at the demand for such labor.

- The new regime could channel migrant labor to sectors or subsectors with little native labor to ensure that migrants are complements to and not substitutes for domestic labor.

- On the demand side, receiving countries need policies that limit the employment of undocumented migrants by offering employers the means to hire legally the workers they need. To promote development and coordinate with the preferences of many ECA migrants to go abroad temporarily, an alternative regime could emphasize circular migration. World Bank surveys for this report found that the majority of migrants would prefer to spend shorter times abroad and then return home (see figure 4.1).

- To ensure that employment under the new regime is temporary and not permanent, incentives could be designed to encourage return home when not employed. For example, unemployment and pension benefits could both be portable and only payable in the country of origin.

- Policies should respect the rights of migrants to be treated with dignity while abroad, including clear and transparent rules regarding remuneration, work conditions, or dismissal procedures. Moreover, migrants' rights to appeal to receiving-country authorities to adjudicate disputes and protect themselves from crime could be communicated and enforced.

Bilateral migration agreements that include some or all of these features could have a number of advantages over many existing policies:

- Agreements could stimulate circular migration, allowing employers in receiving countries to obtain affordable nontraded services while respecting the law, and reduce incentives for potential migrants to use illegal means of entry.

- Such an approach seems commensurate with migrants' preferences to spend shorter periods abroad and the need for receiving countries to obtain labor services but not necessarily absorb a permanent population of migrants.

- Moreover, in the sending country, increased circular migration, encouraged by the lowering of transportation costs, could reduce many of the negative social effects that result from the separation of families during long-term migration[5] and reduce the incidence and degree of "brain drain" from migration-sending countries in ECA.[6]

FIGURE 4.1

Migrants' Preferences for Short- versus Long-Term Migration

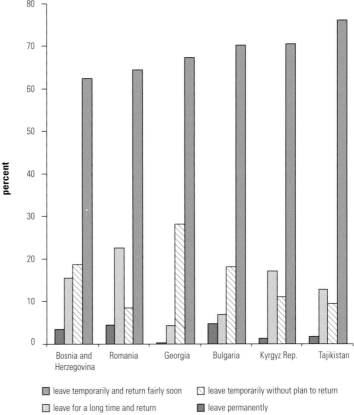

Source: World Bank surveys with returned migrants.

For undocumented migrants, a regime with these features—with incentives for legal migration—could strengthen the rights that migrants receive in the receiving country and allow them to obtain social protection benefits that are out of reach today. Undocumented migrants have no access to adjudicative processes when abroad and hence have no legal recourse to oppose abuse. By drying up the incentives and opportunities for undocumented hiring, legal protections for large stocks of foreign workers could be expanded.

To make the system credible and useful, it may be necessary to increase enforcement against undocumented hiring. The GTAP model described in chapter 3 was used to examine the impact of an increase in the penalty for hiring undocumented labor, combined with an increase in the probability of being caught hiring undocumented labor, which serves as a proxy for better enforcement of such rules.[7]

The results suggest (figure 4.2) that undocumented labor becomes more expensive under these circumstances, thereupon the demand for undocumented migrant workers decreases and interregional labor movements slow down.

The framework proposed in this section is not without its flaws. Nevertheless, its strength is that it allows for the recalibration of incentives for undocumented labor. The benefits of moving to a regime of legal migration for all interested parties cannot be overemphasized.

FIGURE 4.2

Percentage Decrease in Illegal Migration into the EU Owing to Increase in Penalty for Hiring Illegally

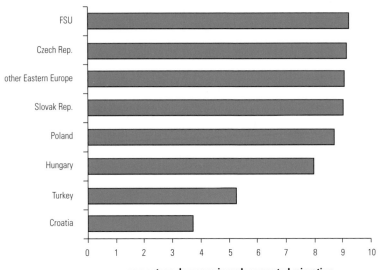

Source: World Bank simulations.

Note: Results are based on an increase in the penalty for hiring undocumented labor by 80 percent from current levels and the probability of being caught hiring undocumented labor at 20 percent, that is, effective enforcement. Other Eastern Europe is Bulgaria, Romania, Estonia, Lithuania, Latvia, and Slovenia.

Endnotes

1. See appendix 4.1 for a more detailed discussion of the integration of migrants in the receiving country.
2. See appendix 4.2 for a more complete discussion of the EU's transitional arrangements for incorporating new CEEC member states into the single labor market.
3. See appendix 4.3 for further information on undocumented migration and some of the risks that it poses to migration-sending and -receiving countries and migrants themselves.
4. Most-favored-nation status is given by one country to another in matters of international trade. This status ensures that the receiving country will receive identical trade access and terms that any third country would receive.
5. For further information on the impact of longer-term migration on communities left behind, see appendix 4.4.
6. To date, there is not a good understanding of the prevalence and impact of brain drain in the ECA region. For a summary of the existing state of knowledge, see appendix 4.5.
7. See appendix 3.2 for a discussion of the model.

Survey Methodology

For the World Bank's ECA migration report, returned migrants were surveyed in six countries: Bosnia and Herzegovina, Bulgaria, Georgia, Kyrgyz Republic, Romania, and Tajikistan. The survey instrument was a comprehensive, 77-item questionnaire that addressed a full range of the returned migrants' experiences before, during, and after migration. Questions covered the financial, social, family, and personal aspects of migrants' experiences both during and after migration. The full questionnaire and survey results will be available on the ECA Web site, www.worldbank.org/ECA.

The survey was designed to provide an impressionistic, rather than representative, picture of returned migrants' experiences. For the purposes of this survey, a "returning migrant" was defined as anyone who has been abroad for more than three months with the purpose of employment, and has hound him/herself in their home country during the survey. The survey also provides some information on the number of migrants who have returned permanently as opposed to those who have expressed desire to migrate again.

Though the same survey instrument was utilized in each of the six countries, local teams relied on slightly different methodologies to select the sample of returned migrants to interview. In most cases, this involved some form of "network" or "snowball" method in which returned migrants were identified through references from other returned migrants or affiliated formal and informal institutions. The preference for this methodology stemmed from the fact that no systematic view, including prior studies on migrant flows and experience or the possibility to use household surveys, were found to support a more comprehensive methodology. In some cases national censuses have allowed for some blueprint on this selection.

Though in most case, efforts were taken to ensure that a national sample is taken and various regions of the six countries were sampled, the extent to which the survey is representative of the universe of returned migrants in these countries cannot be measured. The survey generated relatively large sample sizes—about 1,200 returned migrants in each country—yet the results must be interpreted with caution.

Migration Statistics

APPENDIX TABLE 1.2.1

Population Change in the ECA States, 1989–2004

(beginning-of-year; thousands)

	Total population (1)		Absolute change			Percent change		
	1989	2004	Total	Natural increase	Migration	Total	Natural increase	Migration
Russian Federation	147,400	144,534	−2,866	−8,635	5,769	−1.9	−5.9	3.9
Ukraine	51,707	47,442	−4,265	−3,482	−782	−8.2	−6.7	−1.5
Belarus	10,152	9,849	−303	−332	29	−3	−3.3	0.3
Moldova	4,338	4,247	−91	147	−238	−2.1	3.4	−5.5
Latvia	2,667	2,319	−347	−149	−199	−13	−5.6	−7.4
Lithuania	3,675	3,446	−229	6	−235	−6.2	0.2	−6.4
Estonia	1,566	1,351	−215	−62	−153	−13.7	−4	−9.8
Armenia	3,449	3,212	−236	399	−635	−6.9	11.6	−18.4
Azerbaijan	7,021	8,266	1,245	1,476	−232	17.7	21	−3.3
Georgia	5,401	4,544	−857	242	−1,099	−15.9	4.5	−20.4
Kazakhstan	16,465	14,951	-1,513	1,892	-3,406	−9.2	11.5	−20.7
Kyrgyz Republic	4,254	5,037	783	1,174	−390	18.4	27.6	−9.2
Tajikistan	5,109	6,640	1,531	2,302	−771	30	45.1	−15.1
Turkmenistan	3,518	5,158	1,640	1,269	371	46.6	36.1	10.6
Uzbekistan	19,882	25,707	5,825	7,125	−1,300	29.3	35.8	−6.5
Poland	37,885	38,191	306	973	−667	0.8	2.6	−1.8
Czech Republic	10,360	10,211	−149	−168	19	−1.4	−1.6	0.2
Slovak Republic	5,264	5,380	116	168	−53	2.2	3.2	−1

(Table continues on the following page.)

APPENDIX TABLE 1.2.1 (*continued*)

Population Change in the ECA States, 1989–2004

(beginning-of-year; thousands)

	Total population (1)		Absolute change			Percent change		
	1989	2004	Total	Natural increase	Migration	Total	Natural increase	Migration
Hungary	10,589	10,117	−472	−498	26	−4.5	−4.7	0.2
Albania	3,182	3,103	−80	681	−760	−2.5	21.4	−23.9
Bulgaria	8,987	7,801	−1,185	−497	−688	−13.2	−5.5	−7.7
Romania	23,112	21,713	−1,399	−154	−1,245	−6.1	−0.7	−5.4
Slovenia	1,996	1,996	0	5	−5	0	0.2	−0.2
Croatia	4,495	4,442	−54	−35	−18	−1.2	−0.8	−0.4
FYR Macedonia	1,881	2,030	149	225	−76	7.9	12	−4
Bosnia and Herzegovina	4,435	3,785	−651	..	..	−14.7	..	..
Serbia and Montenegro	10,445	10,662	217	398	−182	2.1	3.8	−1.7

Sources: UNICEF TransMONEE Database and national statistical offices.

Note: .. = negligible.

APPENDIX TABLE 1.2.2

Population by Place of Birth in the FSU, 1989

Place of permanent residence	Persons born in							
	Russian Federation	Ukraine	Belarus	Uzbekistan	Kazakhstan	Georgia	Azerbaijan	Lithuania
Russian Federation	135,549,786	4,595,811	1,408,619	529,814	1,825.035	423,040	478,594	116,115
Ukraine	5,211,922	44,332,132	419,031	137,095	343,730	79,571	84,629	26,258
Belarus	786,672	268,015	8,883,290	14,828	61,894	14,141	11,153	17,403
Uzbekistan	915,978	199,096	27,169	18,108,456	202,204	35,511	26,989	2,577
Kazakhstan	2,450,213	510,702	136,939	139,495	12,714,676	44,485	40,361	10,088
Georgia	191,274	65,974	9,654	4,074	14,685	5,038,710	16,573	954
Azerbaijan	161,999	31,650	7,840	6,910	14,921	24,831	6,604,318	549
Lithuania	173,938	47,453	88,093	4,608	14,391	2,235	2,407	3,299,039
Moldava	248,674	266,585	15,640	5,979	21,091	7,882	3,703	1,041
Latvia	384,423	93,528	116,621	5,241	14,240	3,225	4,827	37,197
Kyrgyz Republic	348,471	53,652	10,056	69,560	125,534	6,597	3,548	784
Tajikistan	234,030	43,446	7,977	86,619	27,788	2,350	4,337	498
Armenia	53,766	13,294	2,297	2,116	4,257	60,756	125,123	322
Turkmenistan	175,788	33,182	9,630	36,860	16,309	2,736	19,916	947
Estonia	300,430	46,322	25,299	2,771	8,072	2,328	2,343	3,386

Place of permanent residence	Persons born in							Persons born abroad and persons not indicating birthplace
	Moldava	Latvia	Kyrgyz Republic	Tajikistan	Armenia	Turkmenistan	Estonia	
Russian Federation	228,795	99,932	260,914	153,806	151,484	140,551	65,485	994,088
Ukraine	186,983	20,965	38,745	36,207	36,498	32,406	10,994	454,868
Belarus	7,502	10,496	4,792	5,305	2,912	5,098	3,246	55,059
Uzbekistan	6,426	3,038	79,663	84,089	12,280	52,226	1,551	52,824
Kazakhstan	27,499	5,274	93,616	21,958	10,756	42,141	2,428	213,830
Georgia	2,243	902	1,486	1,529	37,742	1,466	644	12,931
Azerbaijan	1,830	606	987	1,008	137,027	7,819	243	18,640
Lithuania	1,935	12,247	1,105	1,626	895	3,668	1,663	19,499
Moldova	3,739,090	1,024	1,846	1,379	1,318	1,962	606	17,540
Latvia	4,212	1,974,518	2,115	4,097	1,399	1,811	5,401	13,712
Kyrgyz Republic	2,052	817	3,585,832	11,215	1,701	4,059	353	33,524
Tajikistan	1,830	890	14,926	4,649,781	2,302	5,825	565	9,439
Armenia	668	220	645	1,534	2,570,422	1,977	148	467,231
Turkmenistan	2,608	964	3,755	3,358	4,436	3,204,771	376	7,081
Estonia	1,635	6,467	1,187	904	758	1,056	1,154,585	8,119

Sources: EastView Publications and CIS Statistical Committee, USSR Census Results 1989 CD-ROM.

APPENDIX TABLE 1.1.3

Population by Nationality, 1989–1991 and 1999–2002
(beginning-of-year; thousands)

	Population by nationality				Change from 1989–1991 to 1999–2002	
	(percent)		(thousands)			
	1989–1991	1999–2002	1989–1991	1999–2002	(thousands)	(percent)
CEEC and CIS states						
Russian Federation	100.0	100.0	147,400	145,164	−2,236	−1.5
Russians	81.3	79.8	119,866	115,869	−3,997	−3.3
Tatars	3.7	3.8	5,522	5,558	36	0.7
Ukrainians	3.0	2.0	4,363	2,943	−1,420	−32.5
Other	12.0	14.3	17,649	20,794	3,145	17.8
Ukraine	100.0	100.0	51,707	47,843	−3,864	−7.5
Ukrainians	72.4	78.5	37,419	37,542	123	0.3
Russians	22.0	17.4	11,356	8,334	−3,022	−26.6
Other	5.7	4.1	2,932	1,967	−965	−32.9
Belarus	100.0	100.0	10,200	10,045	−155	−1.5
Belarussians	77.5	81.2	7,905	8,159	254	3.2
Russians	13.2	11.4	1,342	1,142	−200	−14.9
Other	9.3	7.4	953	744	−209	−21.9
Moldova	100.0	100.0	4,338	4,293	−45	−1.0
Moldovans	64.4	69.8	2,795	2,997	202	7.2
Ukrainians	13.8	12.9	600	552	−48	−8.0
Russians	13.0	11.3	562	484	−78	−13.9
Other	8.8	6.0	381	260	−121	−31.9
Latvia	100.0	100.0	2,667	2,377	−289	−10.8
Latvians	52.0	57.7	1,388	1,371	−17	−1.2
Russians	34.0	29.6	906	703	−202	−22.3
Other	14.0	12.8	373	303	−70	−18.7
Lithuania	100.0	100.0	3,675	3,484	−191	−5.2
Lithuanians	79.6	83.4	2,924	2,907	−17	−0.6
Russians	9.4	6.3	344	220	−125	−36.2
Poles	7.0	6.7	258	235	−23	−8.9
Other	4.0	3.5	148	122	−26	−17.7
Estonia	100.0	100.0	1,566	1,370	−196	−12.5
Estonians	61.5	67.9	963	930	−33	−3.4
Russians	30.3	25.6	475	351	−124	−26.0
Other	8.1	6.5	128	89	−39	−30.5
Armenia	100.0	100.0	3,449	3,213	−236	−6.8
Armenians	93.3	97.9	3,218	3,145	−73	−2.3
Russians	1.6	0.5	54	15	−39	−72.1
Azeris	2.6	..	89	..	..	..
Other	2.6	1.6	88	53	−35	−40.0
Azerbaijan	100.0	100.0	7,038	7,953	915	13.0
Azeris	82.5	90.6	5,805	7,206	1,401	24.1
Russians	5.6	1.8	392	142	−250	−63.8
Armenians	5.5	1.5	391	121	−270	−69.0
Other	6.4	6.1	450	484	34	7.5
Georgia	100.0	100.0	5,443	4,372	−1,071	−19.7
Georgians	69.6	83.7	3,787	3,661	−126	−3.3
Russians	6.3	1.6	341	68	−273	−80.1
Other	24.1	14.7	1,314	643	−671	−51.1

APPENDIX TABLE 1.1.3 (*continued*)

Population by Nationality, 1989–1991 and 1999–2002

(beginning-of-year; thousands)

	Population by nationality				Change from 1989–1991 to 1999–2002	
	(percent)		(thousands)			
	1989–1991	1999–2002	1989–1991	1999–2002	(thousands)	(percent)
Kazakhstan	100.0	100.0	16,185	14,953	−1,232	−7.6
Kazakhs	40.4	53.4	6,535	7,985	1,450	22.2
Russians	38.5	30.0	6,228	4,480	−1,748	−28.1
Germans	5.9	2.4	957	353	−604	−63.1
Ukrainians	5.5	3.7	896	547	−349	−38.9
Other	9.7	10.6	1,570	1,588	18	1.1
Kyrgyz Republic	100.0	100.0	4,290	4,823	533	12.4
Kyrgz	52.0	64.9	2,230	3,128	898	40.3
Russians	21.4	12.5	917	603	−313	−34.2
Uzbeks	12.8	13.8	550	665	115	20.9
Other	13.8	8.8	594	427	−167	−28.1
ECA states						
Tajikistan	100.0	100.0	5,109	6,127	1,019	19.9
Tajiks	62.1	79.9	3,172	4,898	1,726	54.4
Uzbeks	23.5	15.3	1,198	937	−261	−21.8
Russians	7.6	1.1	388	68	−320	−82.5
Other	6.8	3.7	350	224	−125	−35.9
Turkmenistan	100.0	100.0	3,534	4,418	884	25.0
Turkmen	71.8	77.0	2,536	3,402	866	34.1
Russians	9.4	6.8	334	299	−35	−10.5
Uzbeks	9.0	9.2	317	407	90	28.3
Other	9.8	7.0	347	310	−37	−10.6
Uzbekistan	100.0	100.0	19,905	24,231	4,326	21.7
Uzbeks	71.0	77.8	14,142	18,861	4,719	33.4
Russians	8.3	5.0	1,653	1,202	−451	−27.3
Tadzhiks	4.7	5.0	934	1,204	271	29.0
Kazakhs	4.1	4.0	808	966	158	19.5
Other	11.9	8.2	2,367	1,997	−370	−15.6
Czech Republic	100.0	100.0	10,302	10,230	−72	−0.7
Czech	94.8	90.4	9,771	9,250	−521	−5.3
Slovak	3.1	1.9	315	193	−122	−38.6
Other	2.1	7.7	217	787	570	263.0
Slovak Republic	100.0	100.0	5,274	5,379	105	2.0
Slovak	85.6	85.8	4,519	4,615	96	2.1
Czech	1.1	0.8	59	45	−15	−24.8
Other	13.3	13.0	696	720	24	3.5
Hungary	100.0	100.0	5,390	5,348	−42	−0.8
Hungarian	97.8	92.7	5,269	4,958	−311	−5.9
German	0.3	0.6	18	32	15	83.5
Croatian	0.1	0.2	7	8	1	12.0
Slovakian	0.1	0.2	6	10	4	62.0
Other	1.7	6.3	89	339	249	278.6
Albania	100.0	−	3,182	−	−	−
Albanian	98.0	−	3,118	−	−	−
Greek	1.8	−	59	−	−	−
Macedonian	0.1	−	5	−	−	−
Other	0.1	−	1	−	−	−

(*Table continues on the following page.*)

APPENDIX TABLE 1.1.3 (*continued*)

Population by Nationality, 1989–1991 and 1999–2002

(beginning-of-year; thousands)

	Population by nationality				Change from 1989–1991 to 1999–2002	
	(percent)		(thousands)			
	1989–1991	1999–2002	1989–1991	1999–2002	(thousands)	(percent)
Bulgaria	100.0	100.0	8,473	7,929	−544	−6.4
Bulgarian	85.8	83.9	7,272	6,655	−617	−8.5
Turkish	9.7	9.4	822	747	−75	−9.2
Roma	3.4	4.7	288	371	83	28.8
Other	1.1	2.0	91	156	65	71.6
Romania	100.0	100.0	22,810	21,681	−1,129	−4.9
Romanians	90.7	89.5	20,683	19,400	−1,284	−6.2
Hungarians	7.2	6.6	1,639	1,432	−207	−12.6
Roma	0.7	2.5	167	535	369	221.1
Ukrainians	0.3	0.3	64	61	−2	−3.9
Other	1.1	1.2	257	253	−4	−1.5
Slovenia	100.0	100.0	1,913	1,964	51	2.6
Slovenes	88.3	83.1	16	1,631	−58	−3.5
Croats	2.8	1.8	53	36	−17	−32.6
Serbs	2.5	2.0	47	39	−8	−17.8
Others	6.5	13.1	123	258	135	109.1
Croatia	100.0	100.0	4,784	4,437	−347	−7.2
Croats	78.1	89.6	3,736	3,977	241	6.4
Serbs	12.1	4.5	582	202	−380	−65.3
Hungarians	0.5	0.4	22	17	−6	−25.8
Others	9.3	5.4	444	242	−202	−45.5
FYR Macedonia	–	100.0	–	2,023	–	–
Macedonians	–	64.2	–	1,298	–	–
Albanians	–	25.2	–	509	–	–
Turks	–	3.9	–	78	–	–
Roma	–	2.7	–	54	–	–
Other	–	4.1	–	84	–	–
CEE-CIS states						
Serbia and Montenegro						
Serbia	100.0	100.0	9,779	7,498	−2,281	−23.3
Serbs	65.9	82.9	6,447	6,216	−231	−3.6
Hungarians	3.5	3.9	344	292	−52	−15
Albanians	17.1	0.8	1,674	60	−1,614	−96.4
Roma	1.4	1.4	140	105	−35	v25.1
Other	29.1	11.8	2,848	885	−1,963	−68.9
Montenegro	100.0	100.0	615	651	36	5.8
Montenegrins	61.9	61.9	380	403	22	5.8
Serbs	9.3	9.3	57	61	3	5.3
Albanians	6.6	6.6	40	43	3	6.2
Other	22.2	22.2	137	144	8	5.7

Sources: Data are from censuses conducted in the CEEC and CIS countries between 1989 and 1991 and again between 1999 and 2002. Nationalities shown for each country are those numerically significant. Actual number of number of nationalities shown for each country differ.

Note: .. = negligible; – = not available.

APPENDIX TABLE 1.1.4

Income Differentials Between ECA Countries and Western Europe, 2000–02

	Per capita GDP PPP (US$)	Percent of that of Western Europe
EU-8		
Slovenia	17,587	61.8
Czech Republic	14,933	52.5
Hungary	12,863	45.2
Slovak Republic	12,133	42.6
Estonia	11,303	39.7
Poland	10,253	36.0
Lithuania	9,530	33.5
Latvia	8,420	29.6
EU accession countries		
Croatia	9,660	33.9
Bulgaria	6,700	23.5
Turkey	6,190	21.7
Romania	6,147	21.6
Other Western Balkans		
FYR Macedonia	6,477	22.8
Bosnia and Herzegovina	—	—
Serbia and Montenegro	—	—

Sources: World Bank, SIMA database, and staff estimates.

Note: — = not available. PPP = purchasing power parity.

APPENDIX TABLE 1.1.5

Income Differentials Between ECA Countries of the CIS and Western Europe and the Russian Federation, 2000–02

	Per capita GDP PPP (US$)	Percent of that of Western Europe	Percent of that of Russian Federation
Russian Federation	7,730	27.2	n.a.
Kazakhstan	5,263	18.5	68.1
Belarus	5,160	18.1	66.8
Ukraine	4,517	15.9	58.4
Azerbaijan	2,887	10.1	37.3
Armenia	2,757	9.7	35.7
Georgia	2,077	7.3	26.9
Kyrgyz Republic	1,607	5.6	20.8
Uzbekistan	1,603	5.6	20.7
Moldova	1,380	4.8	17.9
Tajikistan	900	3.2	11.6

Sources: World Bank, SIMA database, and staff estimates.

Note: n.a. = not applicable.

APPENDIX TABLE 1.1.6
Net Migration by Country for the FSU States, 1989–2003
(thousands)

Country	Russia 1989–2003	Ukraine 1990–2000	Belarus 1990–2001	Moldova 1990–1997	Latvia 1990–2003	Lithuania 1990–2000	Estonia 1989–98
Total	3,796.5	−232.4	110.0	−142.2	−146.5	−57.5	−84.6
Russian Federation	—	−229.3	96.2	−40.8	−80.0	−30.8	−55.8
Ukraine	374.9	—	28.5	−28.2	−19.3	−7.2	−10.5
Belarus	-16.1	-4.2	—	−2.4	−23.3	−12.9	−5.8
Moldova	98.6	17.8	4.1	—	−0.8	−0.1	−0.3
Latvia	118.5	7.8	25.3	0.8	—	1.9	0.0
Lithuania	54.0	3.2	16.2	0.2	−1.6	—	−0.3
Estonia	70.7	3.6	6.6	0.3	0.0	0.3	—
Armenia	224.2	17.6	4.8	0.6	0.1	0.3	0.1
Azerbaijan	398.5	26.7	8.1	0.7	−0.5	0.1	0.0
Georgia	403.1	23.3	7.3	0.9	0.1	0.3	0.4
Kazakhstan	1,703.2	38.7	35.8	1.2	−0.9	0.4	−0.3
Kyrgyz Republic	326.5	6.5	3.4	0.1	−0.1	0.0	0.0
Tajikistan	377.0	16.7	6.1	0.2	0.0	0.1	0.1
Turkmenistan	140.2	5.7	3.9	0.3	0.0	0.1	0.0
Uzbekistan	779.2	82.8	9.7	0.4	−0.2	0.0	0.0
Total FSU	5,052.5	16.9	255.9	−65.7	−126.6	−47.5	−72.5
Germany	−753.7	−25.4	−6.5	−10.7	−6.4	−1.1	−3.6
Israel	−299.1	−157.5	−75.6	−48.1	−4.7	−3.5	−2.0
United States	−132.0	−58.5	−30.5	−13.8	−4.2	−2.2	−1.6
Australia	−4.3	−1.9	−0.8	—	0.0	—	0.0
Canada	−11.5	−3.8	−0.9	—	−0.6	−0.2	−0.2
Poland	−2.3	0.5	−1.3	—	0.0	−0.7	0.1
Sweden	−2.0	−0.1	—	—	0.0	—	−0.3
Finland	−9.8	−0.1	—	—	−0.1	—	−4.4
Other	−41.1	−2.4	−30.3	−2.3	−0.2	0.0	0.2
Total non-FSU	−1,255.9	−249.5	−146.0	−75.0	−19.3	−9.9	−12.1

Source: National statistical offices of the FSU countries.

Note: Data in columns show net migration for each FSU state with countries listed in left column, for the time period indicated.
"—" indicates data not available or not applicable. A zero indicates that net migration rounded to less than 100.

Country	Armenia 1990–2001	Azerbaijan 1990–2003	Georgia 1990–1992	Kazakhstan 1990–2000	Kyrgyz Rep. 1990–1996	Tajikistan 1990–1995	Turkmenistan 1990–1995	Uzbekistan 1990–1998
Total	−60.4	−284.6	—	−1,581.1	−392.1	−357.1	−52.4	−728.3
Russian Federation	−125.6	−252.9	−85.2	−957.6	−278.8	−258.3	−51.2	−542.8
Ukraine	3.5	−2.3	0.9	10.0	1.8	−3.7	2.9	−28.1
Belarus	−3.9	−6.7	−3.3	−21.1	−2.9	−4.7	−1.8	−7.0
Moldova	−0.6	−0.4	−0.4	−1.1	−0.1	−0.2	−0.2	−0.5
Latvia	—	0.1	—	0.0	—	—	—	—
Lithuania	—	0.0	—	−0.1	—	—	—	—
Estonia	—	−0.1	—	0.0	—	—	—	—
Armenia	—	−31.0	−6.0	1.3	0.1	−0.4	−0.5	−2.8
Azerbaijan	60.3	—	−13.7	0.3	−2.6	−0.3	0.1	−13.5
Georgia	10.0	19.7	—	3.0	0.2	0.0	0.3	0.5
Kazakhstan	−1.1	1.3	−1.7	—	−2.1	−11.4	−17.4	−42.5
Kyrgyz Republic	−0.1	1.5	−0.1	4.6	—	−5.7	0.2	17.9
Tajikistan	0.4	0.4	−0.1	13.0	8.9	0.0	7.0	30.6
Turkmenistan	0.9	−0.8	−0.1	24.9	0.0	−7.0	0.0	−7.8
Uzbekistan	1.9	16.4	−0.1	36.3	−22.3	−30.8	9.3	
Total FSU	−33.0	−251.6	−109.6	−883.6	−297.1	−322.3	−51.1	−595.0
Germany	−0.1	−1.1	—	−808.5	−93.8	−19.6	−0.5	−15.2
Israel	−1.4	−25.2	—	−19.9	−5.9	−12.5	−0.7	−53.2
United States	−21.0	−6.3	—	−4.7	−2.7	−2.1	−0.1	−10.4
Australia	—	—	—	—	—	—	—	—
Canada	—	—	—	—	—	—	—	—
Poland	—	—	—	—	—	—	—	—
Sweden	—	—	—	—	—	—	—	—
Finland	—	—	—	—	—	—	—	—
Other	−4.9	−0.4	—	−35.5	−2.9	−0.7	−0.2	−3.2
Total non-FSU	−32.3	−33.0	—	−851.1	−105.1	−34.8	−1.3	−139.5

Remittance Data

APPENDIX TABLE 2.1.1

Remittance Contributions to the Balance of Payments in Selected ECA Countries, 1995 to 2004
(US$ millions)

Country	1995	1996	1997	1998	1999	2000	2001	2002	2003	2004
High migration	114	180	179	470	418	400	407	438	519	393
Bosnia and Herzegovina	—	—	—	2,048	1,888	1,595	1,521	1,526	1,745	1,824
Albania	427	551	300	504	407	598	699	734	889	—
Slovenia	272	279	241	228	226	205	200	214	255	267
Armenia	65	84	136	92	95	87	94	131	168	340
Kazakhstan	116	89	60	72	64	122	171	205	148	167
Belarus	29	351	295	315	193	139	149	140	222	244
Georgia	—	—	284	373	361	274	181	230	239	303
Moldova	1	87	114	124	112	179	243	323	486	—
Intermediate migration	69	98	95	94	96	112	150	206	274	281
Estonia	1	2	2	3	2	3	9	17	40	133
Ukraine	—	6	12	12	18	33	140	207	330	411
FYR Macedonia	—	68	78	63	77	81	73	106	171	—
Croatia	544	668	617	625	557	641	747	885	1,085	1,222
Latvia	—	41	46	49	49	72	113	138	173	229
Kyrgyz Republic	1	2	3	2	9	9	11	37	78	—
Azerbaijan	3	—	—	—	54	57	104	182	171	—
Tajikistan	—	—	—	—	—	—	—	79	146	252

(Table continues on the following page.)

Remittance Contributions to the Balance of Payments in Selected ECA Countries, 1995 to 2004

($ millions)

Country	1995	1996	1997	1998	1999	2000	2001	2002	2003	2004
Low migration	630	678	701	823	667	760	637	568	705	627
Bulgaria	—	42	51	51	43	58	71	72	67	103
Lithuania	1	3	3	3	3	50	79	109	115	308
Russian Federation	2,503	2,771	2,268	1,925	1,292	1,275	1,403	1,359	1,453	2,668
Hungary	152	169	213	220	213	281	296	279	295	307
Turkmenistan	—	4	—	—	—	—	—	—	—	—
Poland	724	774	848	1,070	825	1,726	1,995	1,989	2,655	2,709
Serbia and Montenegro	—	—	—	—	—	—	—	—	1,397	—
Romania	9	18	16	49	96	96	116	143	124	—
Turkey	3,327	3,542	4,197	5,356	4,529	4,560	2,786	1,936	729	804
Czech Republic	191	112	85	350	318	297	257	335	500	—
Slovak Republic	26	21	29	24	20	18	—	24	425	—

Sources: IMF Balance of Payment Statistics; UN International Migration Database; Walmsley, Ahmed, and Parsons 2005.

Note: — = not available. Received remittances = received compensation of employee + received worker's remittances + received migrants' transfers.
High-migration countries have over 180 migrants per thousand population. Intermediate migration countries have between 120 and 180 migrants per thousand population. Low-migration countries have fewer than 120 migrants per thousand population.

Estimations of the Impact of International Remittances on Macroeconomic Growth

This appendix presents background information for the econometric estimation of the impact of international remittances on macroeconomic growth presented in chapter 3 (box 3.1).[1] The intention is to extend the model developed by Chami, Fullenkamp, and Jahjah (2003), which posits that because remittance transfer takes place under asymmetric information and uncertainty, remittances are burdened with a moral hazard problem that limits their ability to contribute to positive business and human capital investment in developing economies, thus leading to negative economic growth. After briefly outlining their model, we show how, using the same general empirical methodology but making slight modifications and adding institution variables, the results could be significantly different from those obtained by Chami, Fullenkamp, and Jahjah.

Using panel data on workers' remittances, per capita GDP, gross capital formation (formerly categorized as gross domestic investment), and net private capital flows (all reported over the period 1970–98), Chami, Fullenkamp, and Jahjah first examine the relationship between worker remittances and per capita GDP growth using standard population-averaged cross-section estimation. The estimated equation is based on

$$\Delta y_i = \beta_0 + \beta_1 y_{0i} + \beta_2 wr_i + \beta_3 gcf_i + \beta_4 npcf_i + u_i$$

where y is the log of real GDP per capita, y_0 is the initial value of y, wr is the log of worker remittances to GDP ratio, gcf is the log of gross capital formation to GDP ratio, and $npcf$ is the log of net private capital flows to GDP ratio. They also use an alternative specification using change in the log of workers' remittances to GDP ratio as an independent variable:

$$\Delta y_i = \beta_0 + \beta_1 y_{0i} + \beta_2 \Delta wr_i + \beta_3 gcf_i + \beta_4 npcf_i + u_i$$

This specification is problematic because a country would need to increase remittances year after year to promote growth, which would end up with a 100 percent share of remittances on GDP in the limit. Therefore, unlike Chami, Fullenkamp, and Jahjah, we look at the level, rather than growth, of remittances to GDP.

Furthermore, as mentioned above, we include institutional quality variables that seem important, based on previous experience. Also, abstracting for missing observations, our dataset adds five years of observations to the data considered by the Chami model and covers the period 1970–2003.

Last, and more important, Chami, Fullenkamp, and Jahjah fail to address the problems associated with running panel estimations. One possible problem arising from the panel specifications is that estimated coefficients may be biased if errors are autocorrelated due to misspecified dynamics. It is very likely that growth is autocorrelated due to business cycle effects. One solution would be to pool observations from peak to peak of the business cycle or take five- or six-year averages of the data. The first option is implausible because it would require previous knowledge of business cycle features for each economy. The second appears to be very arbitrary. Both options also lead to a large loss of information.

Another, more rigorous, alternative is to model these dynamics by introducing the lagged rate of growth of per capita income as an independent variable. This, however, leads to some estimation problems that have to be dealt with by using Dynamic Panel Data (DPD) estimators. In our estimations, we used the annual data and introduced one lag of the rate of growth of per capita GDP. The estimator used in most equations is the Anderson and Hsiao (1981) method. This method estimates the equation in first differences and instrumentalizes the lagged growth of GDPpc by using its lagged level in $t - 2$. This estimation method is superior to the popular Arellano and Bond (1991) generalized method of moments (GMM) estimator for the typical macroeconomic panel datasets as demonstrated by Judson and Owen (1999). Nevertheless, the results of using the GMM estimator are also relevant because we do not have specific Monte Carlo evidence on the appropriateness of each estimator for our panel settings. In both cases we provide a two-step estimator.

Another potential problem that arises is the endogeneity of the remittances variables. This can arise because it is likely that countries experiencing less successful economic performance would receive larger remittances from their émigrés. To deal with this problem, we have estimated the equations instrumentalizing also the remittances variable with its first and second lagged level in the transformed (first difference) equation. This is different from Chami, Fullenkamp, and Jahjah because we believe their results are heavily biased in the absence of this instrumental variables estimator.

In all the estimations we have used the logarithm of the remittances to GDP ratio as the independent variable, as well as the control variables mentioned in the previous estimates. We provide the estimated coefficients and their standard errors, the p-value of a Wald test of joint model significance (high p-values indicate joint significance), the p-value of the Sargan test for instrument validity (high p-values indicate valid instruments) and p-values of autocorrelation tests of orders 1 and 2. Note that autocorrelation of order 1 is expected due to first differencing even if the original-level errors are not autocorrelated unless they follow a random walk. Finally, we provide the long-run dynamic solution for the coefficient on remittances and its standard error, which is to be interpreted as the impact of remittances on growth in equilibrium. We use several specifications depending on the control variables introduced in the regression. We provide, in specifications (1) to (6), the results from the Anderson-Hsiao (AH) estimator. Specifications (7) to (9) present the results from estimating the model using a two-step GMM estimator with robust standard errors.

The results of the analysis are indicated in appendix tables 2.2.1 through 2.2.5. The main result of our analysis is that, although no firm conclusions can be made regarding the effect of remittances on economic growth, models that account for endogeneity concerns indicate that remittances make a positive, albeit modest, contribution to growth.

The cross-section and panel analysis[2] conducted in accordance with the Chami, Fullenkamp, and Jahjah model, over two separate periods, 1970–2003 and 1991–2003, show inconclusive results, but certainly do not find a negative relationship between remittances and economic growth (appendix tables 2.2.1 through 2.2.4). The robustness of the coefficients on remittances depends on model specifications, but in the instances where results are significant, they show a positive effect of remittances on growth. The inclusion of institutional variables also yields inconclusive results, which could be due to the severe endogeneity problems associated with both remittance estimations and the use of subjective institutional indexes. The cross-section analysis conducted as the average over the same two periods leads to a similar outcome. However, although the panel and cross-section estimations (appendix tables 2.2.1 and 2.2.2) produce uncertain results, they do not give any indication that remittances have a negative impact, as suggested by Chami, Fullenkamp, and Jahjah.

Moreover, certain panel and cross-section estimations conducted with data on workers' remittances only, as in Chami, Fullenkamp, and Jahjah, showed a highly robust positive correlation between increases in remittances and GDP growth if institutional quality is accounted for. The consensus in the empirical literature, however, is that data on workers' remittances alone do not fully reflect the amount of money remitted by migrants, and thus the results of these estimations are not reported here.[3]

The results of the dynamic panel estimations are shown in appendix table 2.2.5. We present first the estimate of a simple dynamic model with remittances as the only independent variable and then add different control variables at a time. Specification (9) only includes variables that appeared to be significant in at least one of the previous equations. The inclusion of the Transparency International index and the United Nations Human Development Index (UNHDI) reduce dramatically the number of observations and countries, although this is also the case for the rest of the institutional variables. The result is a shorter panel, especially in the time dimension, in which we end up with four to five consecutive time series per country (this is an unbalanced panel). In that context, the GMM estimator is more reliable than the AH estimator. The Wald test for the AH estimator when these variables are included shows clearly that the model is not significant and is grossly misspecified. For this reason, we recommend looking at the results provided in equations (1) to (3) and (7) to (9).

The main result is that remittances appear to have a positive and statistically significant impact on growth in five out of nine of these specifications. Only in one specification is the impact negative but not significant (when we do not instrumentalize or use control variables). The significant long-run coefficients range from 0.001 to 0.022. This denotes that the estimates cannot be considered very robust. What seems to be more robust, however, is the fact that, if anything, remittances appear to have a positive effect on growth. The other important result is that the impact of remittances appears to be more positive when (a) we control for the potential endogeneity bias in remittances and (b) we consider remittances in conjunction with institutional variables that, in general, also appear to be significant and show the expected sign.

APPENDIX TABLE 2.2.1

Remittances (as Percentage of GDP) and Economic Growth: Cross-Section Estimation Ordinary Least Squares (1970–2003)

Dependent variable: log(GDP per capita growth)	(1)	(2)	(3)	(4)	(5) Quadratic
Log(GDP per capita 1970)	−0.003*	−0.014***	−0.006***	−0.007***	−0.007***
	(0.002)	(0.002)	(0.001)	(0.002)	(0.002)
Log(remittances/GDP)	0.001	-0.000	0.000	0.001	0.001
	(0.001)	(0.001)	(0.001)	(0.001)	(0.001)
(Log(remittances/GDP))^2					0.000
					(0.001)
Log(GCF/GDP)	0.041***	0.028***	0.037***	0.039***	0.039***
	(0.008)	(0.006)	(0.005)	(0.007)	(0.007)
Log(NPCF/GDP)	0.000	−0.003**	−0.002	−0.004	−0.003
	(0.002)	(0.002)	(0.001)	(0.002)	(0.002)
TI Corruption Perception Index		0.004***			
		(0.001)			
UNHDI		0.083***			
		(0.017)			
Voice and accountability			−0.004		
			(0.003)		
Political stability			−0.001		
			(0.003)		
Government efficiency			0.005		
			(0.005)		
Regulatory quality			0.004		
			(0.004)		
Rule of law			0.016**		
			(0.006)		
Corruption			−0.004		
			(0.006)		
ICRG Composite Political Risk Indicator				0.001***	0.001***
				(0.000)	(0.000)
Constant	−0.090***	−0.044**	−0.052***	−0.111***	−0.110***
	(0.021)	(0.022)	(0.016)	(0.023)	(0.023)
Observations	77	69	75	62	62
R-squared	0.44	0.71	0.72	0.55	0.55

Note: GCF = gross capital formation; ICRG = International Country Risk Guide; NPCF = net private capital flows; TI = Transparency International; UNHDI = UN Human Development Index. Robust standard errors in parentheses; * significant at 10%; ** significant at 5%; *** significant at 1%.

APPENDIX TABLE 2.2.2

Remittances (as Percentage of GDP) and Economic Growth: Cross-Section Estimation Ordinary Least Squares (1991–2003)

Dependent variable: log(GDP per capita growth)	(1)	(2)	(3)	(4)	(5) Quadratic
Log(GDP per capita 1970)	−0.001	−0.004	−0.007***	−0.004	−0.004
	(0.002)	(0.005)	(0.002)	(0.003)	(0.003)
Log(remittances/GDP)	0.000	−0.000	−0.000	0.001	0.001
	(0.001)	(0.002)	(0.001)	(0.002)	(0.002)
(Log(remittances/GDP))^2					−0.000
					(0.001)
Log(GCF/GDP)	0.027***	0.024**	0.027***	0.022*	0.022*
	(0.009)	(0.010)	(0.008)	(0.011)	(0.011)
Log(NPCF/GDP)	0.000	0.001	0.000	0.001	0.001
	(0.002)	(0.003)	(0.002)	(0.003)	(0.003)
TI Corruption Perception Index		0.006***			
		(0.002)			
UNHDI		0.003			
		(0.031)			
Voice and accountability			−0.009**		
			(0.004)		
Political stability			0.002		
			(0.004)		
Government efficiency			0.014		
			(0.009)		
Regulatory quality			0.012**		
			(0.006)		
Rule of law			−0.001		
			(0.009)		
Corruption			0.005		
			(0.008)		
ICRG Composite Political Risk Indicator				0.001	0.001
				(0.000)	(0.000)
Constant	−0.069***	−0.059*	−0.021	−0.066**	−0.065**
	(0.026)	(0.030)	(0.022)	(0.030)	(0.031)
Observations	119	104	114	90	90
R-squared	0.13	0.20	0.40	0.17	0.17

Note: GCF = gross capital formation; ICRG = International Country Risk Guide; NPCF = net private capital flows; TI = Transparency International; UNHDI = UN Human Development Index. Robust standard errors in parentheses; * significant at 10%; ** significant at 5%; *** significant at 1%.

APPENDIX TABLE 2.2.3

Remittances (as Percentage of GDP) and Economic Growth: Panel Estimation (1970–2003)

Dependent variable: log(GDP per capita growth)	(1)	(2)	(3)	(4)	(5) Quadratic	(6) Quadratic
Growth GDPpc (t − 1)	0.180***	0.299***	-0.068*	0.017	0.097***	0.018
	(0.020)	(0.057)	(0.038)	(0.028)	(0.020)	(0.028)
Log(remittances/GDP)	0.001**	−0.000	0.003	0.000	0.006***	0.003
	(0.001)	(0.001)	(0.003)	(0.002)	(0.001)	(0.002)
(Log(remittances/GDP))^2					0.001*	0.001**
					(0.000)	(0.001)
Log(GCF/GDP)	0.030***	0.029***	0.065***	0.045***	0.036***	0.045***
	(0.003)	(0.007)	(0.009)	(0.006)	(0.004)	(0.006)
Log(NPCF/GDP)	0.001	0.004*	−0.001	−0.000	0.001	−0.000
	(0.001)	(0.002)	(0.002)	(0.001)	(0.001)	(0.001)
TI Corruption Perception Index		0.001				
		(0.002)				
UNHDI		−0.018				
		(0.018)				
Voice and accountability			0.005			
			(0.009)			
Political stability			0.005			
			(0.005)			
Government efficiency			−0.011			
			(0.007)			
Regulatory quality			0.003			
			(0.006)			
Rule of law			−0.017			
			(0.011)			
Corruption			−0.006			
			(0.008)			
ICRG Composite Political Risk Indicator				−0.000		−0.000
				(0.000)		(0.000)
Constant	−0.080***	−0.074***	−0.184***	−0.117***	−0.097***	−0.120***
	(0.010)	(0.023)	(0.026)	(0.019)	(0.014)	(0.019)
Observations	1,913	297	716	1,108	1,913	1,108
Number of ID	123	80	114	91	123	91
R-squared			0.11	0.06	0.08	0.07

Note: GCF = gross capital formation; ICRG = International Country Risk Guide; NPCF = net private capital flows; TI - Transparency International; UNHDI = UN Human Development Index. Robust standard errors in parentheses; * significant at 10%; ** significant at 5%; *** significant at 1%.

APPENDIX TABLE 2.2.4

Remittances (as Percentage of GDP) and Economic Growth: Panel Estimation (1991–2003)

Dependent variable: log(GDP per capita growth)	(1)	(2)	(3)	(4)	(5) Quadratic	(6) Quadratic
Growth GDPpc (t – 1)	0.143***	0.299***	-0.068*	-0.027	0.078***	-0.027
	(0.026)	(0.057)	(0.038)	(0.034)	(0.027)	(0.034)
Log(remittances/GDP)	0.001	−0.000	0.003	−0.004	0.001	−0.003
	(0.001)	(0.001)	(0.003)	(0.002)	(0.002)	(0.003)
(Log(remittances/GDP))^2					−0.001	0.000
					(0.001)	(0.001)
Log(GCF/GDP)	0.038***	0.029***	0.065***	0.061***	0.056***	0.061***
	(0.005)	(0.007)	(0.009)	(0.008)	(0.007)	(0.008)
Log(NPCF/GDP)	0.002	0.004*	−0.001	−0.000	0.001	−0.000
	(0.001)	(0.002)	(0.002)	(0.002)	(0.001)	(0.002)
TI Corruption Perception Index		0.001				
		(0.002)				
UNHDI		−0.018				
		(0.018)				
Voice and accountability			0.005			
			(0.009)			
Political stability			0.005			
			(0.005)			
Government efficiency			−0.011			
			(0.007)			
Regulatory quality			0.003			
			(0.006)			
Rule of law			−0.017			
			(0.011)			
Corruption			−0.006			
			(0.008)			
ICRG Composite Political Risk Indicator				0.000		0.000
				(0.000)		(0.000)
Constant	−0.102***	−0.074***	−0.184***	−0.194***	−0.155***	−0.194***
	(0.016)	(0.023)	(0.026)	(0.028)	(0.021)	(0.028)
Observations	1079	297	716	807	1079	807
Number of ID	122	80	114	91	122	91
R-squared			0.11	0.10	0.10	0.10

Note: GCF = gross capital formation; ICRG = International Country Risk Guide; NPCF = net private capital flows; TI = Transparency International; UNHDI = UN Human Development Index. Robust standard errors in parentheses; * significant at 10%; ** significant at 5%; *** significant at 1%.

APPENDIX TABLE 2.2.5

Worker Remittances and Growth: Dynamic Panel Estimation (1970–2003)

Dependant variable: growth of GDP per capita Endogenous variable: log (remittances/GDP)	(1) AH	(2) AH-IV	(3) AH-IV	(4) AH-IV	(5) AH-IV	(6) AH-IV	(7) AH-IV	(8) GMM	(9) GMM
Growth GDPpc (t – 1)	0.202^	0.170^	0.132^	0.083^	0.035	0.037^	−0.081	0.039	0.05^
	(0.014)	(0.006)	(0.005)	(0.000)	(0.071)	(0.013)	(0.197)	(0.051)	(0.006)
Log(remittances/GDP Growth)	−0.005	0.002*	0.002	0.001**	0.021**	0.012^	0.012	0.010*	0.002
	(0.010)	(0.001)	(0.001)	(0.000)	(0.090)	(0.002)	(0.022)	(0.006)	(0.002)
Log(GCF/GDP)			0.082^	0.070^	0.086**	0.047^	0.124*	0.056^	0.063^
			(0.004)	(0.000)	(0.035)	(0.008)	(0.075)	(0.018)	(0.002)
Log(NPCF/GDP)				−0.004^	−0.001	−0.002	−0.019	0.000	
				(0.000)	(0.007)	(0.002)	(0.022)	(0.001)	
TI Corruption Perception Index					−0.020*		−0.039		
					(0.011)		(0.026)		
UNHDI					−0.455		0.042		
					(0.657)		(3.037)		
Bureaucracy quality						0.006	0.014	0.005	0.005**
						(0.006)	(0.051)	(0.005)	(0.002)
Corruption						−0.002	−0.007	−0.000	
						(0.004)	(0.026)	(0.005)	
Ethnic tensions						−0.016^	0.046	−0.004	
						(0.006)	(0.045)	(0.004)	
Law and order						0.040^	−0.071	0.007	
						(0.004)	(0.064)	(0.005)	
Democratic accountability						0.004	−0.001	−0.001	
						(0.005)	(0.027)	(0.003)	
Government stability						0.012^	0.012	0.004**	0.002^
						(0.001)	(0.016)	(0.002)	(0.000)
Socioeconomic conditions						0.018^	0.008	0.002	0.002^
						(0.002)	(0.019)	(0.003)	(0.001)
Investment profile						0.005**	0.011	−0.000	
						(0.002)	(0.012)	(0.002)	
Political risk						−0.007^	0.003	0.001	−0.001**
						(0.001)	(0.007)	(0.001)	(0.000)
Observations	2946	2946	2860	1790	217	1017	212	1017	1710
Number of ID	155	155	152	121	65	89	60	89	120
Wald	0.000	0.000	0.000	0.000	0.004	0.000	0.000	0.004	0.000
Sargan	0.083	0.251	0.4290	0.701	0.634	0.450	0.757	0.490	0.233
AR(1)	0.000	0.000	0.000	0.000	0.005	0.000	0.037	0.000	0.000
AR(2)	0.671	0.790	0.819	0.992	0.544	0.538	0.171	0.621	0.374
Long-run remittances coeff.	−0.006	0.003*	0.002	0.001**	0.022**	0.013^	0.010	0.010*	0.002
	(0.012)	(0.002)	(0.002)	(0.000)	(0.011)	(0.002)	0.022	(0.006)	0.002

Note: GCF = gross capital formation; ICRG = International Country Risk Guide; NPCF = net private capital flows; TI = Transparency International; UNHDI = UN Human Development Index. Robust standard errors in parentheses; * significant at 10%; ** significant at 5%; *** significant at 1%.

Specifications (1) to (7) were obtained using the two-step AH estimator and the AH estimator with instruments for the remittances variable. Specifications (8) to (10) were obtained using the two-step GMM estimator of Arellano and Bond (1991) with robust standard errors.

Data Definitions

Workers' remittances and compensation of employees, received (US$): Current transfers by migrant workers and wages and salaries earned by nonresident workers. This new World Development Indicator (WDI) category comprising both workers' remittances and compensation of employees was introduced in mid-2005. Data are in current U.S. dollars. *Source:* Workers' remittances and compensation of employees, received (US$): World Bank World Development Indicators.

GDP per capita (constant 2000 US$): GDP per capita is gross domestic product divided by midyear population. GDP is the sum of gross value added by all resident producers in the economy plus any product taxes and minus any subsidies not included in the value of the products. It is calculated without making deductions for depreciation of fabricated assets or for depletion and degradation of natural resources. Data are in constant U.S. dollars. *Source:* GDP per capita (constant 2000 US$): World Bank national accounts data, and OECD National Accounts data files.

GDP (current US$): GDP at purchaser's prices is the sum of gross value added by all resident producers in the economy plus any product taxes and minus any subsidies not included in the value of the products. It is calculated without making deductions for depreciation of fabricated assets or for depletion and degradation of natural resources. Data are in current U.S. dollars. Dollar figures for GDP are converted from domestic currencies using single-year official exchange rates. For a few countries where the official exchange rate does not reflect the rate effectively applied to actual foreign exchange transactions, an alternative conversion factor is used. *Source:* World Bank national accounts data, and OECD National Accounts data files.

Gross capital formation (current US$): Gross capital formation (formerly gross domestic investment) consists of outlays on additions to the fixed assets of the economy plus net changes in the level of inventories. Fixed assets include land improvements (fences, ditches, drains, and so on); plant, machinery, and equipment purchases; and the construction of roads, railways, and the like, including schools, offices, hospitals, private residential dwellings, and commercial and industrial buildings. Inventories are stocks of goods held by firms to meet temporary or unexpected fluctuations in production or sales, and "work in progress." According to the 1993 system of national accounts, net acquisitions of valuables are also considered capital formation. Data are in current U.S. dollars. *Source:* World Bank National Accounts Data, and OECD National Accounts data files.

Private capital flows, net total (current US$): Net private capital flows consist of private debt and nondebt flows. Private debt flows include commercial bank lending, bonds, and other private credits; nondebt private flows are foreign direct investment and portfolio equity investment. Data are in current U.S. dollars. *Source:* World Bank, Global Development Finance.

Transparency International (TI) Corruption Perception Index (CPI): The TI Corruption Perceptions Index (CPI) ranks countries in terms of the degree to which corruption is perceived to exist among public officials and politicians. It is a composite index, drawing on corruption-related data in expert surveys carried out by a variety of reputable institutions. It reflects the views of business people and analysts from around the world, including experts who are locals in the countries evaluated. *Source:* http://www.icgg.org/.

UN Human Development Index: Data are linearly interpolated by the UN Human Development Report Office. Otherwise, data conform to those used in Human Development Report 2004. *Source:* Unofficial data received as correspondence.

Governance indicators: The Web page http://info.worldbank.org/governance/kkz2002/tables.asp presents the updated aggregate governance research indicators for almost 200 countries for 1996–2002, for six dimensions of governance:

- Voice and accountability

- Political stability and absence of violence

- Government effectiveness

- Regulatory quality

- Rule of law

- Control of corruption.

The data and methodology used to construct the indicators are described in "Governance Matters III: Governance Indicators for 1996–2002" (World Bank Policy Research Working Paper 3106).

ICRG Political Risk Rating: A means of assessing the political stability of a country on a comparable basis with other countries by assessing risk points for each of the component factors of government stability, socioeconomic conditions, investment profile, internal conflict, external conflict, corruption, military in politics, religious tensions, law and order, ethnic tensions, democratic accountability, and bureaucracy quality. Risk ratings range from a high of 100 (least risk) to a low of 0 (highest risk), though lowest de facto ratings generally range in the 30s and 40s. *Source:* Monthly data were collected from www.countrydata.com, and yearly averages calculated by the authors.

Endnotes

1. See Catrinescu et al. (2006) for a more detailed discussion of the estimation of the impact of remittances on growth using these methods.
2. The choice of fixed-effects or random-effects models in each instance was determined by the results of the Hausman test.
3. These are available on request from the corresponding author.

Estimating the Determinants
of Migration in ECA

In this appendix, we construct an econometric model of the determinants of migration in Europe and Central Asia (ECA), and present the results of a statistical estimation of this model.

The Theoretical Model

By releasing the assumption of full employment, the Harris and Todaro framework has been generalized to understand that migration for individual i in the period t from the individual's home country h to potential destination country d is best understood as

$$M_{hd} = \int \left[\frac{I_d(t) - I_h(t)}{I_h(t)} \right] \qquad (3.1.1)$$

where

Ih(t)   represents the discounted present value of the expected real income stream in country h over a potential migrant's planning horizon, and

Id(t)   is the discounted presented value of the expected real income stream in country d over a potential migrant's planning horizon.

Given some of the weaknesses of this basic model to explain and predict migration, we follow the work of Hatton (1995) and Fertig (2001)
as a starting point toward designing an alternative specification. The
model is based on the concepts of individual utility maximization and
migration as a form of investment in human capital. The probability of
migration depends on the difference between expected utility in destination and home countries, where utility is represented by a monotonic
function of expected income, probability of employment, and cost of
migration, which depends on the current stock of immigrants.

$$U_t = \ln(w_d)_t + \gamma \ln(e_d)_t - \ln(w_h)_t - \eta \ln(e_h)_t - z_t \qquad (3.1.2)$$

where w_d, w_h, e_d, e_h are income and probability of employment in the
destination and origin countries, respectively, and z is the cost of
migration.

The formation of expectations of future utility streams follows a
geometric series of past values with the most recent utility streams
given greater weight.

$$U_t^* = \lambda U_t + \lambda^2 U_{t-1} + \lambda^3 U_{t-2} + ..., \qquad 0 < \lambda < 1$$
$$or \qquad\qquad\qquad\qquad\qquad\qquad\qquad\qquad\qquad (3.1.3)$$
$$U_t^* = \lambda U_t + \lambda U_{t-1}^*$$

The immigration rate (M_t) is assumed to be a function of current
and net present value levels of utility from immigration.

$$M_t = \beta(U_t^* + \alpha U_t), \ \alpha > 1 \qquad (3.1.4)$$

where β stands for the aggregation parameter, and α for the extra
weight given to the current utility.

Extending the basic migration model and following Zoubanov (2004)
to account for a nonlinear relationship between the cost of migration
and the current stock of immigrants, the squared current stock of immigrants (MST) from a given origin country is also incorporated. To account
for quality-of-life considerations, the same adaptive expectations structure is used as above. The European Bank for Reconstruction and Development (EBRD) transition index[1] is used to account for the quality of
life in the origin country. As such, the final specification is as follows:

$$\Delta M_t = \beta(\alpha + \lambda)\begin{bmatrix} \Delta \ln(w_d / w_h)_t + \gamma \Delta \ln(e_d)_t - \eta \Delta \ln(e_h)_t - \varepsilon_1 \Delta MST_t \\ -\varepsilon_2 \Delta MST_t^2 + \Delta EBRD_t \end{bmatrix}$$
$$+ \beta(\alpha + \lambda - \lambda\alpha)\begin{bmatrix} \varepsilon_0 + \ln(w_d / w_h)_{t-1} + \gamma \ln(e_d)_{t-1} - \eta \ln(e_h)_{t-1} \\ +\varepsilon_1 MST_{t-1} + \varepsilon_2 MST_{t-1}^2 + EBRD_{t-1} \end{bmatrix} \qquad (3.1.5)$$
$$-(1 - \lambda)M_{t-1}$$

Empirical Specification and Estimation Results

This model is applied to Austria, Denmark, Germany, the Russian Federation, Sweden, and the United Kingdom as destination countries. The samples of countries for estimation and the time period covered are presented in appendix table 3.1.1.

The dependent variable is the change in gross migration rates (inflows from origin to destination country divided by the population stock of origin country). Real wages w_d and w_x are approximated by the per capita income data (in purchasing power parity) of destination and origin countries, respectively. Ignoring labor market participation, the employment rates e_d and e_h are proxied by 100 percent minus the unemployment rate in destination and origin countries, respectively. The model also incorporates distance between the capitals of destination and origin countries[2] as a dependent variable, as well as the EBRD transition index. Appendix table 3.1.2 provides the summary statistics of the variables in the dataset.

An iterated GLS estimator with assumed heteroscedasticity across the cross-sectional units and autocorrelation within each cross-sectional unit with a unit-specific coefficient is used. The choice of the estimator was justified by computing the LR-Test statistic for the hypothesis of homoscedasticity in the original model, which proved that heteroscedasticity is indeed present. Appendix table 3.1.3 summarizes the LR-Test results.

The estimations have mixed results in explaining and predicting migration across the region. Appendix table 3.1.4 summarizes those results and suggests that wage and employment differentials were statistically significant predictors of migration in the expected directions only about half the time. In a number of cases, these differentials

APPENDIX TABLE 3.1.1

Countries Employed in Model Investigating the Determinants of Migration

Destination country	Origin countries	Time frame
Austria	15 origin countries (Albania, Belarus, Bulgaria, Croatia, Czech Republic, Estonia, Hungary, Latvia, Lithuania, Poland, Romania, Russia, Slovak Republic, Slovenia, and Ukraine)	1996–2001
Denmark	16 origin countries (Albania, Belarus, Bulgaria, Croatia, Czech Republic, Estonia, Hungary, Latvia, Lithuania, Moldova, Poland, Romania, Russia, Slovak Republic, Slovenia, and Ukraine)	1992–2002
Germany	16 origin countries (Albania, Belarus, Bulgaria, Croatia, Czech Republic, Estonia, Hungary, Latvia, Lithuania, Moldova, Poland, Romania, Russia, Slovak Republic, Slovenia, and Ukraine)	1994–2003
Russia	12 origin countries (Armenia, Azerbaijan, Belarus, Estonia, Georgia, Kazakhstan, Latvia, Lithuania, Moldova, Tajikistan, Ukraine, and Uzbekistan)	1990–2002
Sweden	16 origin countries (Albania, Belarus, Bulgaria, Croatia, Czech Republic, Estonia, Hungary, Latvia, Lithuania, Moldova, Poland, Romania, Russia, Slovak Republic, Slovenia, and Ukraine)	1992–2002
United Kingdom	4 origin countries (Bulgaria, Hungary, Poland, Romania)	1991–2001

APPENDIX TABLE 3.1.2
Descriptive Statistics

Country	Variable	Number of observations	Mean	Standard deviation
Russia	Migration rate	156	.0048186	.0039413
	Log of per capita income ratio	151	.7880049	.7069455
	Log of employment rate of destination country	144	4.514289	.0373602
	Log of employment rate of origin countries	120	4.538245	.0604201
	Stock of migrants	132	1,047,410	1,402,638
	EBRD transition index	156	2.147179	.7582831
	Distance	156	1,577.333	837.706
Germany	Migration rate	158	.0010321	.0007154
	Log of per capita income ratio	160	1.255495	.6040464
	Log of employment rate of destination country	160	4.51303	.0071116
	Log of employment rate of origin countries	144	4.49148	.0548698
	Stock of migrants	128	60,086.52	81,026.13
	EBRD transition index	160	2.96	.5460401
	Distance	160	960.3813	356.8575
United Kingdom	Migration rate	44	.0000156	7.99e-06
	Log of per capita income ratio	44	1.140287	.2874813
	Log of employment rate of destination country	44	4.525252	.0195157
	Log of employment rate of origin countries	44	4.484731	.0480524
	Stock of migrants	44	22,196.48	26,543.6
	EBRD transition index	44	2.871818	.6664912
	Distance	44	1,751.25	306.4516
Austria	Migration rate	90	.0001618	.0002537
	Log of per capita income ratio	90	1.270075	.4556397
	Log of employment rate of destination country	90	4.565212	.0027299
	Log of employment rate of origin countries	90	4.486468	.0501821
	Stock of migrants	90	12,394.56	17,443.51
	EBRD transition index	90	3.011222	.5368109
	Distance	90	750.3333	455.1169
Sweden	Migration rate	174	.0000268	.0000437
	Log of per capita income ratio	176	1.25652	.5791293
	Log of employment rate of destination country	176	4.524534	.0207685
	Log of employment rate of origin countries	174	4.49469	.0598797
	Stock of migrants	160	2,786.981	4,383.52
	EBRD transition index	176	2.781976	.630339
	Distance	176	1,215.688	473.6677
Denmark	Migration rate	173	.0000305	.0000553
	Log of per capita income ratio	176	1.362795	.5799466
	Log of employment rate of destination country	176	4.539178	.0220577
	Log of employment rate of origin countries	174	4.49469	.0598797
	Stock of migrants	165	701.1152	1,311.389
	EBRD transition index	176	2.781976	.630339
	Distance	176	1,126.25	355.4167

APPENDIX TABLE 3.1.3

LR-Test Results for Groupwise Heteroscedasticity

Country	LR-Test statistic	Country	LR-Test statistic
Russia, $\chi^2(11) = 19.7$	104.825	Austria, $\chi^2(14) = 23.7$	95.302
Germany, $\chi^2(15) = 25.0$	79.599	Sweden, $\chi^2(15) = 25.0$	448.140
United Kingdom, $\chi^2(3) = 7.8$	9.340	Denmark, $\chi^2(15) = 25.0$	389.607

seemed to produce the opposite of the expected effect. These uneven results might reflect the poor quality of migration data.

In general, the results for the Russian model are broadly in line with our hypothesis that the migration rate is positively correlated with expected income differentials and negatively correlated with the expectations of improving quality of life at home. The significant negative effect of the stock of migrants seems to reject the commonly referenced "network" effect in the models for Russia, Austria, and Denmark, suggesting instead the existence of factors such as increased competition in the labor market of the destination country, anti-immigration policy, racial intolerance, and other factors may make migrant stock a poor predictor of future migrant flows. As was expected, distance is negatively correlated with the migration rate in all models.

Once the specification developed by Fertig is dropped, the per capita income ratio and employment rate variables are removed, and only the EBRD index is left to account for the quality of life (appendix table 3.1.5).

APPENDIX TABLE 3.1.4

Signs of the Coefficients in the Models

Migration to	Changes				Lagged levels					
	PCI ratio	E in d	MST	EBRD	PCI ratio	E in d	MST	EBRD	M	D
Russia	+	−	−	+	+	0	−	−	−	−
Germany	0	+	+	0	0	+	−	+	−	−
United Kingdom	−	−	0	0	−	0	0	+	0	0
Austria	0	0	−	0	−	+	0	+	−	−
Sweden	0	+	0	0	0	+	+	−	−	−
Denmark	0	0	0	0	+	+	−	−	−	−

Note: PCI = per capita income; E = employment rate; MST = stock of immigrants; EBRD = EBRD Transition index; M = migration rate; D = distance between destination and origin country; d = Migrants' destination country. If a variable encourages statistically significant migration from h to d, it receives a "+" sign; if negative, a "−" sign; if insignificant, a 0 is assigned.

APPENDIX TABLE 3.1.5

Estimation Results: Dependent Variable ΔM_t

	Russia model		Germany model		UK model	
	Coeff	Z-score	Coeff	Z-score	Coeff	Z-score
Changes						
EBRD index	0.0019455	6.64	0.000062	0.88	−8.46E-06	−4.06
MST	−7.85E-08	−3.77	2.22E-09	0.71	−2.84E-08	−2.63
Squared MST	8.37E-15	4.57	2.49E-14	3.62	2.1E-13	2.12
Lagged levels						
EBRD index	−0.0009978	−5.38	0.0002729	5.27	0.0000017	1.61
Migration rate	−0.4538256	−4.71	−0.4367562	−11.19	−0.0354594	−0.26
MST	−2.64E-08	−10.37	−1.93E-09	−3.70	1.62E-09	1.74
Squared MST	2.74E-15	12.32	8.41E-15	4.62	−1.04E-14	−1.35
Distance	−0.0000191	−7.65	1.44E-08	0.14	9.45E-08	1.88
Wald chi2	466.76		322.15		75.57	
Log likelihood	653.3195		869.0873		473.441	

Estimation Results: Dependent variable ΔM_t

Explanatory variable	Russia model					
	Coeff	Z-score	Coeff	Z-score	Coeff	Z-score
Country-specific effects[a]						
Armenia	0.0033819	3.64	−0.0053404	−1.95	−0.0162904	−3.45
Azerbaijan	0.0016483	3.32	−0.0035908	−2.72	−0.0120918	−3.78
Belarus[b]	0.0068437	5.00			−0.0194683	−3.76
Estonia	0.0088344	6.64	−0.0057415	−1.52	−0.0259414	−3.38
Georgia	0.0037153	5.38	−0.0029113	−1.71	−0.0148168	−3.44
Kazakhstan	0.0168113	5.26	0.024169	5.61	0.017718	6.32
Lithuania	0.0077908	5.37	−0.0067712	−1.82	−0.0279602	−3.69
Latvia	0.0084265	7.61	−0.005681	−1.61	−0.0261036	−3.48
Moldova	−0.0016337	−1.96	−0.0125317	−4.34	−0.0258678	−4.08
Tajikistan	−0.0032731	−2.56	−0.0052925	−2.65	−0.0032557	−2.63
Ukraine[b]	0.0194571	3.02	0.021917	3.55		
Changes						
PCI ratio	0.0056835	11.36	0.0050619	9.13	0.0063701	6.07
Employment destin.	−0.0128993	−8.93	−0.0134857	−8.84	−0.0079046	−1.98
Employment origin	−0.0090613	−12.61	−0.0091548	−12.02		
MST			−2.26E-08	−1.42	−3.66E-08	−2.75
Squared MST			1.31E-15	0.82	3.5E-15	2.95
EBRD index					0.0008346	2.50
Lagged levels						
PCI Ratio	0.0057828	9.28	0.0052635	8.21	0.0025046	3.28
Employment destin.	0.0130283	6.89	0.0112431	5.47	−0.0013986	−0.39
Employment origin	0.015399	17.06	0.0144664	13.56		
Migration rate	−0.6209453	−35.85	−0.5837639	−14.58	−0.4079454	−4.74
MST			−1.03E-08	−3.08	−1.09E-08	−4.27
Squared MST			7.49E-16	2.02	9.17E-16	3.89
EBRD index					−0.0009004	−2.89
Inherent dynamics						
MST	−3.04E-09	−2.13				
Distance			−0.0000042	−4.82	−0.0000115	−4.07
Constant	−0.1334887	−12.07	−0.1024069	−6.47	0.0480387	2.29
Wald chi2	16669.77		14268.97		274.79	
Log likelihood	526.3308		530.5909		643.7139	

a. To prevent multicolinearity, a country dummy for Uzbekistan is not included.

b. In the second and third specifications, respectively, Belarus and Ukraine country dummies were dropped because of colinearity.

Austria model		Sweden model		Denmark model	
Coeff	Z-score	Coeff	Z-score	Coeff	Z-score
9.57E-06	4.37	6.04E-07	0.58	8.01E-07	0.90
−2.21E-08	−4.33	3.52E-09	1.32	4.15E-09	1.05
5.48E-13	4.80	−6.15E-13	−2.67	−8.53E-13	−0.91
0.0000141	4.01	7.61E-07	1.60	1.38E-06	3.10
−0.556848	−5.38	−0.7567089	−14.24	−0.1185468	−2.33
5.52E-09	3.67	4.81E-09	3.56	−5.09E-10	−0.39
6.14E-14	0.75	−4.54E-13	−3.45	4.42E-13	2.08
−1.32E-07	−3.96	−1.31E-07	−7.10	1.40E-09	0.77
98.61		357.77		33.44	
780.9786		1600.348		1689.842	

Endnotes

1. The EBRD transition index is a composite index calculated as an arith-
   metic average of the eight indexes published in the EBRD Transition
   Reports. These include an index of price liberalization, index of foreign
   exchange and trade liberalization, index of small-scale privatization,
   index of large-scale privatization, index of enterprise reform, index of
   competition policy, index of banking sector reform, and an index of
   reform of nonbanking financial institutions. The measurement scale
   ranges from 1 to 4.25 where 1 represents little or no change from a
   planned economy and 4.25 represents the standard of a developed market economy.
2. The City Distance Tool (http://www.geobytes.com/CityDistanceTool.htm)
   was used to calculate the distance between two cities.

Computable General Equilibrium Model of Migration

The computable general equilibrium (CGE) model used is based on the Global Trade Analysis Project (GTAP), which is a comparative-static, multiregional CGE model. To mimic migration, the standard GTAP structure was modified so that the extended model allows for bilateral movement of labor. Unlike the standard GTAP model, the factor labor is now able to cross borders and take part in the production process of foreign firms in different regions similar to production commodities. This migration mechanism generates a country's labor in- and outflow endogenously driven by the different regions' labor demand and supply, and the interregional wage differentials. Accordingly with the interregional differences in labor demand and wage level representing the driving forces of migration, this approach to modeling follows the classical migration theory inspired by Adam Smith and the approach of Harris and Todaro (1970).

In addition to the extensions described above, the model was adjusted to consider illegal migration. Thus, in addition to (legal) domestic and foreign unskilled and skilled workers, employers can hire illegal foreign workers. Illegal workers are assumed to belong to the group of unskilled employees. A full description of the model and its calibration follows.

Description of the Model

GTAP is a comparative-static, multiregional CGE model. It provides an elaborate representation of the economy including the linkages between farming, agribusiness, industrial, and service sectors of the economy. The use of the nonhomothetic constant difference of elasticity (CDE) functional form to handle private household preferences, the explicit treatment of international trade and transport margins, and a global banking sector that links global savings and consumption is innovative in GTAP. Trade is represented by bilateral trade matrixes based on the Armington (1969) assumption. Further features of the standard model are perfect competition in all markets as well as profit- and utility-maximizing behavior of producers and consumers. Usually policy interventions are represented by price wedges. They lead to different prices according to different market stages. Price differentiation adjusts through introduction or change of taxes and subsidies, respectively. Quantitative restrictions or quantitatively induced price adjustments do not exist in the standard version. The framework of the standard GTAP model is well documented in the GTAP book (Hertel 1997) and available on the Internet (http://www.gtap .agecon.purdue.edu/).

Previous (Migration) Extensions of the Model

The standard version of the GTAP model allows for the bilateral exchange of industrial and agricultural products as well as for trade in services. Thus, these components are not only demanded by domestic firms, private households, and the government but also by foreign firms, foreign private households, and foreign governments. In contrast, the remaining input factors—capital, natural resources, land, and labor—are assumed to be regionally fixed. However, when it comes to the analysis of regional integration processes, this means that a border opening for production factors, labor for example, cannot be considered simultaneously with a trade-liberalizing event. Thus, interdependencies between both aspects and resulting economic impacts cannot be observed.

To mimic migration, the standard GTAP structure was modified so that the extended model allows for bilateral movement of labor. Unlike the standard GTAP model, the factor labor is now able to cross borders and take part in the production process of foreign firms in different regions similar to production commodities. This migration mechanism generates a country's labor in- and outflow endogenously driven by the different regions' labor demand and supply, and the interregional wage differentials. Accordingly with the interregional differences in labor demand and wage level representing the driving forces of migration, this approach to modeling follows the classical migration theory inspired by Adam Smith and the approach of Harris and Todaro (1970).

For the implementation of this new feature, the "nested" production structure of the standard GTAP framework was expanded by an additional "nest" (appendix figure 3.2.1). This component is responsible for the split of a country's total labor force into foreign workers and domestic workers. Thus, in contrast to the standard model, firms now choose from a pool of workers composed of both nationals and foreigners.

Appendix figure 3.2.1 represents the basic mechanism regulating the distribution of workers across countries. At the bottom of the circle, a country's total labor force (total LF in r) is divided into workers who decide to stay in their home country (LF in r) and are employed in their home country's economy, and workers who decide to emigrate.

At that point, the workers' decision making is regulated by a CES (Constant Elasticity of Substitution) function. In accordance with the Harris-Todaro theory, the driving force of migration flows is the development of the different regions' wages. Thus, the corresponding parameters reflect the intensity of the workers' reactions to the developments of the wage level across regions. Furthermore, the CES function ensures a distinction between the different nationalities of migrant workers and the resultant different preferences regarding the choice of a host country (equation 3.2.1).

APPENDIX FIGURE 3.2.1
Extended GTAP Production Structure

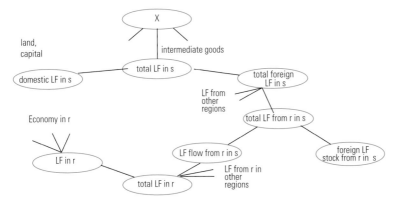

Source: World Bank.

Note: LF = labor force; r = countries; s = countries; X = final product.

$$X_{i,r} = (\alpha * Y_{i,r}^{\eta} + (1 - \alpha) * Z_{i,r}^{\eta})^{1/\eta} \qquad (3.2.1)$$

where

$X_{i,r}$	total labor force in r
α	share of emigrating labor
$Y_{i,r}$	emigrating labor
$Z_{i,r}$	staying labor in r
η	elasticity of substitution

The reason for such preferences can be found in social factors such as geographical and cultural nearness, tradition, and the like. This theory is supplemented by another assumption implying a certain influence of the development of unemployment in different regions. It is assumed that migrants compare the unemployment situation in their home country and potential host country. Accordingly, if the development in the worker's home country is more favorable than in the destination location, the incentive to emigrate declines and vice versa. With unemployment reflecting a disequilibrium situation, a CGE model is not capable of representing unemployment in its standard set-up. Thus, the implementation of unemployment is conducted through application of Okun's law, which states that there exists an inverse relationship between the development of a country's GDP and the country's unemployment rate. This consideration of unemployment can only be regarded as an approximation because other related aspects, such as unemployment benefits, a social security system, and so forth, are not taken into account. With this theoretical background, the migrants who decided to move from r to s (LF from r in s), together with the community of workers from r already living in s (foreign LF stock from r in s), form the total pool of workers coming from r "available" in s (total LF from r in s) while the remaining migrants scatter across the other destinations (LF from r in other regions). Of course, workers from regions other than r will have chosen s as their working destination. Thus, summing up all the immigrants stemming from countries all over the world leads to a pool of foreign labor (total foreign LF in s).

Together with the domestic workers who decided to stay in s (domestic LF in s), this represents the total labor force available to producers in s (total LF in s). The remaining production decisions made are conducted in the "old-fashioned" CGE-GTAP manner. Together with land and capital, labor flows into the production process and builds the value-added nest. The last step to the final product (X) is the combination of value-added and other intermediate commodities.

In addition to this main mechanism, further extensions of the model framework incorporate remittances. Based on figures obtained from the International Monetary Fund, shares of migrants' income that are sent back to their home country or spent in the host country, respectively, are calculated. This enables the consideration of the interregional redistribution of remittances. Thus, outgoing money is subtracted from regional and private household income, while incoming money is added on top of the corresponding income.

New Extensions to the Model

In addition to the extensions described above, the model was adjusted to consider illegal migration. Thus, in addition to (legal) domestic and foreign unskilled and skilled workers, employers can hire illegal foreign workers. Illegal workers are assumed to belong to the unskilled-employees group. Thus, according to the data in appendix table 3.2.1 the ratio between a country's legal and illegal migrant stock and inflow refers to the data for immigrating unskilled labor. In value terms, the percentage share of illegal workers is slightly less because it is assumed that illegal workers face lower wages than legal workers.

A payroll tax of 40 percent was implemented on legal skilled and unskilled employees working in a member state of the EU-15. This payroll tax applies to every production sector.

Furthermore, workers' migration behavior now also depends on the change in a country's or region's quality-of-life index. This index is represented as an exogenous variable and reflects characteristics of a country such as social equity, structural improvement, and the like. It is assumed that workers compare the development of the quality of life in their home country with that in potential destination countries. Similar to the situation concerning the development of unemployment, a quality-of-life improvement in the home country relative to potential host countries weakens the emigration motivation. The parameter determining the strength of the quality-of-life index on workers' migration behavior is adopted from Karemera et al. (2000). That study found a migration elasticity with respect to the development of a country's unemployment rate. Because no migration elasticity considers quality-of-life concerns, this parameter might be an adequate approximation since a country's unemployment situation might reflect a certain part of a region's quality of life.

APPENDIX TABLE 3.2.1
Irregular Migration
(thousands)

Country	Total number of nigrants	Estimated number of irregular migrants		Estimated year	Average % of total migrants
		Max	Min		
North America and Canada					
United States	34,988	10,300		2004	29.44
Canada	5,826	200	100	2003	3.43
High-income Europe					
Greece	534	320		2003	59.87
Portugal	233	100		2003	42.96
Italy	1,634	500		2003	30.59
United Kingdom	4,029	1,000		2003	24.82
Spain	1,259	280		2003	22.24
Belgium	879	150		2003	17.06
Germany	7,349	1,000		2003	13.61
Switzerland	1,801	180		2003	9.99
Netherlands	1,576	163	112	2003	8.72
France	6,277	400		2003	6.37
Ireland	310	10		2003	3.23
Finland	134	1		2003	0.75
Total	26,015	4,104			15.78
ECA countries					
Poland	2,088	600		2000	28.73
Ukraine	6,947	1,600		2000	23.03
Tajikistan	330	60		2002	18.16
Czech Republic	236	40		2003	16.98
Slovak Republic	51	8		1998	15.69
Turkey	1,503	200		2001	13.31
Russia	13,259	1,500	1,300	2000	11.31
Kazakhstan	3,028	300	220	2002	9.91
Belarus	1,284	150	50	2000	11.68
Kyrgyz Republic	572	30		1998	5.24
Uzbekistan	1,367	30		2000	2.19
Lithuania	339	2		1997	0.59

Source: Pew Hispanic Center, IOM, ILO, World Bank, Home Office in UK, ISTAT, Jimenez (2003), Centre on Migration, Policy and Society of the University of Oxford, EU business, Counsil of Europe, Ministry of Labor in Finland, Sadovskaya (2002), Migration Policy Group, Jandl (2003).

Notes: 1. Estimation methods are different for each country. 2. Total number of migrants is at the point in 2000 and is estimated by UN (2003).

Model Design (Regional and Sectoral Aggregation)

The aggregation strategy was dictated by two main requirements: on the one hand, the selection of countries must allow for capturing relevant labor flows and, on the other hand, to keep calculation effort to a reasonable scope, the aggregation must not exceed a certain size. Therefore, all countries representing home regions of most of the immigrants coming to Germany are treated as single individual countries. Obviously, Germany and Poland are among those single regions as well as several other CEECs, Turkey, and the former Sovjet Union. The remaining countries are put together as aggregated regions, either in the group representing the rest of the EU-15, or comprising the rest of the CEECs, respectively (see appendix table 3.2.2)

The 57 industries included in the GTAP database were aggregated to 11 sectors including 6 agricultural sectors. This aggregation was predominantly determined by a sector's relevance in terms of migrant workers' employment and by a sector's labor intensity. Because Germany's vegetables and fruits sector, in particular, and the construction sector account for major shares of seasonal foreign employees, both industries are represented as disaggregated sectors. To be able to observe differences regarding impacts on labor-intensive and less labor-intensive sectors, agricultural production is split up into primary production sectors and processing production sectors. With regard to calculation effort, the same restriction applies as in regional aggregation. Thus, agricultural production is represented in the form of the main agricultural production categories, plant and animal production (see appendix table 3.2.2).

Limitations

In a quantitative analysis it is very difficult to depict any qualitative circumstances. With regard to the migration this becomes particularly

APPENDIX TABLE 3.2.2
Regional and Sectoral Aggregation

Regions	Abbreviation	Sectors	Abbreviation
Germany	D	Plant products (primary)	plant
Rest of the EU-15	EU15	Paddy rice, wheat, cereal grains,	
Austria, Belgium, Denmark, Finland,		oilseeds, sugarcane, sugar beet,	
France, Greece, Ireland, Italy,		Plant products (processed)	plantproc
Luxembourg, Netherlands, Portugal,		Vegetable oils and fats, processed	
United Kingdom, Spain, Sweden		rice, sugar, other food products	
Poland	PL	Vegetables and fruits	vandf
Czech Republic	CZE	Animal products (primary)	animal
Hungary	HUN	Cattle, sheep, goats, horses,	
Slovak Republic	SVK	raw milk	
Rest of candidate countries	CAND6	Animal products (processed)	aniproc
Bulgaria, Estonia, Latvia,		Meat: cattle, sheep, goats, horses,	
Lithuania, Romania, Slovenia		meat products, dairy products	
Croatia	HRV	Other animal products	oap
Former Soviet Union	FSU	Construction	constr
Turkey	TUR	Primary products	prim
Rest of the world	ROW	Manufactures	mnfcs
		Services	svces

Source: own illustration.

apparent when it comes to the representation of migration restrictions. Those restrictions mostly exist as certain bureaucratic procedures, special requirements a potential immigrant has to fulfill, and the like. Due to a lack of quantitative estimations of such rules and formalities, migration restrictions are not considered. The same limitation applies to migration costs. Even though migration costs do represent a quantitative factor, they are not taken into account in the migration part of the model because corresponding data are not available.

Furthermore, data availability imposes major problems on modeling opportunities. Data collection on the share of foreign workers in a country's labor force, migration flows by home and host country, and so forth, turned out to be particularly difficult for the CEECs. Some simulation results may be distorted because of this lack of data. Another difficult task was the introduction of adequate parameters. Because labor migration elasticities with respect to international wage differentials could not be retrieved from the literature for the analysis at hand, these parameters are based on income migration elasticities. There are estimations of migration elasticities with respect to wage differentials on a sectoral or intraregional (for example, rural-urban) basis. But because these are neither specifically estimated for labor movements nor for international migration they did not seem appropriate for application to international labor movements. The same shortcoming applies to the quality-of-life index. As previously described, the parameter for this variable is only an approximation because parameters referring to the influence of a country's quality of life on people's migration behavior could not be obtained from the literature.

Further research is also necessary on technological progress and the resulting development of or advances in labor-saving production processes, particularly with regard to transition countries. Last, in the case of Germany especially, it is essential to focus more extensively on the characteristics of the very complex social security system and its interactions with migration behavior.

Sensitivity Analyses

To verify the robustness of the results on exogenous parameters and shocks a sensitivity analysis was conducted.

There are two ways to carry out such sensitivity tests—Monte Carlo Analysis or Systematic Sensitivity Analysis. Both procedures treat exogenous variables as continuous random variables (Arndt 1996; Arndt and Pearson 2000). The two procedures differ when it comes to the determination of the expected value. Using Systematic Sensitivity Analysis, a sample of solution values within the corresponding integral is selected; Monte Carlo Analysis determines the expected value through a sufficient number of simulations. However, because of the high number of simulations and repetitions necessary, the Monte Carlo method is not practicable. Thus, the Systematic Sensitivity Analysis is used more often. A particularly suitable procedure for the calculation of the integral is the Gaussian Quadrature. The Systematic Sensitivity Analysis available in GTAP is based on this approach and offers two different methods developed by Stroud (1957) and Liu (1997). With these methods, estimates of mean and deviation of endogenous variables are calculated by specifying a distribution for the corresponding exogenous parameters. Furthermore, based on this information and the assumptions concerning the distribution of the parameters, a confidence interval can be determined.

Usually the selection of the parameters to be subject to the sensitivity analysis is geared to the conducted experiments. Thus, for this sensitivity analysis, the parameters to be checked are the ones that significantly influence the development of migration flows and labor demand. The corresponding parameters were simultaneously varied by 50 percent in the course of the Systematic Sensitivity Analysis, assuming that each value is equally likely (uniform distribution). The procedure used here is the procedure developed by Stroud (1957).

The sensitivity analysis showed that for all the examined and reported variables (change in migration flows, welfare, GDP, and so forth), the standard deviations take quite low values. Accordingly, assuming that variables are normally distributed, the corresponding confidence intervals are small. Generally, standard deviations and confidence intervals are larger for those variables to which high shocks are applied. Nevertheless, in most of the cases, the algebraic sign of the results can be classified as reliable at a level of 95 percent. Very few results show only a 68 percent probability. These results are close to zero, so the difference between a positive and a negative value is marginal.

Data and Calibration

The database used is GTAP database 5, comprising 76 regions and 57 sectors. The base year of the database is 1997. Although a 2001 GTAP database has been released, it was not available when the database for the extended model version was prepared, so the 1997 version was used. For detailed documentation of data collection, calibration, and so forth of GTAP database version 5, see Dimaranan and McDougall

(2002) (https://www.gtap.agecon.purdue.edu/databases/archives/ v5/v5_doco.asp). The data necessary for simulating migration were calibrated to this dataset and represent a benchmark global equilibrium situation; that is, the global data of the GTAP database were not modified. The majority of the migration-related data are also from 1997. However, because information on foreign workers by home and host country is difficult to obtain, data from a different year are sometimes used. The share of foreign workers in a country's different production sectors was allocated according to information from OECD (2001). The classification of migrant workers into skilled and unskilled is also based on this information. Because substitution elasticities cannot be endogenously obtained through a calibration process, the substitution elasticities required for the migration-related functions were obtained from secondary literature. However, the elasticities that could be retrieved from the literature represent migration elasticities with respect to the wage development in the country of origin. Elasticities of substitution with regard to migration incentives from wage development in both host and home country at an international level could not be obtained. Thus, the elasticity mentioned above was used as an approximation. The same applies to the elasticities of substitution with respect to the development of unemployment and the change of quality of life in home and host countries. To take account of these inaccuracies, the sensitivity analysis gives information about changes in the results caused by a variation of parameter values.

The Impact of Migrants and the Receiving Society: Integration Policies

The term "integration" is widely used today to denote the process through which a migrant becomes an accepted part of a new society (Penninx 2005). Integration refers to all the processes, activities, and initiatives introduced by host societies that help migrants not only to complete their travel and settle in a host country, but also to find a place in the country, both in physical and in sociocultural terms. The integration process involves such diverse activities as finding housing, jobs, and income; gaining access to educational and health facilities; and adopting new languages and ways of life.

Integration policies are meant to facilitate migrants' participation in host societies by, on the one hand, enabling migrants to live independently and be self-sufficient and, on the other, supporting their active participation in all aspects of the host society's life, including the political process (European Commission 2003). Family reunification, citizenship and naturalization, and antidiscrimination legislation are key elements of traditional approaches to migrant integration, yet these are more specific to permanent immigrants, rather than to the circular or temporary migrants central to this study. Thus, the focus of this appendix is more directly on social inclusion policies. This section will briefly consider the integration processes that apply to temporary migrants, and how the presence of immigrants more broadly affects the receiving society—in this case, the European Union (EU).

Conceptualizing EU Integration Policies

To understand the European integration process, one must first understand the diverse ways in which integration is conceptualized in EU countries. This section highlights two such debates: the falling out of favor of assimilation and migrant conformity, and the variety of entities into which migrants can integrate.

The concept of integration needs to be understood separately from "assimilation" and the implied conformity once expected from migrants. Contemporary democratic societies are complex social orders with diverse cultures, lifestyles, values, and institutional processes, which are constantly in flux. In many societies, however, political pressures to assimilate still persist. In view of the tendency to collapse integration and one-way assimilation, the concept of integration is often replaced with terms such as "inclusion" and "participation." Community organizations, in particular, emphasize the concept of participation, which denotes democratic notions of access, agency, and change, though it does not directly refer to relationships between social groups.

Successful integration requires meaningful interaction between migrants and the receiving society, which means that integration must be conceived of as a two-way process. The host society must ensure that the migrant has the opportunity to participate in economic, social, cultural, and civil life. Conversely, migrants are expected to respect the fundamental norms and values of the host society and participate actively in the integration process, though they are not expected to relinquish their own identity (European Commission 2003).

The speed at which integration occurs varies in different sectors of society. For example, migrants can be integrated in the labor market but excluded from participation in civil society and political processes. Others can be included as citizens and participate in social and cultural interactions, but lack access to education and employment opportunities. Both cases could be considered integration failures, but would require different policy responses. Integration can also involve completely different modes of interaction with the receiving society. For example, typical indicators of integration include the level to which migrants establish social networks or find partners among the majority population. Many others, however, rely on family and kinship networks, or neighbors of the same racial or ethnic background, to create stability and develop roots in the receiving society. Both modes can be considered integration successes, and policies that stifle interaction in any form are likely to be counterproductive.

The experience of migration changes in complex ways depending on the individual's characteristics, including gender, age, racial, ethnic, or religious background. This implies that most policies must address a complex combination of issues. Some policies, however, should target specific factors that disadvantage particular groups. For example, while discrimination on grounds of nationality can lead to racial discrimination, a policy addressing issues of nationality-related discrimination will not affect black and minority ethnic citizens because they are already nationals of the receiving country. At the same time, while racial discrimination may be a major cause of exclusion for black citizens, Muslims in Europe are subject both to religious and racial discrimination.

Generally, the process of integration appears particularly challenging when migrants are perceived as physically, culturally, and religiously different from the host society. For Europe and Central Asia (ECA), this may become more relevant as migrants increasingly move from the southern Muslim belt to non-Islamic countries. At the same time, one positive legacy of the Soviet system is that migrants from ECA Islamic countries may be more attuned to the secular values of the main receiving countries than are migrants with similar religious affiliations from other part of the world.

EU Practices and Policies

EU countries practice a variety of integration schemes. In France, regardless of their ethnic, racial, or religious composition, migrants are expected to be subject to a set of universal social rights and values that presumably bind the whole society together. Austria, Denmark, Germany, and Greece emphasize ethnic ancestry as a basis for membership in society, while countries such as the Netherlands and the United Kingdom traditionally subscribe to a multicultural model of membership and promote pragmatic management of relationships between different ethnic and religious groups (though this has been changing in recent years). The EU Commission has called on the political leadership of Europe to address inherent social divisions and to promote acceptance for diversity and difference in the enlarged union. In the commission's view, the implementation of integration policies that promote at once equality and diversity is the route to a desired social cohesion, based on recognition of the pluralist nature of European society.

Specific policies to counter the particular disadvantages faced by various groups will also operate differently in each EU member state.

While U.K. policy making on diversity and cohesion is characterized by a discourse on race relations, this resonates differently in Germanic countries, where there are few black citizens and immigration mainly originated in Southern Europe. In Scandinavia, most migrants came from Islamic countries, and public attitudes and integration measures there have centered on religious and cultural differences. A problem that many member states share, however, is a reluctance to monitor how different target groups are affected by processes of exclusion. They often monitor social indicators only in relation to nationality (plus gender and age), not race, ethnicity, or religion. This means that there is insufficient information about the social situation of many migrants and ethnic minorities, including their progress toward inclusion.

Many reasons underlie the social and political exclusion, economic deprivation, and disadvantages that migrant populations often face, particularly undocumented migrants. Hence, integration requires a range of different tools to address these disadvantages, including legislation, social inclusion policies, and policies to enhance participation in civil society and democratic decision making. Before turning specifically to social inclusion issues, the following briefly discusses the role of social networks in organizing migrant experience and providing the essential safety net and emotional stability to foreign workers.

The Role of Social Networks

Given the current international mobility in ECA (see chapter 2), social networks play a key role in the flow of information, goods, money, services, and people. Migrants depend on both local and international networks for successful outcomes and personal safety (Vertovec 2003). The well-being of migrants abroad largely rests on the availability of work to generate sufficient income, on a clear and secure legal status, on access to social services and social and health protection, and on their participation in the host society. Integration policies, where available, provide a general structure to the migrant experience and life, yet the social networks that emerge among migrants are often what make it livable.

Temporary and undocumented migrants, who often fall outside formal institutions that assist and organize legal migration flows, rely on social networks to provide an essential social safety net for migrants (World Economic and Social Survey 2004). Research has shown that labor markets in the Russian Federation and Ukraine, for instance, have been closely linked with sending countries through the interpersonal and organizational ties surrounding migrant networks.[1] The majority of migrants who decide to move to Kiev have relatives, family members, or Ukrainian acquaintances in the city (Kennan Institute 2004). Similarly, among Tajik migrants in Moscow, the presence of established networks of people dates back to partnership enterprises developed during the Soviet period in Tajikistan and Russia. In some cases, managers of Tajik plants that ceased production have used their contacts to help their laid-off workers find employment in partner enterprises in Russia. Tajiks continue to work at the fuel and energy complex in Tumen because in Soviet times they had already been employed there as shift workers (IOM 2003).

International standards that provide for the protection of temporary foreign workers' rights in the destination country, established by the International Labour Organization, are not widely ratified. Migrants thus rely on social networks to protect themselves.[2] For instance, research among migrants in Kiev, who came from various parts of the former Soviet Union, has shown that those foreign workers who lacked legal work permits, and who therefore were unable to find employment in the formal sector, came to rely exclusively on the assistance of charitable organizations and family members or other acquaintances from their homeland to make a living. African migrants in Kiev, because of their weaker social safety net, found themselves more often unemployed in comparison to Afghan or Vietnamese migrants, who lived in more closely knit communities and developed a successful system of mutual assistance (Kennan Institute 2004).

While at present migrant networks provide essential support to foreign workers from ECA, they also signal the absence of effective integration programs in host countries that would alleviate the burdens of the migrant experience. Ultimately, this reduces the value of migrants' contributions to host societies. Furthermore, migrant networks are not immune to internal conflicts. Among other problems, they may endanger women and children because, when faced with scarce resources and information, women and children become more vulnerable to abuse from other family members.

Other vulnerabilities pertain to the area of employment, because individuals forced to rely on social networks without alternatives may also be exploited. Such vulnerabilities may arise from the very start of the recruitment process, during travel to the host country, and during the process of finding employment. In ECA, cases proliferate in which recruitment agencies take advantage of migrant workers' limited information about working and living conditions in the host country, misinforming them, charging excessive fees that bear little resemblance to the actual costs of recruitment, and even assisting in smuggling and trafficking (especially of women and children).

The concentration of migrant workers' networks is often linked with the emergence of ethnic migrant neighborhoods, which may lead to the creation of various forms of ghettos. To summarize, some of the common experiences for host communities arising from the presence of a large number of foreign workers include (a) the emergence of "immigrant sectors" in the host country's labor market, (b) the vulnerability of migrant workers to various forms of exploitation in recruitment and employment, (c) the tendency of temporary migration to become longer in duration and bigger in size than initially envisaged, (d) resistance on behalf of the local population to accept the newcomers, as well as (e) the emergence of undocumented foreign workers who, together with local employers, circumvent existing regulations.[3]

Endnotes

1. By way of example, such patterns and processes of network-conditioned migration were extensively and comparatively examined in 19 Mexican communities. See Massey et al. (2004).

2. The problem of protecting temporary foreign workers is a serious one. On the one hand, the sending country does not have any legal jurisdiction outside its territory. The host country, on the other hand, is often reluctant to assume full responsibility unless migrant workers are permanent residents or become citizens. Finally, as reflected in the low ratification percentages of the three global legal instruments developed for the protection of migrant workers, efforts by international organizations to represent and effectively protect the rights and interests of migrant workers have so far had only very limited success.

3. For a detailed discussion of temporary foreign workers programs and their social and economic impact on host societies, see Ruth (2002).

Transitional Arrangement for the Free Movement of Workers from the New Member States

The transitional arrangements for the free movement of workers from the new member states (except Cyprus and Malta) following enlargement of the European Union (EU) on May 1, 2004, allow the EU-15 to decide to postpone the opening of their labor markets for a maximum of seven years.[1] Transitional periods for the free movement of labor have already been granted in other enlargement rounds. What makes the present rules different is that the EU delegated the decision to adopt transitional arrangements to the individual member states. This appendix will briefly discuss the nature and impact of these transitional arrangements, and how they are expected to change in upcoming years.

Since the accession of the EU-8 countries to the EU in May 2004, only seven countries have fully opened their labor markets to the new member states: Ireland, Sweden, and the United Kingdom never had restrictions on workers from the EU-8. Finland, Greece, Portugal, and Spain lifted restrictions in May 2006. Italy ended the transitional arrangements in July 2006, while Belgium, France, and Luxembourg softened their restrictions on workers from the EU-8. Hungary, Poland, and Slovenia apply reciprocal restrictions to nationals from the EU-15 member states applying restrictions. All new member states have opened their labor markets to EU-8 workers.

In May 2006, the second phase of the transitional period started, which allowed member states to continue national measures for up to another three years. At the end of this period (2009), all member states will be invited to open their labor markets entirely. Only if countries can show serious disturbances in the labor market, or a threat of such disturbances, will they be allowed to resort to a safeguard clause for a maximum of two years. From 2011, all member states will have to comply with European Commission rules regulating the free movement of labor.

Available evidence suggests that transitional arrangements after EU enlargement resulted in the diversion of migration flows from the new member states. Figures from the Irish Department of Family and Social Affairs[2] show that Ireland is the most popular destination for migrants from these countries. During the first year after enlargement, over 85,000 migrants from accession states were allocated social security numbers in Ireland, with Polish workers composing almost half the number of newcomers. A report by the U.K. Department of Work and Pensions estimates net flows of approximately 80,000 workers from the eight new member states to the United Kingdom (Portes and French 2005). This number suggests that migrant flows from these states are in excess of those predicted by econometric analyses. Denmark, which opened its labor market in a similar way to Ireland and the United Kingdom, issued 2,048 work permits to workers from the CEECs in 2004. In Sweden, the only country that grants full access to its labor market and welfare system to EU-8 workers, the number of migrants nearly doubled from 2,097 in 2003 to 3,966 in 2004; however, the total is much lower than predicted. Available evidence from Germany, the traditional destination country for migrants, suggests that the number of migrants from the CEECs declined during 2004 to 2005, while the number of residents from new member states dropped by 13.2 percent. The overall picture that emerges from the available data indicates a diversion of migration flows from countries that tightly close their borders (Austria and Germany) to countries with more liberal transitional regimes, particularly English-speaking countries (Ireland and the United Kingdom).

Endnotes

1. According to the transitional arrangements (2+3+2 regulation) the EU-15 can apply national rules on access to their labor markets for the first two years after enlargement. After two years (2006), the European Commission will review the transitional arrangements. Member states that

wish to continue national measures need to notify the European Commission and will be allowed to apply national measures for up to another three years. At the end of this period (2009), all member states will be invited to open their labor markets entirely. Only if countries can show serious disturbances in the labor market or a threat of such disturbances, will they be allowed to resort to a safeguard clause for a maximum period of two years. From 2011, all member states will have to comply with the Community rules regulating the free movement of labor.

2. Data from the Irish Department of Family and Social Affairs, at http://www.breakingnews.ie/printer.asp?j=117490020&p=yy749x6xx&n=117490629&x. Retrieved August 18, 2005.

Undocumented Immigration and Vulnerabilities

The majority of migrant workers find themselves on the low-skilled side of the occupational spectrum. Deception, discrimination, exploitation, and often abuse are employment-related situations commonly and increasingly encountered by poorly skilled and undocumented migrants. Lacking work permits, migrants may experience difficulty finding the employment they aspire to, and must settle instead for low-paying, hazardous, or demeaning jobs. This appendix will briefly describe how undocumented status can influence migrants in all aspects of their lives, including the most extreme example—human trafficking.

Migrants are more susceptible to unemployment and layoffs, unfair labor practices, lesser pay, and other forms of exclusion. A study of Organisation for Economic Co-operation and Development (OECD) countries shows that rates of employment were significantly lower among migrants than among citizens between 2000 and 2001. In Denmark and Switzerland, the migrant unemployment rate for men was over three times the corresponding nonmigrant rate, and unemployment rates for migrant women were over 20 percent in Finland, France, and Italy (OECD 2003). Furthermore, undocumented migrants lack access to public housing, schools, health care, and other social services. Simultaneously, they lose pension funds and social security entitlements at home. This makes them vulnerable to various recruiters and recruitment agencies.

Undocumented status can render migrants vulnerable to other forms of abuse, especially because they lack legal recourse to challenge such abuses. They may be simultaneously invisible to the guardians of the law and subject to excessive forms of policing. Millions of people undergo mistreatment and are subject to xenophobia in part because their presence and labor in foreign countries without papers has been criminalized as "illegal" and subjected to various, often excessive, forms of policing. The undocumented are often denied fundamental human rights and many rudimentary social entitlements, which leaves them in an uncertain sociopolitical situation.

Deciding to Become and Stay Undocumented

Given these disadvantages, why might migrants choose a path of undocumented migration? The legal requirements associated with migration and the enforcement of such provisions constrain and shape migrants' choices. Reports on the process of obtaining work visas and permits in the Russian Federation demonstrate that it is a complicated and expensive endeavor, even where migration quotas or bilateral agreements between countries exist presumably to facilitate the process. Large-scale corruption accompanies this process at every level (Hill 2004). Even though the risks and costs associated with undocumented travel may be high, migrants opt for undocumented entry into host countries when the chances of obtaining legal migrant status are unlikely.

Furthermore, within the current migration regime it appears that some migrants prefer to keep their unauthorized status even if the option of legalizing is open. Those who remain at the fringes of the law gain certain flexibilities, including the option to change employers or negotiate workload and remuneration. This is an issue that deserves serious consideration in specific national contexts, because it contradicts a general truism about undocumented migration being more costly than legal migration. It appears that under the current international migration regime, it is sometimes more expensive to migrants to take part in legal contracts and interactions than to pay the social price of being undocumented migrants. The preference of some migrants for staying undocumented suggests the need to construct multilevel migration policies that include all stakeholders (including employers, migrants, native workers, and the sending country) in the discussion and, at least to some extent, also in the determination of policy parameters.

To foreign nationals from the Commonwealth of Independent States (CIS) countries and Central Asia, for instance, entry into Russia can occur without a visa. Yet, registration with the passport office of the local police station is required upon arrival. While failure to register constitutes an administrative offense and is punishable by a small fee, migrants tend to ignore this regulation. Legalization is viewed as time-consuming and bureaucratic: applications can be rejected and multiple visits to various institutions may be needed, entailing the payment of bribes to various officials. Even after registering, a quarter of migrants continue to be harassed by police who openly ask them for bribes. For Tajik migrants to obtain legal status in Russia, Kazakhstan, or the Kyrgyz Republic, they must either marry a local citizen, legal or fictitious, or alternatively "buy" a passport at a cost of $1,000–2,000 (Olimova and Bosc 2003). The murkiness of today's migration regime exacerbates these problems, because the lack of transparency allows civil servants to take the "rule of law" into their own hands and thus makes migrants vulnerable to their subjective decisions.

Another example confirms the above argument. In Greece, only 50 percent of undocumented migrants applied for residence and work permits in the first migrant regularization program of 1998. Similarly, our survey indicates that many migrants used the same documents in their most recent trip as they had during their first trip. This suggests that even those who had already lived and worked in Greece did not change their legal status or fell out of status after a particular time. It is possible that some migrants purposely did not change their status, particularly if the costs exceeded the benefits in doing so, and given the fact that legal migrants were not permitted to be accompanied by family members. Additionally, such migrants may have lacked necessary information to apply, or feared retribution for exposing their undocumented status.

While the above examples make an undocumented status appear slightly less inconvenient, they do not take away from the fact that illegality exposes migrants to numerous vulnerabilities. Even so, in these cases, it seems the social cost of becoming legal exceeds the economic inconvenience of illegality.

Migrant Vulnerability at Its Extreme: Human Trafficking

The emergence of the human smuggling and trafficking industries are perhaps the most worrying consequences of the mismatches between labor supply and demand and the economic incentives to migrate vis-à-vis the legal means for doing so.[1] With more than 175,000 persons trafficked annually, Europe and Central Asia (ECA) is the second largest source of trafficked persons in the world after Southeast Asia.[2] Victims of human trafficking largely come from the Balkans and the poorer countries of the CIS (in particular Albania, Bulgaria, Lithuania, Moldova, Romania, and Ukraine).

Trafficking is distinguishable from smuggling, although sometimes the two activities may merge or smugglers may collaborate with traffickers. The smuggling of migrants, while often undertaken in dangerous or degrading conditions, involves migrants who have consented to the course of action. Trafficking victims, conversely, have either never consented or, if they initially consented, their consent has been rendered meaningless by the coercive, deceptive, or abusive actions of the traffickers. Trafficking involves the ongoing exploitation of the victims to generate illicit profits for the traffickers. The majority of such victims in ECA are females who are trafficked to work in the sex industry. However, male victims and adolescents are also forced to labor in the building industry, agriculture, or small-scale production; are brought into households; or are set to beg in the streets. In some Balkan countries, such as Albania, Bosnia and Herzegovina, and Serbia and Montenegro, minors of Roma origin in particular were a large percentage, if not the majority, of victims assisted by the IOM in the region (Surtees 2005).

Most of the trafficking networks operating in Europe are believed to be Albanian, Russian, or Turkish (Clert and Gomart 2004). While criminal groups in these countries are known for their drug trafficking, the high profits obtained through human trafficking, as compared with the relatively low risk in running such operations, make this activity highly attractive.

Trafficking of humans typically starts at the place of origin. Traffickers target those who are interested in finding employment abroad but are unable to make the journey independently or perceive a high risk in doing so. Recruitment most often involves the promise of a high-paying job, marriage to a Western European, or kidnapping. Most such arrangements are made informally. Interestingly, 60 percent of victims of trafficking in Southeast Europe were contacted through someone they knew (Laczko and Gramegna 2003). Recruitment through job advertisements and job agencies is less common in countries where awareness-raising campaigns have already addressed the use of such techniques (as in Bulgaria). As a result, increasingly, new recruitment strategies are employed, including female recruiters who are often victims themselves or former victims, and recruitment by couples. Trafficking increasingly occurs within a façade of legality, where victims are trafficked with legal documents and cross borders at legal border crossings (Surtees 2005).

The risks and costs involved in human trafficking mean that the typical victim is someone whose situation at home is relatively poor. Typically these conditions include poverty, unemployment or under-employment, a difficult or abusive family background, and experience with political instability, violence, or discrimination. As a consequence, a substantial portion of trafficked victims are young, female adults, with low education levels.

Trafficking magnifies the disadvantages suffered by undocumented migrants. By definition, they are exploited, so will not earn as much as legal or other undocumented migrants. Exposure to a variety of inhumane living and working conditions is common. These include, but are not limited to, mental violence, including blackmail, insult, manipulation, humiliation, and threats; physical violence, including beating and threats with physical violence; or sexual attack, including rape. Along with limited sphere of movement, trafficked persons find themselves highly isolated; they lack the vital social networks available to other undocumented workers and are often under constant surveillance by traffickers.

Apart from human rights violations, trafficked victims face serious health risks, such as exposure to sexually transmitted diseases including HIV/AIDS, and other communicable diseases such as tuberculosis and hepatitis; reproductive health problems such as sexual abuse and violence, unwanted and unsafe motherhood, and complications associated with teenage pregnancies; physical traumas from severe beatings; and psychological and mental health disorders, including substance abuse or misuse. Political concern for the public health implications of human trafficking in ECA was spelled out in the Budapest Declaration of 2003.[3] For those without access to health care, these cases will go untreated and sufferers will lack access to necessary information. In migration-receiving countries, the result is a heightened risk of infection among the native population. The link between human trafficking and the sex trade means that the prevalence of HIV/AIDS and other sexually transmitted diseases is a particular area of concern. Given that most migrants will, at least periodically, return to their home countries, these risks apply equally to source countries.

Those who have fallen victim to human trafficking find it much harder to return home and would be expected to have less surplus income to remit back home. More directly, the families of the victims may have to pay financially, socially, or psychologically for the consequences of their relatives' abuse. The family may have to meet the costs of the necessary medical and psychological care for returned migrants, some of whom may be unable to work again. Families may also suffer trauma and guilt or face social stigma. If the migrant returns with a communicable disease, such as HIV or tuberculosis, family members risk infection. In cases of death, there will be a permanent loss of potential family income, as well as personal loss.

Endnotes

1. According to the UN Protocol to Prevent, Suppress and Punish Trafficking in Persons, Especially Women and Children, Supplementing the Convention on Transnational Organized Crime, UN, Palermo 2000, the "trafficking in persons" is the exploitation of others for (a) prostitution or other forms of sexual exploitation, (b) forced labor or service, (c) slavery or practices similar to slavery, (d) servitude, or (e) the removal of organs.
2. http://www.unfpa.org/news/news.cfm?ID=48.
3. Trafficking in human beings and health implications. Seminar on Health and Migration, June 9–11, 2004. Session II B—Public Health and Trafficking: When Migration Goes Amok.

Incentives for Criminality in Migration

Criminality, defined for the purposes of this report as any transaction that is illegal or a constituent of the informal economy, is present in almost all types of migration and in most stages of migration (that is, in the countries of origin, and in transit and destination countries). Criminality ranges in its level of severity from bribing the passport-issuing agency to obtain a travel passport, to entering into a marriage with a citizen of the destination country to receive citizenship. Incentives for these types of criminality arise partly from the lack of legal channels for migration. The most violent and grave forms of criminality are exercised by organized criminal groups that traffic and smuggle human beings and drugs. An incentive for this type of criminality is usually enormous profits derived from human and drug trafficking.

Migrant smuggling and human trafficking are often an integral part of the illegal economy that is connected with other forms of illegal business (Phongpaichit, Piriyarangsan, and Treerat 1998). It has been reported that human trafficking and drug trafficking routes are often the same. Estimates indicate that up to 175,000 persons are trafficked from Central and Eastern Europe and the Commonwealth of Independent States (CIS) annually (Organization for Security and Cooperation in Europe 1999).

This appendix reviews some of the incentives for criminality in migration.

Economic Disparity

The wage gap between poorer countries in Europe and Central Asia (ECA) and typical migrant destination countries is enormous. For example, an average salary in the Kyrgyz Republic is $48 per month.[1] Labor migrants working in low-wage jobs in the United States reported making $1,500–2,000 per month. Men working in the construction industry earn at least twice as much.[2] Such a wage difference serves as a powerful incentive to seek jobs abroad. In the absence of legal channels for migration, people migrate illegally.

Demand for Cheap Labor in Destination Countries

There is substantial demand for inexpensive labor in high-income and many middle-income economies. Unskilled migrants often work in jobs that the native population or legal migrants would not take at the wages being offered. In most cases, such jobs pay below the minimum wage and provide no overtime payment or benefits. The growing demand for cheap labor may result in illegal activities, such as employment of illegal immigrants or migrants with no proper work authorization, if there are not sufficient legal channels for matching the demand with the supply of unskilled labor.

However, some have found that while there is demand for cheap labor in the Western European countries, greater homogeneity, smaller territories, and a strict registration system make it more difficult for illegal immigrants to find jobs and live in Europe. Thus, a larger share of illegal migrants in Europe may be women trafficked for sexual exploitation (Shelley 2003).

Political Instability or Ethnic Conflicts in Countries of Origin

In some cases, economic disparity is not the main push factor for migration; political instability or ethnic conflicts (or both) force individuals to flee their home countries. This category of migrants often turns to illegal migration to escape persecution or conflict. In such cases, migrant smuggling is an overlapping issue between migration and human rights. Koser (2001), for example, examines asylum seekers as another major source of human smuggling, often falling between that uncomfortable dichotomy of "freedom fighter" and "evil smuggler." He argues that one should not put too fine a point on the distinction between human smuggling as a migration issue and human trafficking as a human rights issue. Asylum seekers straddle this distinction in that they are often escaping human rights violations by seeking out smugglers but then also encounter additional human rights violations along the way.

Restrictive Immigration Regime in Destination Countries

Stricter border control may not be an effective way to combat smuggling of undocumented immigrants. Opponents of restrictive immigration regimes argue that "as more restrictive policies increase the obstacles to crossing borders, migrants increasingly turn to smugglers rather than pay the growing costs of unaided attempts that prove unsuccessful" (Koser 2001, pp. 207–8). Moreover, tougher immigration control will only enrich smugglers and traffickers because fees, and consequently debts, to be paid by would-be immigrants rise dramatically. As Koslowski (2001, p. 208) puts it, "if potential migrants are willing to pay the additional costs while at the same time stiffer border controls prompt more migrants to enter into the market, border controls will most likely increase the profits of human smuggling and entice new entrants into the business."

Conclusion

Overall, it is likely that migration from poorer ECA countries into wealthier ones will continue as economies of sending countries deteriorate and the demand for low-wage labor in receiving countries remains high. Because channels for legal labor migration are limited, irregular migration is likely to prevail. The consequences of this migration are serious for the countries concerned, as well as for labor migrants themselves. The International Organization for Migration (2001, p. 11) reports, "99 percent of labor migration in the Eurasian Economic Union formed of Tajikistan, Kyrgyz Republic, Kazakhstan, the Russian Federation, and Belarus is irregular. Due to their irregular situation, most labor migrants do not benefit from the same protection rights other regular citizens enjoy and are thus more vulnerable to exploitation by underground employers" (IOM 2001, p. 11).

Endnotes

1. National Statistics Committee of the Kyrgyz Republic, [http://www.stat.kg/Eng/Annual/Labor.html#Top1], accessed on August 15, 2005.
2. Interviews with Kyrgyz labor migrants in the United States, December 2005 to January 2006.

Migrants, Their Families, and Communities "Left Behind"

The impact of migration is felt nowhere as keenly as in the family. Migration alters not only kin relationships and the size and composition of families, but also affects predominant gender roles and responsibilities, the care of the elderly and children, the education of children, reproductive patterns, and even patterns of social and political participation and civic engagement of citizens. The consideration of "family migration" has consistently been neglected in European scholarship and policy debates. This appendix briefly attempts to fill this gap by investigating how the absence of family members, as well as their return, is dealt with by the family and the larger community.

Migrants and Their Families

For some families in Europe and Central Asia (ECA), sending a family member to work abroad is one of the few options available to avoid poverty or improve quality of life and social status. The fact that migration is often perceived as a family coping strategy is expressed in the frequency of survey answers; many migrants desire to "save money for the education of children" or "buy a house upon return." In all of the researched cases, the decision to work abroad is overwhelmingly economic. Yet, at the same time, there is little mention of any reasons for migration related to increasing the earning capacity of migrants (to learn new skills, to acquire a new profession) and thus improve their economic situations in the long run. This suggests that migration may not necessarily be part of a consciously defined long-term investment plan but rather a reaction to the pressures to satisfy everyday needs. In the absence of secure employment alternatives, strategic employment planning, and more tactical migration management in countries of origin, migrants prioritize improving their immediate economic situation.

The departure of any family member transforms the family structure and its economics, which may have far-reaching effects for the structure of society as a whole. Many of these implications—including the country's fertility rates and number of divorces—are gendered.

Women who are left behind have developed a number of strategies to cope with the absence of partners. In countries and areas where recent wars took many male lives, three or four generations of women may live together as a coping strategy. With the overall decline in household incomes in ECA and the growing number of women in poverty as a "push" factor on the one hand, and the demand for domestic labor abroad as a "pull" factor on the other, households often resort to financial strategies that stretch across national divides. The increase in recent decades in the demand for female labor in the home care services (domestic work, care of children) of Northern European and North American countries has put new pressure on women to look for employment.

Such efforts have also changed the structure of family care relationships. Caring at a distance involves relying on older children, grandparents, and relatives; however, such arrangements are contingent on the socioeconomic conditions and other reasons that underlie migration. The current immigration regime in Europe, in particular, makes it hard for many migrant families to have recourse to other family members to help with care, because restrictions exist on the number of family members allowed to join the migrant in the destination country.

The migration of women has boosted family incomes, but also contributes to reshaping gender relationships as women become more active as decision makers. Furthermore, there has been little study in ECA on the impact of the migration of women on children they leave behind. Children of emigrants tend to receive less supervision; they lag behind in their education and often do not receive regular medical care. For example, it has been suggested that migration has been a significant factor in declining school enrollment of children in Moldova and Bulgaria. Moldova has also seen an increase in the

number of street children in the larger urban areas. Children aban-
don their families for various reasons: feeling disconnected, lacking
attention, and even because of hunger and abuse. Specialists in
Moldova fear that among other negative repercussions, inadequate
education (both at school and at home) will have long-term negative
implications for human development in the country. Separation from
parents can disturb the psychological and social development of children and in the long run can contribute to a deterioration of the stock
of human capital in the society.

Returning Home and Reintegration

Return migration has emerged recently in international debates as a
central topic when development opportunities for countries of origin
are discussed. Despite the impact of remittances on consumption and
investment, return migration is seen as essential for human development and positive social change, the circulation of knowledge and
ideas, and the benefits of skills return. There are various factors that
affect the potential of migrant return to improve development. These
include the number and concentration of returnees in a particular
period, the duration of their absence from home countries, the social
class of migrants, their motives for return, the degrees of difference
between countries of destination and origin, the nature of acquired
skills and experiences, the organization of return, and the political relationships between the countries of immigration and return. The devel-
opmental impact of return also depends heavily on a healthy business
environment in the country of origin, characterized by a sound legal
framework, an effective banking system, honest public administration,
and a functioning physical and financial infrastructure.

From the individual's perspective, the return experience may not
be universally positive. Some migrants may find that their country or
families are not as they remembered. For others, changes in the labor
market in their absence, or the weakening of important social networks, reduce the quality of job opportunities. A migrant's condition
on return will reflect the income, experiences, and skills earned or
gained while abroad. Migrants who have been away for a longer
period are likely to return with more cash and experience, but may
find it more difficult to adjust to their own, perhaps greatly changed,
communities.

Some migrants return after they have accomplished the objectives
they left to pursue; this has a positive impact on their attitude to
return. Furthermore, the more returning migrants respond to posi-

tive socioeconomic developments that attract them home, the greater the chance for innovation. Other migrants return home after a relatively short stay abroad because they are disappointed with the actual conditions of life and work in the destination country. They may not be able to bear the psychic cost of separation from family and loved ones or familiar environments, or the difficulties interacting with people who speak a different language and have a different culture and ways of doing things. Finally, some migrants return home because of unforeseen and undesirable changes such as health problems or family crises at home. Those migrants who make a conscious decision to return and who have planned ahead emerge as most valuable to their home communities in terms of the invested interest and the human capital they are able to transfer to their country of origin.

Surveys with returned migrants conducted for this report point to a general improvement in household living standards in Bulgaria, Bosnia and Herzegovina, and Romania despite the difficulties encountered by family members when the migrant is away. This means that migrants have reported they are now better able to finance their household expenses, buy clothing, pay utility bills, purchase electrical appliances, buy a new car, and even travel abroad.

More crucial, however, is the extent to which the country of origin is prepared to offer reintegration strategies for returning migrants and to nurture their newly acquired skills and capital. Options include making social benefits portable (discussed in chapter 4) and designing programs that support returning migrants in making informed decisions about the use of their resources. Many ECA migrants have expressed their desire to start businesses of their own, yet almost all point to investment constraints and a lack of trust in formal institutions, such as banks, as discouraging factors. Training programs and access to microcredit facilities are also in high demand. Such programs should make special provisions to target women in particular—research shows that women make the most effective use of remittances.

Brain Drain in the ECA Region

This appendix provides a brief overview of the quantity and type of "brain drain" resulting from the migration of skilled workers from Eastern Europe and the former Soviet Union since transition.

Past Efforts at Estimating the Importance of Brain Drain in ECA Countries

In an attempt to estimate the importance of brain drain in developing countries (Carrington and Detragiache 1999), experts from the International Monetary Fund explained that their justification for excluding the former Soviet Union and Eastern European countries from their study was the lack of reliable data. Four years later, the availability of data has not significantly improved and the exact nature of brain drain is still not well understood. Studies undertaken during the last 10 years have come to somewhat contradictory conclusions. The absence of a generally accepted definition of "highly skilled migration" is also a problem, as is the lack of reliable information on migrants' job qualifications, both in the countries of origin and the destination (with the sole exception of the United States [Straubhaar and Wolburg 1999]).

Moreover, estimates of the importance of highly qualified migration tend to depend on the approach adopted. Taking into account the point of view of the country of origin or of destination may affect any conclusions regarding the exact nature of the phenomenon. For example, Albanian migrants to the United States have generally been viewed in the United States as highly qualified (Kosta 2004), while they were seen as relatively poorly qualified in Greece or Italy. From an Albanian point of view, emigrants are perceived as belonging simultaneously to both unskilled and highly skilled groups (Galanxhi et al. 2004). Therefore, any conclusions regarding migration and possible brain drain will necessarily depend on the country of reference.

Generally speaking, highly skilled migration from the ECA countries flows toward the Western and Northern European countries, as well as toward Canada and the United States. Migratory flows from one ECA country to another are not characterized by a large proportion of highly skilled migrants, even though some students regularly do come to the Russian Federation. The nature of the phenomenon differs from one country of origin to another, in both the numbers and proportions of highly skilled emigrants. Both of these measures are comparatively low in the former Yugoslavia and Albania as compared with Bulgaria, Poland, and Romania.

Previous studies on brain drain have distinguished between student migration, migration of researchers and scientists, and migration of other highly skilled persons (such as managers, engineers, artists, athletes and clergy).

Student Migration

About 100,000 foreign students from the ECA region were enrolled in tertiary education in industrial countries in 1998–99, according to UNESCO. Among them, 37,000 foreign students from ECA countries (including Poland, 7,800; Russia, 5,400; Croatia, 4,600; Serbia and Montenegro, 4,300) were studying in Germany and 21,100 (including Russia, 6,100; Bulgaria, 2,400; Romania, 2,100) in the United States. However, student statistics in the United States clearly show that the Russian community was not the largest group of student migrants, in fact, not even one of the five largest groups. Graduate students from China, the Republic of Korea, India, and Taiwan (China) constitute most of the migrant student population in the United States. In Europe, even though the enlargement of the European Union in 2004 effectively increased student mobility, the increase in student migration from the ECA was rather small.

Migration of Active, Highly Skilled Populations

The proportion of highly qualified persons in each migration flow varies according to factors such as the type of migration ("political" emigrants are generally not particularly qualified), the selectivity of emigration (the socioeconomic structure of the aspiring emigrant population), the match between the level of the educational system and the labor market in the country of origin, and the average level of education in the country of origin. It is important to remember that enrollment in tertiary education is generally very high in ECA countries. The gross enrollment ratio (appendix table 4.5.1) shows considerable variation in the level of education according to country. Of course, those countries with a high level of education (such as Belarus, Bulgaria, Lithuania, Russia, Slovenia, or Ukraine) are more likely to have highly skilled people among emigrants than countries with fewer university graduates (such as Armenia, Azerbaijan, or Albania). However, the impact of brain drain (that is, the problems caused by the emigration of the highly skilled) may be more evident in countries with a relatively low proportion of highly skilled persons.

A country's size also plays a role in highly skilled emigration and brain drain. A report from the World Bank (2006) recently stated that countries with more than 30 million inhabitants, such as Russia, were not massively affected by brain drain. According to this report, the proportion of emigrants in the former Soviet Union (FSU) should amount to something between 3 percent and 5 percent of the total number of persons having completed tertiary education. In recent years, the high proportion of tertiary-educated persons in Russia and other Commonwealth of Independent States (CIS) countries has largely compensated for the emigration of highly qualified persons. Smaller countries, such as Bulgaria, have been more likely to suffer from the negative impact of brain drain.

Migration of Scientists

The frequent attempts to estimate migration undertaken by scientists have often been subject to debate. Russian sources suggest that the emigration of scientists is not a problem in CIS countries. The Ministry of Education and Research has considered the emigration of researchers from Russia as "normal." It is harder for the Russian government to deal with the fact that young researchers prefer to work in the private sector, where wages are higher.[1]

Nonetheless, it is no surprise that the youngest and best researchers have been the most likely to leave the country. Academics often left

APPENDIX TABLE 4.5.1

Gross Enrollment Ratio, Tertiary Level, by Country, 1998–99 and 2002–03

(regardless of age, as a percentage of the population of official school age for that level)

Country	Men		Women	
	1998–99	2002–03	1998–99	2002–03
Albania	10.9	11.7	17.2	20.9
Armenia	20.7	23.3	25.2	27.4
Azerbaijan	20.0	18.6	12.4	14.4
Belarus	41.6	51.7	55.4	72.1
Bulgaria	34.5	35.9	52.9	42.2
Croatia	29.6	36.1	34.2	42.8
Czech Republic	25.7	34.3	26.5	36.8
Estonia	42.3	50.1	60.0	83.4
Georgia	30.4	38.3	34.1	37.5
Kazakhstan	22.0	38.7	25.5	50.7
Kyrgyz Republic	29.8	38.5	30.9	45.9
Lithuania	36.1	56.2	55.0	87.5
Poland	38.5	49.6	53.1	70.6
Moldova	25.8	25.7	33.1	34.0
Romania	20.4	31.3	22.1	38.7
Russian Federation	—	59.1	—	79.3
Serbia and Montenegro	31.1	—	37.0	—.
Slovak Republic	25.2	31.0	27.9	36.4
Slovenia	45.3	58.4	60.7	79.0
Tajikistan	20.3	24.4	7.1	8.3
FYR Macedonia	19.3	23.6	24.7	31.6
Ukraine	44.1	56.5	50.5	67.2
Uzbekistan	—	17.5	—	13.9

Source: UNESCO, http://stats.uis.unesco.org/ReportFolders/reportfolders.aspx.

Note: — = Not available.

the country during the 1990s to continue their work abroad. This has significantly diminished the quality of research, especially in the natural sciences such as mathematics, where such research flourished during the Cold War. UNESCO's *1998 World Science Report* (UNESCO 1998) estimated that the number of Russian scientists involved in research and development (R&D) fell from 900,000 to 500,000 from 1991 to 1995. Izvetzia (March 20, 2002) was more cautious, estimating the number of researchers who emigrated after the fall of the Iron Curtain at 200,000. Armenia saw a similar decrease in scientists involved in research (from 15,000 to 3,000) and in Ukraine, approximately 15,000 specialists with higher education degrees (not only scientists) have left the country each year.[2] Bulgaria was estimated to have lost annually 50,000 qualified scientists and skilled workers (Chobanova 2006) following the collapse of the Warsaw Pact; the main destinations were the United States, Canada, and Germany.

The cooperative programs in R&D between Western European countries and FSU member countries set up during the last 10 years were an attempt to remedy the pattern of emigration. However, programs favoring research in Central and Western Europe were not able to stop the decline of the research infrastructure and capabilities of FSU countries. Even so, according to an international survey carried out in 10 Eastern European countries, they did have a positive impact, with the brain drain turning out to be less serious than previously feared (INCO 1997).

A Polish survey on scientists who emigrated clearly demonstrated that the opportunity to work with new technologies was not the main reason behind emigration between 1995 and 1999. Most emigrant researchers explained that a salary increase was the reason that best explained their decision (Koszalka and Sobieszczanski 2003). The recent move on the part of the Russian government to improve the wages of researchers was an attempt to solve the salary-related emigration problem.[3] However, wage differentials between Russia and industrial countries are still significant. If they remain high, researcher emigration will likely continue.

Highly Skilled Emigrants in Six Countries of Origin

Surveys undertaken for this project provide an estimate of highly skilled emigration in six countries (appendix table 4.5.2). The proportion of persons having completed higher education (master of arts or other degree) among return migrants varied according to sex and country of origin. Because of the different return rates observed between highly skilled and low-skilled emigrants, those proportions imperfectly reflected the exact nature of the phenomenon.

However, these results clearly showed the high level of qualification among migrants in countries such as Georgia (53 percent of female

APPENDIX TABLE 4.5.2
Proportion of Return Migrants Having Completed Higher Education (Bachelor or Master's Degree)
(percent)

Country	Female	Male
Bosnia and Herzegovina	11.0	9.5
Bulgaria	31.5	25.0
Georgia	52.7	37.7
Kyrgyz Republic[a]	30.3	20.0
Romania	11.5	12.8
Tajikistan[b]	28.8	17.2

Source: World Bank staff.

a. University degree.
b. Master's degree or higher.

return migrants held a university degree). FSU countries and Bulgaria were also characterized by high levels of return migrants who had completed university, while Bosnia and Herzegovina and Romania showed a low proportion of highly skilled migrants. Perhaps cross-country differences could have been partially explained by the respective education systems and tertiary education enrollment statistics (see appendix table 4.5.1). Moreover, female return migrants were more frequently highly qualified than males. Such a result could have been partially explained by the fact that work opportunities abroad (particularly in Russia) were probably less numerous for lower-qualified women. It is also possible that emigration strategies differed according to the education levels of the partners: in a couple with a woman whose qualifications are higher than the man, the gain resulting from female emigration would tend to be higher than from male emigration.

The Effects of the Brain Drain in Countries of Origin

According to a number of theoretical approaches summarized by, among others, Straubhaar and Wolburg (1999) and Abu-Rashed and Slottje (1991), the emigration of skilled labor, contrary to that of unqualified workers, clearly has a positive impact on the global income of destination countries. The effect on "donor" countries of highly skilled migration is not so clear.

It is generally agreed that the international mobility of highly qualified labor is positive. However, in the case of brain drain, which implies an irreplaceable loss to the stock of highly skilled populations in the country of origin, the overall impact is hard to estimate. One important implication of brain drain frequently mentioned in the case of Africa is that a part of the investment in education in the country of origin is not replaced once migrants leave. Consequently, a shortage of skills becomes evident, leading to the impossibility of ensuring economic growth. However, the aforementioned high level of enrollment in tertiary education and universities in most ECA countries may help offset this situation in the future.

Emigration on the part of highly skilled labor also leads to an aging of the more highly qualified population at home (it is the younger workers who emigrate), and to a rapid decrease in the development of sectors such as R&D. This has been observed in Russia following the departure of top researchers, who not only go abroad but also move to work in other sectors of the economy.

However, negative effects may occasionally be counterbalanced by a decrease in unemployment in the country of origin or by an increase in remittances from highly skilled emigrant labor, which can partially or totally compensate for any losses from emigration. Straubhaar and Wolburg (1999), in fact, argue that brain drain can improve economic efficiency from an international perspective. Therefore, the main issue to be resolved is how to compensate for certain negative aspects of brain drain in the countries of origin without diminishing the overall positive effect.

Easing Temporary Migration as an Answer to Brain Drain

Brain drain probably cannot be avoided in ECA countries, but its negative impact on research and industrial development may be attenuated by implementing measures aimed at making it worthwhile for highly trained professionals to stay home or to come back. Many programs encouraging the return of highly skilled migrants have been implemented in African countries. In the ECA region, programs promoting R&D in the countries of origin will probably play an important role in the future.

Maintaining the Quality of R&D

Maintaining the quality of R&D in countries of origin is also an important factor when attempting to avoid brain drain. To reach this objective, it is important to replace emigrants with competent locals at the same rate as they depart. Specialization abroad is a good thing, and job opportunities for emigrants may exist in both scientific and economic domains. The simplification of investments and business in the country of origin is an important factor in using highly skilled labor emigration to the advantage of the country of origin.

Networking Between Migrants and Nonmigrants

Another aspect frequently mentioned is the need to encourage the creation of networks between emigrants and their countries of origin, for instance, by providing information to migrants. Such networks would allow the dissemination of professional and scientific knowledge and know-how through contacts between emigrants and researchers who have stayed in the home country. Networking between migrants and nonmigrants has already become more frequent with the rising development of communications services.

The Role of Remittances

Remittances have a positive impact on highly qualified migration. This is the case even when surveys show that highly educated persons send less money than those with lower qualifications (see chapter 3, "Migrants' Remittances"). A differential between remittances sent by highly skilled and other emigrants can be easily explained by factors such as specific spending behaviors abroad, the kind of migration (individual or family), the financial necessities of the family at home, and the expectations concerning the duration of migration. Remitted money can have an immediate impact on economic development in countries of origin when it is used for investments. However, as mentioned in chapter 3 of this report, only one-fifth of remitted money corresponds to an investment in material capital, and 14 percent to investment in human capital (education of children). Among the investments in material capital, the portion of investment in business is small (about 6 percent of the total amount of remittances). Therefore, to improve the economic impact of highly skilled migration for the country of origin, it would also be useful to provide incentives to invest.

Conclusion: The Nature of Migration within ECA Countries and Between ECA Countries and the Industrial World— Brain Drain, Brain Gain, or Brain Waste?

Surveys in CIS countries (Tajikistan and Kyrgyz Republic) have clearly demonstrated that, during their stay in Russia, highly skilled migrants frequently worked in sectors requiring a low qualifications (such as agriculture, transportation, or construction). Therefore, emigration may lead to "brain waste," that is, a downward adjustment of migrants' aspirations to reconcile with the divergent characteristics of the Russian labor market (appendix figure 4.5.1). Brain waste, a negative effect of migration flows, has also been observed, to a lesser extent, in Western Europe, in border countries (principally Austria [Fassmann, Kohlbacher, and Reeger 1995]), and among Russian migrants to Israel (Hansen 2006). Highly skilled migrants, especially women, working in domestic sectors or in nonqualified (and seasonal) work are frequently observed in Western Europe. Swiss data show that highly qualified migrants from ECA countries, and particularly from the former Yugoslavia and countries of the FSU, are much more affected by brain waste (that is, the fact that a job requires less qualification than their skills) than migrants from Western Europe (appendix figure 4.5.1). Obstacles encountered in the Western labor market (such as infrequent recognition of diplomas) may increase such brain waste.

Industrial societies are progressively moving toward a tertiary economy with a high level of added value. Therefore, the demand for highly qualified immigrants will probably increase. Furthermore, during recent decades, migratory flows have increasingly been composed of highly skilled migrants. Such highly skilled migration will probably also increase in the future.

APPENDIX FIGURE 4.5.1

Proportion of Migrants with Tertiary Education from ECA Countries and from the Main Western Communities Who Are Active in Work Requiring Low Skills

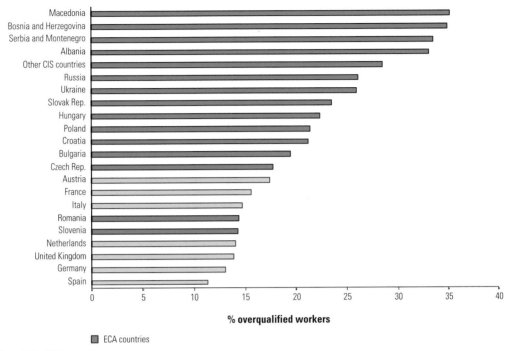

% overqualified workers

■ ECA countries

Source: Swiss 2000 census.

Even so, labor market segmentation is still evident, leading to a demand for relatively unqualified immigrants, which can cause brain waste. Enlargement of the European Union in May 2004 and the consequent free movement of workers may turn out to be a factor influencing the ratio between brain waste and brain gain.

In short, highly skilled migration is a reality that cannot be avoided. The extent to which countries of origin are capable of using it to their own advantage depends on a variety of factors. The issue for the next decade will therefore be how highly skilled migration can become a positive factor in the development of countries of origin, rather than a negative phenomenon resulting in waste.

Endnotes

1. See a report from the French Senate on Russian education (www.senat .fr/rap/r04-274/r04-2746.html).
2. State Committee of Statistics of Ukraine.
3. President Putin decided at the beginning of 2006 to increase wages (from the equivalent of US$800 to up to the equivalent of US$1,000).

Bibliography

Abu-Rashed, J., and D. J. Slottje. 1991. "A Theoretical Analysis of the Beneficial Effects of the Brain-Drain Phenomenon." *Canadian Journal of Development Studies* 12: 357–66.

Adams, R. H. 1989. "Workers' Remittances and Inequality in Rural Egypt." *Economic Development and Cultural Change* 38 (1, October): 45–71.

Adams, R. H.. 1991. "The Effects of International Remittances on Poverty, Inequality, and Development in Rural Egypt." Research Report 86, International Food Policy Research Institute, Washington, DC.

Adams, R. H. 1993. "The Economic and Demographic Determinants of International Migration in Rural Egypt." *Journal of Development Studies* 30 (1): 146–67.

Adams, R. H. 1998. "Remittances, Investment, and Rural Asset Accumulation in Pakistan." *Economic Development and Cultural Change* 47 (1), 155–73.

Adams, R. H., and J. Page. 2003. "International Migration, Remittances, and Poverty in Developing Countries." Policy Research Working Paper 3179, World Bank, Washington, DC.

Adams, R. H. 2004. "Remittances and Poverty in Guatemala." Policy Research Working Paper 3418, World Bank, Washington, DC.

Adelman, I., and J. E. Taylor. 1990. "Is Structural Adjustment with a Human Face Possible? The Case of Mexico." *Journal of Development Studies* 26: 387–407.

Adelman, I., and J. E. Taylor. 1991. "Multisectoral Models and Structural Adjustment: New Evidence from Mexico." *Journal of Development Studies* 28 (1): 154–63.

Adelman, I., J. E. Taylor, and Stephen Vogel. 1988. "Life in a Mexican Village." *Journal of Development Studies* 25: 5–24.

Alvarez-Plata, P., Brücker H., and B. Siliverstovs. 2003. "Potential Migration from Central and Eastern Europe into the EU-15: An Update (Final Report)." Report for the European Commission, DG Employment and Social Affairs, DIW, Berlin.

Anderson, T. W., and C. Hsiao. 1981. "Estimation of Dynamic Models with Error Components." *Journal of the American Statistical Association* 76: 598–606.

Andrienko, Y., and S. Guriev. 2003. *"Determinants of Interregional Mobility in Russia: Evidence from Panel Data."* Working Paper 551, William Davidson Institute, University of Michigan, Ann Arbor.

Andrienko, Y., and S. Guriev. 2005. "Understanding Migration in Russia: A Policy Note." Policy Note, World Bank, Washington, DC.

Arellano, M., and S. Bond. 1991. "Some Tests of Specification for Panel Data: Monte Carlo Evidence and an Application to Employment Equations." Review of Economic Studies 58: 277–97.

Armington, P. 1969. "A Theory of Demand for Products Distinguished by Place of Origin." *International Monetary Fund Staff Papers* 16: 159–78.

Arndt, C. 1996. "An Introduction to Systematic Sensitivity Analysis via Gaussian Quadrature." Center for Global Trade Analysis, Department of Agricultural Economics, Purdue University, Lafayette, IN.

Arndt, C., and K. Pearson. 2000. "Implementing Systematic Sensitivity Analysis Using GEMPACK." Center for Global Trade Analysis, Department of Agricultural Economics, Purdue University, Lafayette, IN.

Baganha, M. 1998. "Immigrant Involvement in the Informal Economy: The Portuguese Case." *Journal of Ethnic and Migration Studies* 24 (2): 367–85.

Baganha, M. I. 2003. "From Closed to Open Doors: Portuguese Emigration under the Corporatist Regime." *e-Journal of Portuguese History (e-JPH)* 1 (1, Summer), Brown University, Providence, RI. http://www.brown.edu/Departments/Portuguese_Brazilian_Studies/ejph/.

Baganha, M. I., and P. Perreira. 2000. "Portuguese Migration." Photocopy.

Baganha, M. I., J. C. Marques, and G. Fonseca. 2000. *"Is An Ethclass Emerging in Europe? The Portuguese Case."* Lisbon: Luso-American Development Foundation.

Baganha, M. I., J. Ferrão, and J. M. Malheiros. 1998. "Immigrants and the Labour Market: The Portuguese Case." In *Metropolis*, Metropolis International Workshop–Lisbon, Luso-American Development Foundation, 89–120.

Barisik, A., A. Eraydin, and A. Gedik. 1990. "Turkey." In *Handbook on International Migration*, ed. J. Serow, C. Nam, D. Sly, and R. Weller. New York: Greenwood Press.

Barrett, A. 1999. "Irish Migration: Characteristics, Causes and Consequences." Discussion Paper 97, Institute for the Study of Labor (IZA), Bonn, Germany.

Barrett, A., and P. J. O'Connell. 2000. "Is There a Wage Premium for Return-ing Irish Migrants?" Discussion Paper 135, IZA, Bonn, Germany.

Bauer, T. K., and K. F. Zimmerman. 1999. "Assessment of Possible Migration Pressure and Its Labour Market Impact following EU Enlargement to Central and Eastern Europe." Research Report 3, IZA, Bonn, Germany.

Berrocal, L. (1983).*Marche du Travail et Mouvements Migratoires: L'euromigra-tion Espagnole*. Brussels, Belgium: Editions de l'Université de Bruxelles.

Bijak, J., A. Kicinger, K. Saczuk, D. Kupiszewska, M. Kupiszewski, and B. Nowok. 2004. "Long-Term International Migration Scenarios for Europe, 2002–2052." Paper prepared for the Second Conference of the EAPS Working Group on International Migration in Europe, Rome, November 25–27. http://www.cefmr.pan.pl/events/materials/2004-11-26_rome_cefmr.pdf.

Bleubu, A. 2004. "Romanian to Spain: Motivation, Networks and Strate-gies." Paper presented at the Conference on New Patterns of Labor Migra-tion in Central and Eastern Europe, organized by the Public Policy Center in Cluj Napoca, Romania.

Boeri, T., and H. Brücker. 2001. *The Impact of Eastern Enlargement on Employ-ment and Labour Markets in the EU Member States*. Brussels: European Com-mission.

Bokozada, Q. 2005. *Assessment of Standard of Living of Labour Migrants*. Dushambe, Tajikistan: Zerkalo.

Bover, O., and P. Velilla. 1999. "Migrations in Spain: Historical Background and Current Trends." Discussion Paper 88, IZA, Bonn, Germany. ftp://repec.iza.org/RePEc/Discussionpaper/dp88.pdf.

Braichevska, O., H. Volosiuk, O. Malynovska, Y. Pylynskyi, N. Popson, and B. A. Ruble. 2004. *Nontraditional Immigrants in Kiev*. 7–33. Washington, DC: Kennan Institute, Woodrow Wilson International Center for Schol-ars.

Breen, R. 1984. "Education and the Labour Market: Work and Unemploy-ment among Recent Cohorts of Irish School Leavers." General Research Series Paper 119, Economic and Social Research Institute, Dublin.

Brücker, H. 2002. "Can International Migration Solve the Problems of Euro-pean Labour Markets?" In *UNECE Economic Survey of Europe*, 2, 109–42.

Brücker, H., and B. Siliverstovs. 2004. "The Macro Determinants of Interna-tional Migration in Europe: Evidence from Germany." Paper presented at the Conference Immigration Issues in EU-Turkish Relations, Bogazici Uni-versity. http://www.econ.boun.edu.tr/cee/cee/BrueckerMigration.pdf.

Bruecker, H. 2005. *"Eu-Osterweiterung: Uebergangsfristen fuerhen zu Umlenkung der Migration nach Grossbritannien und Irland."* DIW Wochenbericht Nr. 22/2005.

Burda, M. C. 1993. "The Determinants of East-West German Migration: Some First Results." *European Economic Review* 37 (2–3, April): 452–61.

Burdelnii, E. 2004. "In Search of New Guidelines for East-West European Migration in the Light of European Union's 'Wider Europe – Neighbour-hood' Policy (the case of the Republic of Moldova)." Paper presented at the Conference on New Patterns of Labor Migration in Central and Eastern Europe, organized by the Public Policy Center in Cluj Napoca, Romania. http://www.cenpo.ro/files/03%20Migration.pdf.

Callan, T., and H. Sutherland. 1997. "Income Supports in Ireland and the UK." In *Income Support and Work Incentives: Ireland and the UK*, ed. T. Callan. Policy Research Paper 30, Economic and Social Research Institute (ESRI), Dublin.

Carrington, W. J., and E. Detragiache. 1999. "How Extensive Is the Brain Drain?" *Finance and Development* 36 (2, June). http://www.imf.org/exter nal/pubs/ft/fandd/1999/06.

Caselli, F., and S. Tenreyro. 2005. "Is Poland the Next Spain?" Discussion Paper 668, Centre for Economic Performance (CEP), London. http://cep.lse.ac.uk/pubs/download/dp0668.pdf.

Catrinescu, N., M. Leon-Ledesma, M. Piracha, and B. Quillin. 2006. "Remittances, Institutions and Economic Growth." Discussion Paper 2139, IZA, Bonn, Germany.

Cazorla, J., D. D. Gregory, and J. P. Neto. 1979. "El Retorno de los Emigrantes al sur de Iberia." *Revista de Sociologia* 11: 65–85.

Chami, R., C. Fullenkamp, and S. Jahjah. 2003. "Are Immigrant Remittance Flows a Source of Capital for Development?" Working Paper 03/189, International Monetary Fund (IMF), Washington, DC.

Chies, L. 1994. *Das Migrationsproblem in der Europäischen Gemeinschaft: Theoretische und empirische Analyse der Bestimmungsfaktoren un Folgen internationaler Arbeitskräftewanderungen*. Frankfurt: Lang.

Chobanova, R. 2006. "The Brain Drain Study: Emigration Flows of Qualified Scientists." In *The Brain-Drain – Emigration Flows for Qualified Scientists*, ed. W. Hansen. MERIT, University of Maastricht, Netherlands.

Clert, C., and E. Gomart. 2004. "Human Trafficking in South East Europe: Beyond Crime Control, an Agenda for Social Inclusion and Development." Internal Scoping Paper, World Bank, Washington, DC.

Coenders, M., M. Lubbers, and P. Scheepers. 2004. "Majorities' Attitudes towards Minorities in Western and Eastern European Societies: Results from the European Social Survey 2002–2003." Report 4 for the European Monitoring Centre on Racism and Xenophobia, University of Nijmegen, Netherlands.

Contini, B., and C. Villosio. 1998. "Analysis of Wage Flexibility and Mobility in the UE." R&P, Report for the European Commission.

De Luna Martinez, J. 2005. "Workers' Remittances to Developing Countries: A Survey with Central Banks on Select Policy Issues." Policy Research Working Paper 3638, World Bank, Washington, DC.

De Soto, H., P. Gordon, I. Gedeshi, and Z. Sinoimeri. 2002. "Poverty in Albania: A Qualitative Assessment. Technical Paper 520, Europe and Central Asia, Environmentally and Socially Sustainable Development Series, World Bank, Washington, DC. http://www-wds.worldbank.org/servlet/ WDSContentServer/WDSP/IB/2002/10/12/000094946_0210010401175 8/Rendered/PDF/multi0page.pdf .

Desai, R. M., L. M. Freinkman, and I. Goldberg. 2003. "Fiscal Federalism and Regional Growth: Evidence from the Russian Federation in the 1990s." Policy Research Working Paper 3138, World Bank, Washington, DC.

Dimaranan, B. V., and R. A. McDougall. 2002. *Global Trade, Assistance, and Production: The GTAP 5 Data Base*. Center for Global Trade Analysis, Purdue University, Lafayette, IN.

Drinkwater, S., P. Levine, and E. Lotti. 2002. "The Economic Impact of Migration: A Survey." Paper presented for the second workshop of the Fifth Framework Programme Project European Enlargement: The Impact of East-West Migration on Growth and Employment, Vienna, December.

Durand, J., E. A. Parrado, and D. S. Massey. 1996. "Migradollars and Development: A Reconsideration of the Mexican Case." *International Migration Review* 30 (2): 423–44.

Dustmann, C., and I. Preston. 2005. "Racial and Economic Factors in Attitudes towards Migration." Working Paper 2542, Center for Economic and Policy Research (CEPR), Washington, DC.

Economic and Social Research Council. 2002. "Survey of Fujianese Chinese." University of Oxford, London.

el-Qorchi, M., S. M. Maimbo, and J. Wilson. 2002. *The Hawala Informal Funds Transfer System: An Economic and Regulatory Analysis*. Washington, DC: IMF and World Bank.

Epstein, J. M., and R. Axtell. 1996. *Growing Artificial Societies: Social Science from the Bottom Up*. Washington, DC and Cambridge, MA: Brookings Institution and MIT Press.

Eriksson, T. 1989. "International Migration and Regional Differentials in Unemployment and Wages: Some Empirical Evidence from Finland." In *European Factor Mobility: Trends and Consequences*, ed. I. Gordon and A. P. Thirlwall. New York: St. Martin's Press.

Eurobarometer. 2005. "Public Opinion in the European Union." 63. http://ec.europa.eu/public_opinion/archives/eb/eb63/eb63.4_en_first.pdf.

European Commission. 2003. "Communication from the Commission to the Council, the European Parliament, the European Economic and Social Committee, and the Committee of the Regions on Immigration, Integration, and Employment." http://europa.eu.int/eur-lex/en/com/cnc/2003/com2003_0336en01.pdf.

European Commission. 2006. "Report on the Functioning of the Transitional Arrangements Set Out in the 2003 Accession Treaty (Period 1 May 2004–30 April 2006)." EC, Brussels.

Faini, R. 1994. "Workers Remittances and the Real Exchange Rate." *Journal of Population Economics* 7: 235–45.

Faini, R., and A. Venturini. 1993. "Trade, Aid and Migration: Some Basic Policy Issues." *European Economic Review* 37: 435–42.

Faini, R., and A. Venturini. 1994a. "Migration and Growth: The Experience of Southern Europe." Discussion Paper 964, CEPR, Washington, DC.

Faini, R., and A. Venturini. 1994b. "Italian Emigration in the Pre-war Period." In *Migration and the International Labour Market, 1850–1913*, ed. T. Hatton and J. Williamson. London: Routledge.

Faini, R., and A. Venturini. 2001. "Home Bias and Migration: Why Is Migration Playing a Marginal Role in the Globalization Process?" Working Paper 27/2001, Centre for Household, Income, Labour, and Demographic economics (CHILD), Torino, Italy. http://www.child-centre.it/papers/child27_2001.pdf.

Fassmann, H., J. Kohlbacher, and U. Reeger. 1995. "Forgetting Skills at Borderline: Foreign Job-Seekers on the Viennese Labour Market." *Studi Emigrazione* 117: 78–89.

Fertig, M. 2001. "The Economic Impact of EU-Enlargement: Assessing the Migration Potential." *Empirical Economics* 26: 707–20.

Fertig, M., and C. Schmidt. 2000. "Aggregate Level Migration Studies as a Tool for Forecasting Future Migration Streams." In *International Migration: Trends, Policy and Economic Impact*, ed. S. Djajic. London: Routledge.

Ford, R. 1994. "Current and Future Migration Flows." In *Strangers and Citizens: A Positive Approach to Migrants and Refugees*, ed. S. Spencer. London: Rivers Oram Press.

Freeman, G. 2000. "Political Science and Comparative Immigration Politics." Photocopy. http://www.tulane.edu/~dnelson/PEMigConf/Freeman.pdf.

Furman, D. E. 1996. "On the Future of the Post-Soviet Region." In Cooperation and Conflict in the Former Soviet Union: Implications for Migration, ed. J. R. Azrael, E. A. Payin, K. F. McCarthy, and G. Vernez, 166–78. Conference Proceedings CF130. Santa Monica, CA: RAND. http://www.rand.org/publications/CF/CF130/CF130ch13.pdf.

Galanxhi, E., E. Misja, D. Lameborshi, M. Lerch, P. Wanner, and J. Dahinden. 2003. "Migration in Albania: Population and Housing Census 2001." Tirana, Albania and Neuchâtel, Switzerland: Institute of Statistics of Albania (INSTAT) and the Swiss Forum for Migration and Population Studies (SFM). www.instat.gov.al/repoba/english/Researches/anglisht/migration/migration25fevrie05.pdf.

Gale, D., and L. S. Shapley. 1962. "College Admissions and the Stability of Marriage." *American Mathematical Monthly* 60: 9–15.

Garnier, P. 2001. "Foreign Workers from Central and Eastern European Countries in Some OECD European Countries: Status and Social Protection." In *Migration Policies and EU Enlargement*. Paris: OECD.

Geary, P. T., and C. McCarthy. 1976. "Wage and Price Determination in a Labour Exporting Economy: The Case of Ireland." *European Economic Review* 8: 219–33.

Geary, P. T., and C. Ó. Gráda. 1989. "Post-war Migration between Ireland and the United Kingdom: Models and Estimates." In *European Factor Mobility: Trends and Consequences*, ed. I. Gordon and A. P. Thirlwall, 53–58. New York: St. Martin's Press.

Glytsos, N.P. 1988. "Remittances in Temporary Migration: A Theoretical Model and Its Testing with the Greek-German Experience." *Weltwirtschaftliches Archiv* 124 (3): 524–49.

Glytsos, P. N. 1993. "Measuring the Income Effects of Migrant Remittances: A Methodological Approach Applied to Greece." *Economic Development and Cultural Change* 42 (1, October): 131–68.

Glytsos, P. N. 1995. "Problems and Policies Regarding the Socio-economic Integration of Returnees and Foreign Workers in Greece." *International Migration* 33 (2): 155–76.

Glytsos, P. N. 1998. "Le Migration comme Moteur de l'Integration Rée-gionale: l'example des Transferts de Fonds." In *Migrations, Libre-Échange et Intégration Régionale dans le Bassin Méditerranéen*. Paris: OECD.

Glytsos, P. N., and L. Katzeli. 2001. "Greek Migration: The Two Faces of Janus." Paper presented at the CEPR Conference, "European Migration: What Do We Know?" in Munich. In *European Migration: What Do We Know?* ed. K. Zimmermann. Oxford: Oxford University Press.

Hansen, W., ed. 2006. *"The Brain-Drain – Emigration Flows for Qualified Scientists."* MERIT, University of Maastricht, Netherlands. http://www.merit.unimaas.nl/braindrain/.

Harris, J., and M. P. Todaro. 1970. "Migration, Unemployment, and Development: A Two-Sector Analysis." *American Economic Review* 60: 126–42.

Harrison, A., T. Britton, and A. Swanson. 2004. "Working Abroad – The Benefits Flowing from Nationals Working in Other Economies." Report of the OECD Round Table on Sustainable Development, OECD, Paris. http://www.oecd.org/dataoecd/30/20/32297831.pdf.

Hárs, A. 2003. "Channeled East-West Labour Migration in the Frame of Bilateral Agreements." FLOWENLA Discussion Paper 13, Hamburg Institute of International Economics, Hamburg, Germany. http://www.hwwa.de/Projects/Res_Programmes/RP/Mobility/Flowenla/Flowenla13.pdf.

Harton, J., and N. Vriend. 1989. "Post-war International Labour Mobility: The Netherlands." In *European Factor Mobility: Trends and Consequences*, ed. I. Gordon and A. P. Thirlwall. New York: St. Martin's Press.

Hatton, T. and J. Williamson, eds. 1994. *Migration and the International Labour Market, 1850–1913."* London: Routledge.

Hatton, T. J. 1995. "A Model of U.K. Emigration, 1870–1913." *Review of Economics and Statistics* 77 (3, August): 407–15.

Hatton, T., and J. Williamson. 1998. *The Age of Mass Migration*. New York: Oxford University Press.

Hatton, T., and S. W. Price. 1999. "Migration, Migrants and Policy in the United Kingdom." Discussion Paper 81, IZA, Bonn, Germany. http://www.iza.org/index_html?lang=en&mainframe=http%3A//www.iza.org/en/webcontent/publications/papers&topSelect=publications&subSelect=papers.

Heleniak, T. 2005. "The Causes and Consequences of Fertility Decline in the Former Soviet Union and Central and Eastern Europe." Paper presented at the conference, "Health and Demography in the States of the Former Soviet Union," Harvard University, April 29–30.

Hertel, T. W. 1997. *Global Trade Analysis: Modeling and Applications*. Cambridge, MA: Cambridge University Press.

Hill, F. 2004. "Eurasia on the Move: The Regional Implications of Mass Labor Migration from Central Asia to Russia." Presentation at the Kennan Institute, Washington, DC, September 27. http://www.brookings.edu/views/op-ed/hillf/20040927.pdf.

Hille, H., and T. Straubhaar. 2001. "The Impact of the EU-Enlargment on Migration Movements and Economic Integration: Results of Recent Studies" In *Migration Policies and EU Enlargement*. Paris: OECD.

Hollifield, J. 1992. *Immigrants, Markets, and States: The Political Economy of Post-war Europe.* Boston: Harvard University Press.

Hunt, J. 2000. "Why Do People Still Live in East Germany?" Discussion Paper 123, IZA, Bonn, Germany.

IMF. 2003a. *Balance of Payments Compilation Guide.* Washington, DC: IMF. http://www.imf.org/external/pubs/ft/bopcg/1995/bopcg.pdf.

IMF. 2003b. *Balance of Payments Statistics Yearbook, 2003.* Washington, DC: IMF.

INCO. 1997. "Surveying the Brain Drain from Eastern Europe." International Cooperation (INCO), European Commission. http://ec.europa.eu/research/intco/pdf/097e.pdf.

IOM. 2001. "Deceived Migrants from Tajikistan: A Study of Trafficking in Women and Children." Dushanbe, Tajikistan: International Organisation for Migration (IOM). http://www.untj.org/files/reports/Deceived%20Migrants%20from%20Tajikistan-A%20Study%20of%20Trafficking%20in%20Women%20and%20Children.pdf.

IOM. 2002. *International Legal Norms and Migration: An Analysis.* Geneva, Switzerland: IOM.

IOM. 2004. *Legal Guide for Migrants to Russia.* Geneva, Switzerland: IOM.

IOM. 2005a. *Labor Migration in Central Asia, Russia, Afghanistan and Pakistan.* Geneva, Switzerland: IOM.

IOM. 2005b. *World Migration 2005: Costs and Benefits of External Migration.* Geneva, Switzerland: IOM.

Izquierdo, E. A., and F. Munoz-Perez. 1989. "L'Espana, pays d'immigration." *Population* 44 (2): 257–89.

Jandl, M. 2003. "Estimates on the Numbers of Illegal and Smuggled Immigrants in Europe." Presentation at the Eighth International Metropolis Conference, September 17. http://www.net4you.com/jandl/Metropolis 2003.pdf.

Jandl, M. 2004. "Market-Based Instruments in Migration Control Policies." Presentation at the Ninth International Metropolis Conference, September 30. http://www.net4you.com/jandl/development-visa-regime.pdf.

Jimenez, M. 2003. "U.S. Starting to Embrace Illegal Workers." *Globe and Mail* (November 17).

Judson, R. A., and A. L. Owen. 1999. "Estimating Dynamic Panel Data Models: A Guide for Macroeconomists." *Economics Letters* 65 (1): 9–15.

Karemera, D., V. I. Oguledo, and B. Davis. 2000. "A Gravity Model Analysis of International Migration to North America." *Applied Economics* 32: 1745–55.

Karras, G., and C. U. Chiswick. 1999. "Macroeconomic Determinants of Migration: The Case of Germany, 1964–1988." *International Migration* 37 (4): 657–77.

Katseli, L. T., and N. P. Glytsos. 1989. "Theoretical and Empirical Determinants of International Labour Mobility: A Greek-German Perspective." In *European Factor Mobility: Trends and Consequences,* ed. I. Gordon and A. P. Thirlwall. New York: St. Martin's Press.

Kaufmann, D., A. Kraay, and M. Mastruzzi. 2003. "Governance Matters III: Governance Indicators for 1996–2002." Policy Research Working Paper 3106, World Bank, Washington, DC.

Keenan, J. G. 1981. "Irish Migration: All or Nothing Resolved?" *Economic and Social Review* 12: 169–86.

Kondis, B. 1990. *The Greeks of Northern Epirus and Greek-Albanian Relations.* Athens: Hesita Publishers & Booksellers.

Koser, K. 2001. "The Smuggling of Asylum Seekers into Western Europe: Contradictions, Conundrums, and Dilemmas." In *Global Human Smuggling: Comparative Perspectives*, ed. D. Kyle and R. Koslowski, 58–73. Baltimore: Johns Hopkins University Press.

Kosta, B. 2004. "Albania: Looking Beyond Borders." In *Migration Information Source* (August). Brussels: Migration Policy Institute (MPI). http://www .migrationinformation.org/Profiles/display.cfm?ID=239.

Koszalka, L., and J. Sobieszczanski. 2003. "Brain Drain – Brain Gain: Introduction and Short Overview of the Situation in Eastern Europe." Presented to Conférence internationale sur l'enseignement et la recherche supérieure, Education International, Dakar, October 30 to November 1. www.ei-ie.org/hiednet/english/Downloads/2003_hied_Dakar_paperNSZZ.pdf.

Lackso, F., and M. A. Gramegna. 2003. "Developing Better Indicators of Human Trafficking." *Brown Journal of World Affairs* 10 (1, Summer/Fall): 179–94.

León-Ledesma, M., and P. Matloob. 2001. "International Migration and the Role of Remittances in Eastern Europe." Discussion Paper 01/13, University of Kent, Canterbury.

Lianos, T. 1972. "The Migration Process and Time Lags." *Journal of Regional Science* 12 (3): 425–33.

Lianos, T. 1975. "Flows of Greek Out-Migration and Return Migration." *International Migration* 13 (3): 119–33.

Lianos, T. 1980. "Movement of Greek Labor to Germany and Return." *Greece Economic Review* 2 (1): 71–77.

Lianos, T. 1997. "Factors Determining Migrant Remittances: The Case of Greece." *International Migration Review* 31 (1): 72–87.

Lianos, T., A. H. Sarris, and L. T. Katseli. 1996. "Illegal Immigration and Local Labour Markets: The Case of Northern Greece." *International Migration* 34 (3): 449–84.

Linn, J. F. 2004. "Economic (Dis)Integration Matters: The Soviet Collapse Revisited." Paper prepared for the conference on Transition in the CIS: Achievements and Challenges at the Academy for National Economy, Moscow, September 13–14.

Liu, S. 1997. "Gaussian Quatrature and its Applications." PhD dissertation, Department of Agricultural Economics, Purdue University, Lafayette, IN.

Lopez, C. 2004. "Globalization, Migration, and Development: The Role of Mexican Migrant Remittances." Photocopy, Inter-American Development Bank, Washington, DC.

Lucas, R. E. B. 1985. "Migration amongst the Botswana." *Economic Journal* 95: 358–82.

Lucas, R. E. B. 2005. "International Migration and Economic Development: Lessons from Low-Income Countries." Stockholm: Expert Group on Development Issues (EGDI), Swedish Ministry for Foreign Affairs. http://www.egdi.gov.se/pdf/International_Migration_and_Economic_Development.pdf.

Lundborg, P. 1991. "Determinants of Migration in the Nordic Labor Market." *Scandinavian Journal of Economics* 93: 363–75.Martin, P. L. 1991. *The Unfinished Story: Turkish Labour Migration to Western Europe.* Geneva: ILO.

Martin, P. L. 2003. "Managing Labor Migration: Temporary Worker Programs for the 21st Century." International Institute for Labour Studies, ILO, Geneva, Switzerland. http://www-ilo-mirror.cornell.edu/public/english/bureau/inst/download/migration3.pdf.

Massey, D. S., and E. Parrado. 1994. "Migradollars: The Remittances and Savings of Mexican Migrants to the USA." *Population Research and Policy Review* 13 (1): 3–30.

Massey, D. S., G. Hugo, A. Kouaouci, A. Pellegrino, and J. E. Taylor. 1993. "Theories of International Migration: A Review and Appraisal." *Population and Development in Review* 19: 431–66.

Massey, D., L. Goldring, and J. Durand. 1994. "Continuities in Transnational Migration: An Analysis of Nineteen Mexican Communities." *American Journal of Sociology* 99: 1492–1533. As quoted in S. Vertovec. 2003. "Migration and Other Modes of Transnationalism: Towards Conceptual Cross-Fertilization." *International Migration Review* 37 (3): 641–65.

Mayda, A. M. 2005. "Who Is against Immigration? A Cross-Country Investigation of Individual Attitudes toward Immigrants." *Review of Economics and Statistics* 88 (3): 510–30.

Molle, W., and A. van Mourik. 1989. "A Static Explanatory Model of International Labour Migration to and in Western Europe." In *European Factor Mobility: Trends and Consequences,* ed. I. Gordon and A.P. Thirlwall. New York: St. Martin's Press.

Moulier-Boutang, Y., and J.-P. Garson. 1984. "Major Obstacles to Control of Irregular Migrations: Prerequisites to Policy." *International Migration Review* 18 (3, Autumn): 579–92.

Muellbauer, J., and A. Murphy. 1988. "UK House Prices and Migration: Economic and Investment Implications." Research paper, U.K. Economics Series, Shearson Lehman-Hutton, Oxford.

Ó Gráda, C. 1986. "Determinants of Irish Emigration: A Note." *International Migration Review* 20 (3): 651–56.

Ó Gráda, C., and B. M. Walsh. 1994. "The Economic Effects of Emigration: Ireland." In *Emigration and Its Effect on the Sending Country,* ed. B. J. Asch. Santa Monica, CA: Rand.

O'Rourke, D. 1972. "A Stock and Flows Approach to a Theory of Human Migration with Examples from Past Irish Migration." *Demography* 9 (2): 263–74.

O'Rourke, K. 1992. "Why Ireland Emigrated: A Positive Theory of Factor Flows." *Oxford Economic Papers* 44 (2): 322–40.

OECD. 1999. "Proposed Action Plan 2000 for Activities to Combat Trafficking in Human Beings." Office for Democratic Institutions and Human Rights, OECD, Warsaw.

OECD. 2001. *Migration Policies and EU Enlargement*. Paris: OECD.

OECD. 2003. *Trends in International Migration: SOPEMI 2002 Edition*. Paris: OECD.

OECD. 2004. *Migration for Employment: Bilateral Agreements at a Crossroads*. Paris: OECD.

OECD. 2005. *Trends in International Migration*. Paris: OECD.

Olimova, S., and I. Bosc. 2003. "Labour Migration from Tajikistan." Dushanbe, Tajikistan: IOM (in cooperation with the Sharq Scientific Research Center). http://www.iom.int/jahia/webdav/site/myjahiasite/shared/shared/mainsite/published_docs/studies_and_reports/Tajik_study_oct_03.pdf.

Ozden, C., and M. Schiff, eds. 2006. *International Migration, Remittances, and Brain Drain*. Washington, DC and Hampshire, U.K.: World Bank and Palgrave Macmillan.

Parsons, C. 2005. "Trade and Migration in ECA: A Survey of Preliminary Results." Photocopy, World Bank, Washington, DC.

Passel, J. S. 2005. "Estimates of the Size and Characteristics of the Undocumented Population." Pew Hispanic Center, Washington, DC. http://pewhispanic.org/files/reports/44.pdf.

Penninx, R. 2005. "Elements for an EU-Framework for Integration Policies." In *Managing Integration: The European Union's Responsibilities towards Immigrants*, ed. R. Sussmuth and W. Seidenfeld, 74–83. Gütersloh, Germany: Bertelsmann Stiftung/MPI

Pereira, P. T. 1994. "Portuguese Emigration, 1958–1985." *Empirical Economics* 19: 647–57.

Phongpaichit, P., S. Piriyarangsan, and N. Treerat. 1998. *Guns, Girls, Gambling, Ganja: Thailand's Illegal Economy and Public Policy*. Chiang Mai, Thailand: Silkworm Books.

Poalelungi, O. 2003. Interview with Mrs. Olga Poalelungi, Director Adjunct for the Department of Migration, Moldova, Aug 28. Social Development Unit, ECSSD, World Bank, Washington, D.C.

Poot, J. 1995. "Do Borders Matter? A Model of Interregional Migration in Australasia." *Australasian Journal of Regional Studies* 1: 159–82.

Portes, J., and S. French. 2005. "The Impact of Free Movement of Workers from Central and Eastern Europe on the UK Labour Market: Early Evidence." Working Paper 18, Department for Work and Pensions, Her Majesty's Stationery Office, Corporate Document Services, Leeds, U.K.. http://www.dwp.gov.uk/asd/asd5/WP18.pdf.

Rapoport, H., and F. Docquier. Forthcoming. "The Economics of Migrants' Remittances." In *Handbook on the Economics of Reciprocity, Giving, and Altruism*, ed. L.-A. Gerard-Varet, S.-C. Kolm, and J. M. Ythier. Amsterdam: North Holland.

Reyneri, E. 1979. *La Catena Migratoria*. Bologna: Il Mulino.

Reyneri, E. 1998. "The Role of the Underground Economy in Irregular Migration to Italy: Cause or Effect?" *Journal of Ethnic and Migration Studies* 24 (2, April): 313–31.

Roberts, B., and K. Banaian. 2004. "Remittances in Armenia: Size, Impacts, and Measures to Enhance Their Contribution to Development." USAID, Yerevan, Armenia. http://pdf.usaid.gov/pdf_docs/PNADB948.pdf.

Rodrik, D., and A. M. Mayda. 2005. "Why are Some People (and Countries) More Protectionist than Others?" *European Economic Review* 49 (6, August): 1393–1430.Ruhs, M. 2002. "Temporary Foreign Workers Programmes: Policies, Adverse Consequences and the Need to Make Them Work." Perspective on Labour Migration 6, Social Protection Sector, International Migration Programme, International Labour Office (ILO), Geneva, Switzerland. http://www.ilo.org/public/english/protection/migrant/download/pom/pom6e.pdf.

Sadovskaya, E. 2002. "Migration Trends in Eastern Europe and Central Asia: Kazakhstan." ILO, Geneva

Sala-i-Martin, X. 1996. "Regional Cohesion: Evidence and Theories of Regional Growth and Convergence." *European Economic Review* 40: 1325–52.

Shelley, L. 2003. "The Rise and Diversification of Human Smuggling into the United States." In *Essays in Honour of Alice Yotopoulos-Marangopoulos: Human Rights Crime-Criminal Policy, Volume B*, ed. A. Manganas, 1191–1204. Athens: Nomiki Bibliothiki Group, p. 1198.

Sjaastad, L. A. 1962. "The Costs and Returns of Human Migration." *Journal of Political Economy* 70 (5): 80–93.

Stark, O., and D. Levhari. 1988. "Labor Migration as a Response to Relative Deprivation." *Journal of Development Studies* 1: 57–70.

Stark, O., and J. E. Taylor. 1989. "Relative Deprivation and International Migration." *Demography* 26: 1–14.

Stark, O., and J. E. Taylor. 1991. "Migration Incentives, Migration Types: The Role of Relative Deprivation." *Economic Journal* 101 (408, September): 1163–78.

Stark, O., and R. E. B. Lucas. 1988. "Migration, Remittances, and the Family." *Economic Development and Cultural Change* 36 (3, April): 465–81.

Stark, O., J. E. Taylor, and S. Yitzhaki. 1986. "Remittances and Inequality." *Economic Journal* 96 (383, September): 722–40.

Straubhaar, T. 1986a. "The Causes of International Migration: A Demand Determined Approach." *International Migration Review* 20 (4): 835–55.

Straubhaar, T. 1986b. "The Determinants of Workers' Remittances: The Case of Turkey." *Welwirtschaftliches Archiv* 122: 728–39.

Straubhaar, T. 1988. *On the Economics of International Labor Migration*. Bern, Switzerland: Haupt.

Straubhaar, T., and M. R. Wolburg. 1999. "Brain Drain and Brain Gain in Europe: An Evaluation of the East-European Migration to Germany." *Jahrbücher für Nationalökonomie und Statistik* 218 (5–6): 574–604.

Stroud, A. H. 1957. "Remarks on the Disposition of Points in Numerical

Integration Formulas." *Mathematical, Tables and Other Aids to Computation* 11 (60, October): 257–61.

Surtees, R. 2005. *Second Annual Report on Victims of Trafficking in South-Eastern Europe.* Geneva, Switzerland:IOM. http://www.iom.int/jahia/webdav/ site/myjahiasite/shared/shared/mainsite/published_docs/studies_and_re ports/second_annual05.pdf.

Taylor, J. E. 1986. "Differential Migration, Networks, Information and Risk." In *Research in Human Capital and Development, Volume 4, Migration, Human Capital, and Development,* ed. O. Stark, 147–71. Greenwich, CT: JAI Press.

Taylor, J. E., and T. J. Wyatt. 1996. "The Shadow Value of Migrant Remittances, Income and Inequality in a Household-Farm Economy." *Journal of Development Studies* 32 (6): 899–912.

Taylor, J. E., J. Mora, R. Adams, and A. Lopez-Feldman. 2005. "Remittances, Inequality and Poverty: Evidence from Rural Mexico." Working Paper 05-003, Department of Agricultural and Resource Economics, University of California, Davis, CA. http://repositories.cdlib.org/cgi/viewcontent .cgi?article=1068&context=are.

Todaro, M. P. 1968. *"An Analysis of Industrialization, Employment, and Unemployment in LDCs."* Yale Economic Essays 8 (2): 329–402.

Todaro, M. P. 1969. "A Model of Labor Migration and Urban Unemployment in Less Developed Countries." *American Economic Review* 59 (1): 138–48.

UNESCO. 1998. *World Science Report 1998.* Paris: UNESCO.Unger, K. 1981a. "Determinants of the Occupational Composition of Returning Migrants in Urban Greece." Paper presented at the First European Conference on International Return Migration, Rome, November 11–14.

United Nations. 2000. "Protocol to Prevent, Suppress and Punish Trafficking in Persons, Especially Women and Children, Supplementing the United Nations Convention on Transnational Organized Crime." Palermo: United Nations. http://www.ohchr.org/english/law/pdf/protocol traffic.pdf.

United Nations. 2001. *Replacement Migration: Is it a Solution to Declining and Ageing Populations?* Population Division, Department of Economic and Social Affairs. New York: United Nations. http://www.un.org/esa/popu lation/publications/migration/migration.htm.

United Nations. 2002. *International Migration 2002.* New York: United Nations.

United Nations. 2004. *World Economic and Social Survey 2004.* Department of Economic and Social Affairs. New York: United Nations.

United Nations. 2005. "Migration in an Interconnected World: New Directions for Action." Report of the Global Commission on International Migration (GCIM). Switzerland: GCIM. http://www.gcim.org/attache ments/gcim-complete-report-2005.pdf.

Venturini, A. 1988. "An Interpretation of Mediterranean Migration." *Labour* 2 (1): 125–54.

Venturini, A. 2004. *Postwar Migration in Southern Europe, 1950–2000: An Economic Approach.* Cambridge, U.K., and New York: Cambridge University Press.

Brücker, H., G. Epstein, B. McCormick, G. Saint-Paul, A.Venturini, A. , , K. Zimmermann. 2002. "Managing Migration in the European Welfare State." In *Immigration Policy and the Welfare System*, ed. T. Boeri, G. Hanson, and B. McCormick. Oxford, U.K., and New York: Oxford Economic Press.

Verhaeren, R. H. 1986. "Politiques d'immigration en Europe." *Revue Problemes Politiques et Sociaux* 530: 1–40.

Vertovec, S. 2003. "Migration and Other Modes of Transnationalism: Towards Conceptual Cross-Fertilization." *International Migration Review* 37 (3): 641–65.

Walfdorf, B. S., and A. Esparza. 1988. "Labor Migration to Western Europe: A Commentary on O'Loughlin, 1986." *Environment and Planning A* 20 (8): 1121–24.

Walmsley, T. L., S. A. Ahmed, and C. R. Parsons. 2005. "The GMig2 Data Base: A Data Base of Bilateral Labor Migration, Wages, and Remittances." GTAP Research Memorandum 6, Center for Global Trade Analysis, Purdue University, Lafayette, IN.

Walsh, B. M. 1974. "Expectations, Information, and Human Migration: Specifying an Econometric Model of Irish Migration to Britain." *Journal of Regional Science* 14: 107–20.

Winter-Ebmer, R., and K. Zimmermann. 1999. "East-West Trade and Migration: The Austro-German Case." In *Migration: The Controversies and the Evidence*, ed. R. Faini, J. de Melo, and K. Zimmermann, 296–327. Cambridge, U.K.: Cambridge University Press.

World Bank. 1999. "Update on Poverty in Kyrgyz Republic." Report 19425-KG, World Bank, Washington, DC.

World Bank. 2000a. "Albania Interim Poverty Reduction Strategy Paper." Washington, DC, World Bank.

World Bank. 2000b. "Republic of Tajikistan Poverty Assessment." Report 20285-TJ, World Bank, Washington, DC. http://www-wds.worldbank .org/servlet/WDSContentServer/WDSP/IB/2000/08/14/000094946_000 80105305244/Rendered/PDF/multi_page.pdf .

World Bank. 2002a. "Armenia Poverty Update." World Bank, Washington, DC.

World Bank. 2002b. "Georgia: Poverty Update." Report 22350-GE, Poverty Reduction and Economic Management Unit, Europe and Central Asia Region, World Bank, Washington, DC. http://www-wds.worldbank .org/external/default/WDSContentServer/WDSP/IB/2002/03/01/00009 4946_02021604020221/Rendered/PDF/multi0page.pdf.

World Bank. 2003a. "Kyrgyz Republic: Enhancing Pro-Poor Growth." Report 24638-KG, World Bank, Washington, DC.

World Bank. 2003b. "Moldova Country Brief 2003." World Bank, Washington, DC. http://wbln0018.worldbank.org/ECA/eca.nsf/2656afe00bc5f 02185256d5d005dae97/ed6b6063a1e08a3585256d5d00684811?Open-Document.

World Bank. 2003c. "Poverty Assessment." World Bank, Washington, DC.World Bank. 2003. *Global Development Finance 2003: Striving for Stabil-*

ity in Development Finance. Washington, DC: World Bank. http://siteresources.worldbank.org/INTRGDF/Resources/GDF_vol_1_web.pdf.

World Bank. 2005. "Moldova Country Economic Memorandum: Opportunities for Accelerated Growth." World Bank, Washington, DC. http://siteresources.worldbank.org/INTMOLDOVA/Resources/cem05.pdf.

World Bank. 2006. *Global Economic Prospects 2006: Economic Implication of Remittances and Migration.* Washington, DC: World Bank. http://www-wds.worldbank.org/external/default/WDSContentServer/IW3P/IB/2005/11/14/000112742_20051114174928/Rendered/PDF/343200GEP02006.pdf.

Zarate, G. A. 2002. "The Hidden Benefits of Remittances to Mexico." Photocopy. State University of New York, Cortland.

Zoubanov, N. 2004. "Assessing Determinants of Migration in the European Union. An Empirical Inquiry." *E-journal* (October), ISSN 1505-1161. http://venus.ci.uw.edu.pl/~rubikon/forum/kolia.htm.

Index